QUALITATIVE RESEARCH
AND
TRANSFORMATIVE RESULTS

A PRIMER FOR STUDENTS AND MENTORS
IN THEOLOGICAL EDUCATION

"This book highlights the potential of qualitative research practice in enhancing the seminary's connectedness with context and responsiveness to church and society. Theological education should facilitate field-based research projects that carefully analyse contextual issues and realities leading to transformative ministries—which is often than not, lacking in most seminary curricula. There is a need to develop this kind of research culture and competency among seminary faculty and students. This book is a valuable resource for theological educators committed to the task of equipping transformational leaders for the church and the world."

Theresa Roco-Lua, EdD
General Secretary, Asia Theological Association

"There are a number of textbooks on the more generic issues relating to Qualitative Research (QR) but also those that particularly relate to psychology, social sciences, etc. Some of these are too comprehensive and detailed (as e.g. *the Handbook of Qualitative Research* by SAGE) whereas the others are too narrowly focused on an aspect of QR (as e.g. David Silverman's *Interpreting Qualitative Data* or David Morgan's *Focus Group as Qualitative Research*). This text book falls in between these. Its roots lie in the author's own experience of research in India, UK, and USA but the work itself is significant for two other reasons: (i) It combines both the conceptual and practical aspects of QR but in a style, scope and format that is accessible and applicable without much fuss; (ii) It exceptionally assumes the praxis of theology as the particular source and object of research. For these reasons, it will particularly be useful for practical theologians interested in investigating problems around them "in the world" and those that are auditing their preparedness for research."

David Immanuel Singh, PhD
Research Tutor, University Link Tutor & PhD Stage Leader
Oxford Centre for Mission Studies (OCMS), UK

"This is a very useful qualitative field research guide for theological education, written with both student researcher and faculty mentor in mind. Its well-organized chapters conclude with a reflection box that illustrates and provokes. Jessy Jaison is well aware of the variety of methods available in the global discipline; yet she is also in touch with contextual challenges in the majority world and is committed to helping minimize the relevance gap between mission academia and church mission practice."

Ian Payne, PhD
Principal, Educational Consultant, Professor in Theology
South Asia Institute of Advanced Christian Studies, Bangalore, India

"Qualitative research in theological education? Yes, in order that the seminaries of the twenty-first century will not devolve into "cemeteries" but will engage with and reflect on how ministry and mission today can be effective and relevant for a changing world. If we want transformation of church and society, then Dr. Jessy Jaison helps us develop research capacities that will be up to that task!"

Amos Yong, PhD
Director of Center for Missiological Research
Professor of Theology & Mission
Fuller Theological Seminary, California, USA

"In this book Jessy Jaison explains very clearly the different main approaches to qualitative social research. Chapters on the main theoretical issues are followed by one on the ethics of social research, and then several on data gathering, research design, and the professional skills and personal qualities needed for successful social research. Jessy Jaison makes a prolonged appeal to Christians, theological educators and students of theology to take seriously the importance of understanding the contexts in which they work. This book will be helpful to students of theology working at undergraduate and postgraduate levels who wish to undertake some social research competently, as well as Christian practitioners who wish to understand better the social and church contexts in which they work."

Brian Marshall, PhD
Retired Theology Professor and Associate Dean for Student Experience in the Faculty of Humanities and Social Sciences
Oxford Brookes University, Oxford, UK

"This book brings a fresh perspective to qualitative research in human sociocultural environments. It is about "facilitating a critical approach to all manner of research" and encouraging keen minds to "ask the essential questions for constructive change and growth." The author demonstrates how qualitative approaches can contribute to theological thinking that reflects the presence of God. She seeks to ensure that people are able to recognize Christ's presence (incarnation) and their appropriate response based on their identity with *Imago Dei*. The breadth of approach and value of these methods encourage researchers to enable people to embrace a biblical perspective with its attenuating theological implications in any cultural environment."

R Daniel Shaw, PhD
Sr. Prof. Anthropology & Translation
Fuller Graduate School of Intercultural Studies, California, USA

QUALITATIVE RESEARCH
AND
TRANSFORMATIVE RESULTS

A PRIMER FOR STUDENTS AND MENTORS
IN THEOLOGICAL EDUCATION

Jessy Jaison

SAIACS Press
2018

Qualitative Research and Transformative Results
A Primer for Students and Mentors in Theological Education

Copyright © Jessy Jaison 2018

ISBN: 978-93-86549-10-5

Published by SAIACS Press
an imprint of SAIACS Publications

South Asia Institute of Advanced Christian Studies (SAIACS)
Box 7747, Kothanur, Bangalore 560 077, India
saiacspress@saiacs.org
www.saiacs.org

CONTENTS

List of Figures

ACKNOWLEDGMENTS

The preceding action to constructive changes is asking difficult questions, followed by specific steps initiating the change. Theological education with its ongoing culture of research, hence, should be asking questions like: Are we doing what we are called to do with the enormous amount of learning that is being facilitated in theology campuses? How persuasively are students drawn to the church and mission as a result of their research projects? Do our research endeavours truly embrace the wisdom of God both in theory and practice? Thus, we assume a cohesive hermeneutic of suspicion towards positive change.

This book is designed as a helpful tool for the students of theology, informing, engaging and encouraging them in their pursuit of qualitative research. Through eight chapters, it resolutely addresses crucial areas around transformative research practice for theology schools. The number of practical theological researchers who explores meaningful connections between theology and the world is on steady increase and yet many researchers lack information and guidance about the actual direction of research. At least in part, this book seeks to address this need.

I thank God Almighty for bestowing His grace, wisdom and strength on this writing project. The genuine requests from my research students for a book of this nature have been the key motivator. Heartfelt gratitude to each of them whose challenges and invaluable insights breathed life to every section of this book. Special word of appreciations to Fuller Theological Seminary and the Global Research Institute at the School of Intercultural Studies (SIS) for providing necessary guidance and support during my writing. Academic interactions with the faculty and PhD scholars at the School of Intercultural Studies were highly beneficial in the writing process. Thanks to Dr. Scott Sunquist, the Dean and Dr. Amos Yong, the Director of Centre for Missiological Research for making my research endeavour at Fuller Seminary most effective.

Dr. Amos Yong's earnest support and mentoring through this research has impacted this project significantly. I am deeply grateful to Dr. Daniel Shaw for initiating regular conversations on the development of thought for the book. Thanks to Mrs. Georgia Grimes Shaw for extending her expert editing support to someone whom she has never met! Sincere gratitude is also due to Dr. Theresa Roco-Lua, Dr. Daniel Shaw, Dr. Ian Payne, Dr. Brian Marshall and Dr. Immanuel Singh for reading through the manuscript, sending in suggestions for improvement and writing endorsement notes for the book. SAIACS Press and the staff at the publishing department deserve special words of appreciation for their excellent services in making this dream come true.

Among those who deserve special thanks are my parents, colleagues, and friends. I am indebted to Dr. Alexander Philip, the Executive Director of New India Evangelistic Association (NIEA) and the leadership of New India Bible Seminary for relieving me to be away for this project. Special thanks to Jaison Thomas, my husband, for being the unparalleled source of support through years of life and ministry together. To Abraham and Aquil, my beloved sons for their joy, love and fun that made the duration of the research and writing most peaceful. A big note of thanks to Abraham for helping out with the diagrams in this book.

I present this book on Qualitative Research to theology students and research mentors envisioning that every theology school would assume its rightful transformative posture between church and the society. It is my prayer that the research element will be vigorous in every program, course and assignment so that scholarship and service will be meaningfully integrated.

INTRODUCTION

THEOLOGICAL EDUCATION BETWEEN ACADEMY AND WORLD

THE QUALITATIVE DOMAIN

SECTION CONTENTS:
- A Constructive Critical Appraisal on Research Practices in Theological Education
- The Context of Learning in Theology Schools
- The Plethora of Difficult Questions
- Self-Evaluation Questions for Theology Schools on Research Practices
- The Need for Focused Qualitative Research in Theological Education
- Purpose Statement of the book

A Constructive Critical Appraisal on Research Practices in Theological Education

How meaningful are the current practices of qualitative research in theological education in instilling and advancing the mission of God in our world today? Are we still lacking basic insights on the conduct of transformative qualitative research in theological education? This book extends an ardent invite to theology researchers to deepen their expertise in transformative qualitative researching and theology schools to review their research/learning practices against their espoused aims.

The initial premise of this book recognizes that research is already an essential component across the academic programs in theological education. However, it aims to address certain issues around this proposition. Are students equipped to conduct research in their own real contexts of ministry? Have they been facilitated to make sense of their theological convictions in real-life situations? What does a typical research or thesis submitted to a theology school accomplish, apart from being a great reference-resource within the academy? Are the countless field-based research projects significantly impacting the contexts of their inquiry? Are these studies and their results known and used by the churches/missions in those contexts? Practitioners in mission actually wonder why several semesters or years of research and reflection are required if these are not reaching back to the people and the contexts concerned.

My recent work *Towards Vital Wholeness in Theological Education* presented certain procedural considerations for theology schools in the path of wholeness in training[1] as given in Figure 1.

Figure 1: Pivotal Procedural Considerations Towards Wholeness in Theological Education

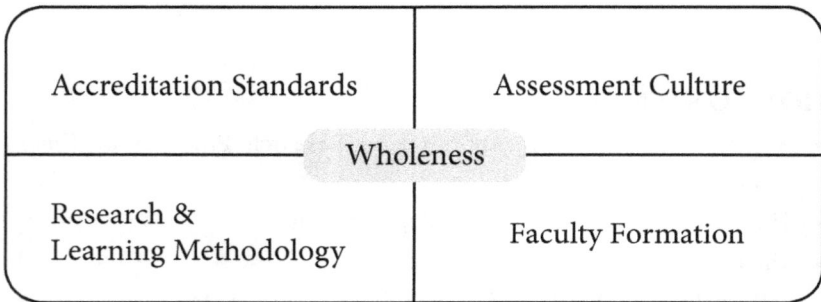

Accreditation Standards	Assessment Culture
Wholeness	
Research & Learning Methodology	Faculty Formation

Research and learning methodology is identified as a crucial area for theology schools in their prospect of transformative education.

The Context of Learning in Theology Schools

Theology schools all over the world practice some form of practicum or field study. Such endeavours are commonly labelled as *research,* and certainly, they make the major trajectory in higher education. Nonetheless, in spite of the prevalence of research practice, critical questions can be raised: Are we doing it well? What are we achieving in terms of the existential call on theology schools? How adequately do our research projects contribute in bridging the gap between the seminary, church and mission, or do they serve to the further distancing of scholarship and context of life? Are graduates committedly following up on their contextual research projects in various degrees towards enhancing the field mission? Questions like these are hard-core yet, no claims are made in this book to have suggested comprehensive answers to these. Overall, the purpose is to initiate thinking and strategic discussions on

---

[1] Jessy Jaison, *Towards Vital Wholeness in Theological Education: Framing Areas for Assessment* (Cumbria: Langham Global Library, 2017), 180.

where we are with the qualitative research practice in theology schools. Three radical commitments at the backdrop of this are:

- Enhancing *vital wholeness*[2] in the teaching–learning practice and responsiveness in the way theological education is done by enunciating the conceptual and practical frame of qualitative research
- Strengthening of the *church-seminary-society* relationship and pastoral formation through transformative research practices, with specific focus on the qualitative domain
- Setting of an *outcome-impact question* on the amount of research happening in theology schools and the tangible results in the mission of the church

Beyond the general aim to serve the intensifying needs for a handy resource on qualitative research in theological education, this book places several elements on the desk for theological leadership and the faculty to pause and ponder on. Each chapter ends with a *Reflection Box* to facilitate practical thinking. It also might set some agenda for discussion as to how formal theological schools can grow deeper to impact the context of the church and her mission and how all of this corresponds to the latest discussions on the non-formal pastoral training and on-line education where training mostly happens in the context of the learner.

Complexities accompany the influx of students in higher education and research. Lack of personnel for focused mentoring and examination, *technicalities of writing* overlooks the vision of *transformative learning*, lack of commitment on the part of faculty and researcher in developing a coherent research mindset, repetitions (just with slight variations) in the subject area and context of study, increasing issues of plagiarism, research projects going uncommunicated with the grounds of mission of the church, are a few to mention. There is felt need for resources, insights and support as we facilitate calibration of this area. Theology schools sometimes even confuse between study methods and research methodology. While a course on 'Study Methods' might orient the student to the specifics of reading-writing methods, referencing, bibliographies and presentations in the specific context of a school/ university, 'Research Methodology' should be equipping the student on the path of critical thinking, analysis, continuing learning, and, ultimately towards significant contributions in life and ministry.

Therefore, we need to take heed to the most difficult questions on the philosophy and practice of theological education raised by churches and missions. These can direct our path to enhanced transformative research and learning.

---

[2]   Research dimension in training was one among the four potential areas for advancing wholeness in training. See Jessy Jaison, *Towards Vital Wholeness in Theological Education: Framing Areas for Assessment* (Cumbria: Langham Global Library, 2017).

The Plethora of Difficult Questions

- What makes many ministers and lay people testify to the irrelevance of theology or theological education today?
- Why do a large number of theology graduates not get ready for ministry when they graduate?
- Why do students seem hesitant to take up challenges in the ministry they are allotted for?
- Why are many theology graduates quite unable to break the barriers in conversational engagements with people of other faiths even after having spent years in theology schools?
- Why does a theology student who is confident in presenting excellent academic papers, struggle when it comes to addressing people with real-life issues in a congregation or society?
- Why do many graduates appear to be ignorant about the needs and challenges of the society around them?
- Why are graduates who join pastoral ministry found in an endless pursuit of *what they are supposed to do* rather than *what the congregation needs*?
- Why do theology graduates generally tend to remain insensitive or irresponsive to the changes, stagnations and setbacks in mission that are right in front of their eyes?
- Why do theology schools let the churches and missions send their candidates to non-formal trainings elsewhere, for vision formation and lately, for pastoral and leadership training?
- Who is missing the mark; the school, student or the sending agency?

We should also be asking questions for self-evaluation on the research practices in theology schools.

Self-Evaluation Questions for Theology Schools on Research Practices

- How is the term *research* perceived in theological education? Do schools define its expected outcomes in summative and formative terms?
- How adequately does a student get equipped in research and on-going learning through the academic programs in theology schools?
- Is the *research orientation* given in theology schools adequate to equip the student to conduct a qualitative inquiry with confidence?
- Do we have an academic system that is open enough to releasing the student to observe his/her context, get immersed in real life, make initial judgment on relevant issues and address them?

- What percentage of the research projects addresses real issues of people in context, particularly to impact a real future?
- What changes would have happened in the scenario of mission if the findings of the mission-ministry research projects were consistently followed up in the contexts of their inquiries?
- What accountability measures does our educational system have when schools fail to follow up on the findings of research were taken into action? Whose needs are being met and what is achieved?
- When faculty lack expertise in the mentoring and examination process, how would that affect the mission of the school, future of the student and the growth of the church? How should we handle these issues?

The Need for Focused Qualitative Research in Theological Education

Transformative learning has the research component at its core; it breathes life to education. It is about pursuing divine wisdom in human context. However, ironies pertaining to training are:

- training practices grow rigid even as theologies keep emerging and ministry contexts grow increasingly diversified;
- curriculum remain stagnant while poignant challenges in mission are on the rise;
- decades-old, ready-made answers are taught when real-life queries of students go unheeded;
- *content* becomes the focus although consultations endlessly dwell on the *context*;
- in spite of the limitless information amassed, in many cases, research results are not substantially taken back to the contexts of the inquiry.

There is still a long way to go in addressing the multiple gaps in learning and practice. A school that overlooks the need for self-learning and on-going practices of research is like a ship that strives to get across the river with its anchor still fixed to the shore. Students gain deep learning by tackling life's actual questions and, teachers offer the best of their teaching by setting the model of servant leadership in whatever context they serve. Transformative learning happens only when study becomes student's personal pursuit to reach a specific goal. Students who are overly depending on teachers' knowledge will have struggle in self-learning, reflection and action. Referring to the need of assessment and the critical interactions between the practitioners and the academic faculty, Smith suggests a privileged voice for the practitioners in the academic learning exercises, which is highly relevant in terms of qualitative research undertakings.

Theological schools will not be able to do good assessment of their academic programs unless they recognize the critical need to give a privileged voice to the practitioners-those who actually do the ministry for which the degree program is designed. This applies equally to the formation of women and men for religious leadership as it does for social work and medicine. While denominational officials and church bodies can certainly have either unreasonable or misinformed expectations of the full character of academic programs and culture, they are an indispensable source of insight and encouragement. Taking assessment seriously necessarily means that we recognize the critical place of field supervisors in both the learning of students and the evaluation of their learning. The critical piece in assessment, then, is the conversation between the practitioners and the academic faculty, which ultimately leads to the meaningful capacity of practitioners to inform the shaping of an academic program.[3]

We need to take a fresh look at the locale of research curriculum in theology schools. Ott states in his voluminous handbook on theological education, "Special challenges demand special competencies"[4]. Two factors that make any training sensible are: the ability to see the special challenges and the commitment to develop special competencies to resolve them. Does our curriculum nurture critical knowing by research practices stimulated and formed in the academic programs? This critical knowing could be defined however as the "striving not just for knowledge in books, but knowledge about how to live out in the world."[5] Empirical research integration in learning process offers a transformative feed to the theology students who face several new waves of change in the world where they live. Their world is becoming more and more virtual and detached, and, until they reach out, dialogue and participate with, connections will only be a mirage. Gnanakan wrote on the need for research in theological institutions,

> We will need to encourage much more independent research. Unfortunately "spoon-feeding" has continued even at post-graduate levels defeating the whole purpose of their degrees which were intended to enhance the students' appreciation of a particular field. In some cases, there does not seem to be any difference between the MDiv and the MTh Degree programs. If post-graduate study has to do with independent research, then all that is required is a supervisor or mentor and the available library resources for research. Sprawling campuses and large buildings will hardly matter as

3   Gordon T Smith, 'Faculties that listen, Schools that Learn: Assessment in Theological Education' 229-245 in Malcom L Warford (ed) *Practical Wisdom on Theological Teaching and Learning* (New York: Peter Lang, 2004), 238.

4   Bernhard Ott, *Understanding and Developing Theological Education*, Cumbria: Langham, 2016, 7.

5   Limatula Longkumer, "Theological Education as Critical Engagement" 115-122 chapter in *Communion on the Move: Towards a Relevant Theological Education*. Ed by Wati Longchar, P Mohan Larbeer (Bangalore: BTESSC, 2015), 121.

it is what is within those edifices that will help or hinder the student's stimulation for research.[6]

In order to revive the philosophy of a school regarding the research integration in curriculum, first, the school has to engage in a critical research on its own practice.

In the broader spectrum of academy–world relationship, the underlying scheme of the book advocates to explore newer patterns in areas such as: Student's learning to happen in the real ground of church's mission in the world, Concrete designs of the interchange of learning and action that help church and the theology schools flourish reciprocity in worship, work and wisdom in the world, Deliberate acceptance of the church and missions in the academic domain of theology schools to share, critique, guide, aid for research, and to serve as an accountability partner in the research practices, and, Assessing the outcome and impact of the research endeavours in each theology school to help determine *why we do what we do* and *how should we do what we do* and, most importantly, *to what end we do what we do.*

Purpose Statement of this Book

This book, therefore, suggests that qualitative research practices, designed and carried out intentionally, have the inherent potential to bridge the unfavourable gap between the theology academia and church's mission in the world today. A basic puzzle for theology schools is regarding the impact of their research projects on the real contexts of human needs and dilemma. It is estimated that adding value and direction to the qualitative research undertakings in theological education can bring about tangible results in academy–world bridging and thus a phenomenal growth in the mission of the church in contexts that make the grounds for the inquiries. Aiming at an audience that consists of students, faculty and academic–administrative leadership in theology schools, the book is primarily divided into the conceptual and practical aspects that are vital to current discussion. It is intended that this book provides the researchers and mentors with a clear vision of the transformative practice of qualitative research and motivate them to conceive and employ this methodology as a highly potential connector between the academy and the world.

The proposition here is that the careful design and implementation of qualitative research, beside all other forms and dimensions of learning, is central to the formation of the students in theological thinking, social skills in ministry, and transferable personal competencies and practical wisdom. Hence, the following chapters

- provide theoretical and practical bases of qualitative researching in theological education, addressing themes such as methodological foundations, primary

---

[6] Ken R Gnanakan, "Postgraduate Theological Degrees" 53-60 *AETEI Journal* Vol. 9 No. 1 Jan-June 1996, 55-56.

genres, ethical principles, theoretical frame, literature review grid, designing of research, methods of data gathering, data analysis, essential research skills and mentoring;

- appreciate the effectuality of qualitative research in exploring complex situations in human life holistically and competently;
- show that qualitative study is used not as an easier option, but a highly rigorous as well as relevant method in addressing the problems of the multi-layered social world;
- draw attention to pertinent aspects of transformative thinking and learning as a life pursuit; and, most importantly,
- invite those engaged in theological education to take active steps to evaluate the current practices and to ensure that all research and learning is for the church, in the world.

The chapters in this book contain initial thoughts aimed to provoke further thinking on effective qualitative researching rather than a comprehensive body of knowledge on the topic. The thoughts presented are not exclusive in terms of the scientific side of research, but supplementary to the existing knowledge and the practices. Admittedly, important of all, is the call for a review of our research practices for purpose and effectiveness and this is done side by side with the laying out of foundational guidelines for students to follow.

CHAPTER 1

THE QUALITATIVE METHODOLOGY
TERMS AND FOUNDATIONAL GRID

SECTION CONTENTS:

- Theology Researcher as a Thinking Practitioner
- Research: A General Introduction
  - Natural Sciences and Humanities
  - Theoretical and Practical Research
  - The Empirical Milieu in Theological Research
- Social Research: The Qualitative and Quantitative Types
- Enhancing Deeper Learning: Educational Indicators
- Shaping Research in the Methodology of Practical Theology

Theology Researcher as a Thinking Practitioner

Researchers are typically classified as either thinkers or practitioners. These stereotypes present thinkers as producers of exclusively theoretical research that advances knowledge, corrects errors in the existing knowledge, or critiques concepts or formulates new theories. And, practitioners as those limit their inquiry to exploring contexts, generating field information, surfacing issues and investigating assumptions and so on. Although terms like theory and practice can help us comprehend the domains of knowledge in ideological and real-world senses, researchers and mentors sometimes tend to advance unhealthy tensions between both. Holding academics, faith and ministry in balance in a scholarly inquiry is the challenge for the theology researcher, while, for the mentor, it is facilitating this sort of a transformative learning practice. Wisdom, faith and practice must go hand in hand for the theologian. One separated from the other can be utterly damaging.

Perspectives can shift when the inquirer starts connecting the *purely theoretical* to the *essentially practical* levels in research. For instance, an arduous *argument against eating food offered to an idol* takes on a careful reconsideration when the researcher personally visits a Hindu community where all food is offered to idols or where the essential connection made between the missionary and the context happens at a fellowship meal where such food is served. For another example, excavating the theological implications of the *koinonia* theme in M. M. Thomas'[1] thinking will be different from the actual working out of it in a complex socio-religious setting. Exclusive theoretical processing of information is not the same as gaining essential practical insights about a human social reality. Thus the task of the theology researcher is handling knowledge and experience in critical balance. There are unheard stories, unspoken dilemmas, unimaginable problems that keep calling researchers to critically review what they initially thought the realities were and what they assumed the hermeneutic should have been. This leads one to a refreshed reading of the scripture, empathetic understanding of human struggles, critical hermeneutical analyses and a correlative reflection exercise before suggesting solutions or formulating theories.

Chapters in this book, hence, present the process of qualitative social research in enabling the theology researcher to handle the theory-practice grid in balance and how illuminating it can be for the inquirer and his/her Christian ministry. Ideas presented communicate to the researcher as well as the mentor simultaneously in two basic directions: providing information for qualitative research undertakings, and, provoking thinking about solid connections between the church, mission and the academy. The first two chapters cover more ground on the conceptual foundations of qualitative research and therefore, could be heavy-reads for beginners. Through eight chapters this book calls for the incorporation of qualitative thought-action processing in making transformative theological education.

Research: A General Introduction

Research is re-search into something—seeking newer dimensions of knowledge, identifying issues, bridging gaps, building theories in the existing body of knowledge. It is the product of inquisitive minds that seek to raise critical questions and make systematic analyses where the task is not just ploughing the ground, rather, particularly digging for gold. In other words, academic research is not about going broadly on several important matters, rather, focusing on a specific problem, studying in depth.

---

[1]   M. M. Thomas was a World Ecumenical Leader from Kerala, India, who served the World Council of Churches from 1968 to 1975 and wrote over 60 books including, *The Christian Response to Asian Revolution* (London: SCM, 1966); *The Acknowledged Christ of Indian Renaissance* (London: SCM, 1969); and *Salvation and Humanization: Some Crucial Issues of the Theology of Mission in Contemporary India* (Madras: CLS, 1971).

Social science identifies the three major methodological approaches of Positivist Social Science, Interpretive Social Science and Critical Social Science.[2]

This chapter outlines the development of qualitative researching as a distinct methodology in deeper learning. The terms and their meanings given below provide us with helpful signals for impending sections.

- Research Methodology: Overall logical procedure in the inquiry
- Research: Inquiry, study, project, process
- Research Approach: The particular path taken in research
- Research Methods: Specific techniques and tools used to collect the data
- Researcher: The student, interviewer, observer, inquirer
- Research participant: Interviewee, respondent, object, sample, informant, the observed
- Empirical Research: Research using direct empirical/experiential evidences
- Sample: Specific cases in the population selected for the research endeavour
- Data Collection: Process of gathering information to address the research problem
- Variable: A concept that varies (e.g., 'marital status' is a variable that has different attributes)
- Attributes: Categories of a variable (married, unmarried, single, divorced etc. are attributes of the variable 'marital status')
- Stimuli: Any means such as questions, pictures, objects etc. used to stimulate the generation of data from the research participants
- Hypothesis: A statement of assumption or prediction to be tested in quantitative method; used also in qualitative (e.g., Grounded Theory)
- Model: A clearly defined overall framework that shows the working of a phenomenon
- Concept: An idea deriving from a given model
- Theory: The sum of interconnected sets of concepts used to define and explain the reality

Natural Sciences and the Humanities

There are natural sciences like Agriculture, Biology, Chemistry, Geology, Physics, Mathematics and social sciences such as Economics, Geography, History, Political Science, Psychology and Sociology. Humanities division consists of Religion, Philosophy, Arts and Literature. The idea that scientific methods are not compatible

---

[2] Refer for details, W. Lawrence Neuman, *Social Research: Qualitative and Quantitative Approaches*, 2nd Edition, (Boston: Allyn & Bacon, 1994), 55-77.

with humanities subjects is prevalent in the positivist line of thought in research. We also see novice researchers in practical theological disciplines often getting confused with the expression *scientific research methods*. The method of science is understood as systematic, provable and testable. Basically, research is known as the logical and systematized form of analysis of a phenomenon for the accumulation of reliable knowledge. Attitude of science has been traditionally known by characteristics such as, logical, generalizable, abstract, public and empirical, that which rests on the data we can sense. Science in its conventional bearing has no inherent interest in individual cases since the goal is logically meaningful generalizations.

Research, in its simple definition, is the method of analysis that involves a careful, critical and logical investigation in seeking facts. However, the study of beliefs, behaviour and experiences of people as closely related to the dimensions of sociology, psychology and organization, instigated a whole different wave of research practices emerged in across the humanities arena in its own logic. In the social sciences, the term methodology applies to how one conducts the research. The processes, principles and procedures by which a problem is addressed is also dependent on the researcher's questions, interests, assumptions and goals. Heitink used Swanborn's summary of the traditional differences of natural sciences and human sciences[3] as shown below.

Figure 2: Differences between Natural Sciences and Human Sciences

Natural Sciences	Human Sciences
Quantitative	Qualitative
Positivistic	Naturalistic
"From the outside in"	"From the inside out"
Spectator Perspective	Participant Perspective
Objective	Subjective
Explanation	Understanding
Causal explanations	Attribution of meaning
From facts and numbers	Through those surveyed
Structure-directed	Process-directed
Surveys and experiments	Participatory observation, unstructured interviews, documents
Variable language	Common language
Hard	Soft

3   Gerben Heitink, Trans. By Reinder Bruinsma, *Practical Theology: History, Theory, Action Domains* (William B Eerdmans: Michigan, 1999), 222-223.

In spite of these divisions, however, attempts to link the logical frontiers (rationalism) and its experimental frontiers (empiricism) are accepted to be valid scientific social research. Ultimately, the scientific method is "one and the same in the branches (of science) and that method is the method of all logically trained minds."[4] Therefore, the contention here is that the natural sciences and humanities are not to be set one against the other. We see them as logical methods appropriated to the body of knowledge and to the types of research questions designed.

Theoretical and Practical Research

Research is the activity of the logical minds that seek to make connections between the world of ideas and the world of phenomena. Generally across academia, *theoretical research* is referred to as conceptual research, library research, basic research or fundamental research. Common synonyms for *practical research* are, applied research, field research or empirical research, based on the distinctive ways in which the inquiry is conducted. When theoretical research aims at a new bit of theoretical knowledge or a new development in the existing concepts, the practical research focuses on change and improvement in a situation where practical applicability of knowledge is of prime value. The key focus in theoretical research is the formulation of theory, rather than seeking practical solutions to a problem, in spite of the fact that certain theories can have intrinsic problem-solving baselines. In principle, nevertheless, the theoretical researcher is satisfied as he/she is able to broaden the area of knowledge by generating, improving, comparing or contrasting theories, or bringing to light the ignored theories. The academic discipline of theology is producing great research projects on various aspects of Christian faith and living. Theories of considerable practical application too are developed through exegetical research, literary critiques and hermeneutical analyses. Martin Luther's outstanding example illustrates how the thorough inquiry in the Scriptures and the traditions of the church could impact a paradigm shift in the walk and talk of the then world and ever since.

However, while theoretical research generally remains to be a rational investigation between concepts, the practical/field study proceeds from an empirical investigation of contexts, persons or events. While the theoretical approach attempts to *develop or critique theories in the formation of church liturgy*, practical research would turn more towards *exploring the impact of liturgical symbols and practices on the worshipping community*. The latter focuses on identifying the practical issues and advocating practical remedies. Nonetheless, many have wrongly perceived that practical research has no conceptual underpinnings. In reality, practical research

---

[4]   C R Kothari, *Research Methodology: Methods and Techniques* (New Delhi: Vishwa Prakashan, 1990), 11.

proceeds from and critically explores on the body of existing knowledge, certainly supported with relevant conceptual foundations. It achieves meaning and coherent reflection through the careful analysis of the existing theoretical frame and the existing theoretical constructs. Standing aloof from the literary and conceptual undergirding, practical research lacks authenticity. As far as theological education is concerned, the normative theoretical base of the scripture is running all through the reflection and analysis. Every other theoretical concept and construction is viewed through this lens.

It is therefore, contended that since knowledge is found in the frames of theory and practice, both are valid and they complement each other in their own logic and advantages. Emphasizing one over the other therefore does not comply with a lucid scientific approach. Furthermore, both these types are now being progressively combined in academic research.

Scholars attempt to make sharp distinctions between the theoretical and practical frames of research probably due to the differences in the procedures involved. Theoretical research is customarily more dependent on texts, records, or similar sources, which if once gathered, then the researcher can carry out the study at home or in the library in isolation. To get familiar with the philosophical currents in the field of study and to apprise the historical development and shifts in the relevant concepts, the researcher would be immersed in critical reading and writing for months. Practical or field research is more concerned with gathering qualitative data from places and people and hence, normally demands extensive travelling and the tedious process of scheduling appointments with the research participants. Experience proves that both types are worthwhile as well as demanding. For example, formulating fundamental theories on Islamic and Christian theological interaction could be as challenging as exploring practical strategies towards Muslim-Christian social harmony in a given place. Practical research works with an immediate situation or selected group of people, normally aiming some level of problem-solving. Russell Bernard speaks with reference to anthropology, "Research is a craft…Research isn't *like* a craft. It *is* a craft…It takes practice, practice and more practice."[5]

The challenge therefore is exploring the possibility of integrating theory and practice in the research practices in theological education. Theology schools are already discussing within themselves how not to teach theology as abstract theory and how to employ unconventional methodologies in theological study. This is all about teaching theology in response to human queries, contemporary situations or the most challenging quests of the church today. When learners are taken out of their

---

[5] H Russell Bernard, *Research Methods in Anthropology: Qualitative and Quantitative Approaches,* 4th Edition, (New York: Altamira Rowman and Littlefield Publishers, 2006), 1.

social contexts for the duration of training that prevents transformation and growth, because it obstructs the ability to see and connect. Newer patterns of internship models to bring church and seminary to a position of mutual learning and serving each other toward the same goal are dimensions toward integration. This proposal in no way seeks to let go of the cognitive aspect in learning, but carefully attends to how not to lose the practical dimension in training. By purpose, this book focuses on the transformative theory-practice reinforcement in learning and towards which, the subsequent sections discuss the empirical milieu in research.

The Empirical Milieu in Theological Research

The term *empirical*, denoting *research using empirical evidences* has been derived within the board scenario of practical studies. This term, which has won much attention in theological studies in recent decades, is used in the current discussion synonymously with practical research and at times, with reference to qualitative methodology. The word *empiricism* derives from Greek *empeiria*, which means *experience*, referring to a way of gaining knowledge by direct and indirect experience or observation. This is the approach that derives knowledge from observed phenomena from actual experience rather than from theories or fixed understandings. Given the simplest definition, it is identifying a problem and reflecting it on the five W's (what, when, where, who, why) and the two H's (how, how much).

As explained elsewhere, those who perceive empiricism as an approach in opposition to the logical frontiers (the rational modes in theoretical research, i.e., systems of belief regulated by reason) fail to see how these function as two sides of the same coin. They are not dichotomies rather they are methods of knowledge that help to make sense of the social realities by building bridges between theories and human experience. Scholars in social research have observed,

> If empirical findings outrun logical constructions (theories, laws), science is at a loss; logical construction would have to catch up before the new empirical findings can be put in their place. Conversely, if logical constructions go ahead of empirical investigation that may not be regarded as so serious, because, there will always be a scope for something to come up in the empirical realm to fill the new branch of logical development and provide an interpretation for part of the structure that was not interpreted before.[6]

Hence we recognize that the advancement of knowledge is a continuing interplay between logical constructions and empirical frontiers. Empiricism proceeds from knowledge by first-hand experience of social reality, investigating the patterns of

---

[6]   T S Wilkinson & P L Bhandarkar, *Methodology and Techniques of Social Research* (Bombay: Himalaya Publishing House, 1996), 5.

relationship between events. Empirical research is gaining greater acceptance today than ever before, probably due to the felt urgency in academia to make sensible responses to the emergent cultural, epistemological and perspectival challenges of the twenty-first century. However, discussions continue regarding the reliability and credibility of empirical evidence in investigating particular aspects of the social world such as attitudes, feelings, authority, emotions, and opinions. Experts like Neuman[7] introduced several techniques in social research developed to observe and measure such aspects of the social world.

Like any other stream of academics, theological studies also operate across a wide range of research approaches, both theoretical and practical. This is because, theological education is "...holistic and a life-long process of nurturing and transforming the people in communities. It is a living practice, a living experience, a process which includes the attitudes, values, and relations of both students and teachers. It stresses wholeness, integrity, and interrelatedness."[8] Theological studies cover a number of departments such as Biblical Studies, Church History, Theology, Missions, Religions, Counseling, Psychology, Christian Ministry, Homiletics, Christian Education and so on. While *textual research* takes on the synchronic, diachronic, hermeneutical and exegetical methods, *historical research* follows historical comparison, chronological analysis, historiography and biographies. Linguistic research, anthropological research and cross-cultural mission research are particularly significant in mission studies. Creditably, in all of these, practical research has won a unique regard and logical standing in the past four decades.

Empirical research in theological education intends to amalgamate knowledge with real life through first hand experience with social reality. The approach is taken on the fact that to claim any knowledge of the context in which the church and society exist, experiential engagement is crucial. The researcher in theological education has to learn by experiencing the current realities and addressing the relevant issues. This knowing is grounded in actual experiences, perceptions and the deepest queries of people. However, doing this sort of inquiries in theology would presuppose hermeneutical skills in advancing critical reflections on the scripture. The practical theology researcher seeks wisdom from other departments in theology and relevant correlations with other academic disciplines towards achieving a rounded view of the reality. In this critical task of integration, students sense a tension between class room and real life and, that makes them grow into the role of a reflective practitioner who functions on firm theological grounding. The first

---

[7]   W. Lawrence Neuman, *Social Research: Qualitative and Quantitative Approaches*, 2nd Edition, (Boston: Allyn & Bacon, 1994), 6.

[8]   Limatula Longkumer, 'Theological Education as Critical Engagement' 115-122 in *Communion on the Move: Towards a Relevant Theological Education*, Wati Longchar and P Mohan Larbeer (eds.), (Bangalore: BTESSC, 2015), 118.

venture into empirical research might open up the avenue for real-life knowledge to the students that remained unknown to them before. This critical pedagogy of engagement enhances hands-on learning where: new discoveries are found, life's deepest questions are encountered, theoretical knowledge is put to hard tests with human situations/experiences, biblical interpretations are revisited for deeper clarity, theological values are deliberated against the research findings and newer patterns of thinking and models of ministry are formed.

Van der Ven suggests five principles that should inform the research practices in theology as:

- researcher's prejudices come into play throughout the research process;
- empirical researcher participates in the life world of those human beings whose praxis is studied;
- an historical dimension is involved in all research endeavours;
- research participants' multi-dimensional life context needs to be taken into account; and
- researcher has to take an ideological-critical point of view about societies.[9]

Generally, empirical research is conducted to answer a specific question/problem, or sometimes, test an assumption. When data is acquired in numbers/specific measurable formats, it is said to be *quantitative*; when narrative, it is *qualitative*. We will now explore more on the qualitative and quantitative approaches in social research.

Social Research: The Qualitative and Quantitative Types

Social Research designates a collection of methods people use to produce knowledge systematically. It is an exciting process of discovery, but requires persistence, personal integrity, tolerance for ambiguity and interaction with others. Social researchers creatively combine theories with facts in a systematic way to understand, describe, analyse and explore social life. They attempt to find patterns of regularities in social life on the basis of logical and empirical observations. The task involves the intellectual interaction between ideas and evidences in correcting, extending, revising or testing observations through data collection and analysis. Thomas Kuhn's ideas about paradigm shift[10] in 1962 helped in a certain extent to demystify what was known, until then, to be the unmistakable pursuit of scientific inquiry carried by detached professionals. Social science steadily introduced the powerful movement

---

[9]   J A Van der Ven, 'Empirical Methodology in Practical Theology: Why and How?' *Practical Theology in South Africa*, 9 (1), 29-44 (1994).

[10]   Thomas Kuhn, *The Structure of Scientific Revolutions* (Chicago: Chicago University Press, 1962).

of qualitative research that challenged the long-standing claims of positivist science and technology as *having all reliable knowledge.*

Social research methodology has two major sub-divisions: Qualitative and Quantitative. Although field-based sociologists and anthropologists engaged in qualitative inquiry earlier, it was in 1970s when this methodology gained a distinct currency in multiple forms of social research. In qualitative research, says Mason,

> You will be working out the intellectual and practical implications and consequences of all elements in the unfolding research process, and in all the research decisions you make. This emphasis is a continual activity, in both thinking and doing, in my view not only is essential to the production of good qualitative research, but also potentially places qualitative researchers in a rather special position as particular kinds of research practitioners.[11]

Qualitative research is both complementary to, and transcendent of, conventional scientific inquiry. According to Lincoln and Guba,

> Qualitative methods are stressed within the naturalistic paradigm not because the paradigm is anti-quantitative but qualitative methods come more easily to the human-as-instrument…Indeed there are many opportunities for the naturalistic investigator to utilize quantitative data-probably more than are appreciated.[12]

Considering qualitative and quantitative methods as complementary strategies, Auerbach and Silverstein list the significant characteristics of the qualitative research as:

- it directly investigates subjective experience;
- it incorporates meaningful stories in addition to measurable variables;
- it allows for naturalistic observation and description, rather than testing general laws;
- it is a tool for studying diversity;
- it uses research participants as expert informants and it involves reflexivity and the explicit use of researcher's subjectivity and values.[13]

Qualitative method follows its own logic in handling the social phenomena. Oliver writes;

> Positivist perspective tends to assume that the research methods of the natural sciences may generally be applied to the social sciences, including education. Positivism

---

[11]   Jennifer Mason, *Qualitative Researching* (Thousand Oaks, CA: Sage, 1996), 164.

[12]   Y S Lincoln and E G Guba, *Naturalistic Inquiry*, (Beverly Hills, CA: Sage, 1985), 198-199.

[13]   Adapted from Carl F Auerbach and Louise B Silverstein, *Qualitative Data An Introduction to Coding and Analysis*, (New York: New York University Press, 2003), Chapter 3. 22-284.

tends to be associated with the use of quantitative data. Interpretivism is associated with a number of perspectives used in research including phenomenology, interactionism, feminism, ethnography and action research. Such perspectives tend primarily to employ qualitative data.[14]

Since the qualitative approach is based on the interpretivist social tradition, it focuses more on generating theories as an essentially different methodological tradition from the positivist, rational, linear paradigms in quantitative research. The qualitative methodology follows methods including ethnomethodology, phenomenology, hermeneutics, and symbolic interactionism. However, there is no strict rule that empirical research should only employ qualitative methods. The researchers can effectively integrate quantitative methods as the topic and the research question require. According to Mason, the qualitative research "usually does some form of quantification, but statistical forms of analysis are not seen as central".[15] This approach in social research seeks to understand, interpret, reflect, evaluate, and/or discuss a sociological reality, using themes, concepts, motifs and taxonomies. The strength of qualitative research lies in the informality of communication and the iterative (repetitive, recursive and systematic) nature of the data process. Ethnography, cultural analyses, autobiography, historical research, gender studies and studies in religions are examples of this.

Qualitative research offers flexibility to use various methods for data generation, which include official records and document analyses, observation techniques, photographs, videos and narrative methodologies and many more. *Method* in qualitative research is more than a practical technique in data gathering; it refers to the process of data generation through a variety of analytical and interpretive activities. Fundamentally, the qualitative approach as a comprehensive and rigorous procedure has to:

- Be systematically and rigorously conducted
- Be strategically conducted, yet flexible and contextual
- Involve critical self-scrutiny by the researcher, or active reflexivity
- Produce social explanations to intellectual puzzles
- Produce social explanations which are generalizable in some way or which have a wider resonance
- Not be seen as a unified body of philosophy and practice, whose methods can simple be combined unproblematically
- Be conducted as an ethical practice, and with regards to its political context.[16]

---

[14] Paul Oliver, *Writing Your Thesis* (Sage publications: London), 2008), 22-23.

[15] Jennifer Mason, *Qualitative Researching* (London: Sage, 1996), 4.

[16] Extracted from Jennifer Mason, *Qualitative Researching* (London: Sage, 1996), 5-6.

Researchers sometimes use the wrong reasons in their choice for qualitative approach. Schwandt puts it clearly thus,

> Sadly, some researchers seem drawn to qualitative inquiry for the simple fact that they do not wish to "deal with numbers". This is tragic. First, it is based on faulty reasoning-there is nothing inherent in the epistemologies of qualitative inquiry that prohibits the use of numbers as data. Second, such a stance can be based in the illusion that so-called qualitative inquiry is somehow easier to do than so-called quantitative inquiry....These inquiry tasks simply require different kinds of awareness, knowledge and skills.[17]

He went on explaining that it is not the hard and fast labeling of epistemologies that matters to us, "rather, we are confronted with choices about how each of us wants to live the life of a social inquirer."[18] For instance, take the three epistemological stands in qualitative research–Interpretivism, Hermeneutics and Social Constructionism. The interpretivist standpoint argues that the human social action is intrinsically meaningful and therefore, our inquiry must enable us to understand and interpret the meanings that constitute an action. The *philosophical hermeneutic* sets itself against the interpretivist notion that humans *produce* understanding and argues that "understanding is not, in the first instance, a procedure or rule-governed undertaking; rather, it is a very condition of being human. Understanding *is* interpretation."[19]

The hermeneutical task is not simply about freeing oneself from biases but rather, engaging one's biases concretely in the learning process, exploring the path to take ahead in thinking and action. The social constructionist epistemology in qualitative research is based on the view that knowing is active in human life and we always construct knowledge at a backdrop of the lived realities of perceptions and practices. Qualitative data typically follows a process of induction to develop a new theory which is grounded in the original data and normally, it is much more voluminous than the quantitative data. It seeks detailed written commentaries, the methods demonstrate causal relationships and are guided by practical measurements rather than fixed theories. Generally, qualitative research is used to address a specific problem, enhance understanding for certain areas of study, combine detailed research with case studies or at times, test a hypothesis. Often, the theories proven can work in a real world environment rather than just in a controlled situation.

---

[17] Thomas A Schwandt, 'Three Epistemological Stances for Qualitative Inquiry 292-331 chapter 7 in *The Landscape of Qualitative Research: Theories and Issues* (2nd Edition), Norman K Denzin and Yvonna S Lincoln (eds) (Thousand Oaks: Sage 2003), 320.

[18] Schwandt, 'Three Epistemological Stances for Qualitative Inquiry' in *The Landscape of Qualitative Research'*, 2003, 320.

[19] Schwandt, 'Three Epistemological Stances for Qualitative Inquiry' in *The Landscape of Qualitative Research'*, 2003, 30.

The quantitative approach is concerned with quantifying social phenomena in a rational, positivist and linear pattern. This enables one to quantify social issues, collect and analyse numerical data, and focus on the links among a smaller number of attributes across many cases. Methods are based on the positivist model of testing out theories in the natural sciences. In quantitative data, inferential statistical methods may be employed to develop possible causal connections between variables. While quantitative tools are analysed, usually there is little for detailed discussion in the full-length research report. Attempting to measure, enumerate, codify and explain a topic, quantitative social research uses variables and statistics effectively in the religious, economic, political and sociological disciplines. Meticulous and quantifiable fact-gathering techniques are statistically analysed.

This research approach follows fixed methods that are scientifically validated and makes claims on reliability in producing the same result if study is repeated in the same conditions. Statistical analyses, content analyses, surveys, experiments, data mining, structured observation, structured interviews are common methods. Research in positivist paradigm aims to be objective and value-free. Data is collected and research report presented in the logical structures in line with the scientific propositions. The positivist-quantitative research report usually contains the sequence: "theory (deduction)---------hypothesis (operationalization)-------- observations/data collection (data processing)---------data analysis (interpretation)- -------findings (induction)."[20]

Tensions sustain between the qualitative-quantitative debates. Qualitative research is termed by some as unscientific and the researchers are called soft scientists or journalists. They discard the possibility for any qualitative research to authentically verify the truth statements, which come in the form of opinions or personal bias. Denzin and Lincoln reports the sharp criticisms by positivists who opined on newer qualitative paradigms thus, "ethnographic poetry and fiction signal the death of empirical science, and there is little to be gained by attempting to engage in moral criticism."[21] Unhealthy criticisms cause multiple setbacks in the production of knowledge and the social developmental prospects. Padgett puts it this way, "some quantitative designs provide grass-roots views (e.g., household surveys) and many a qualitative study has become unhinged from its context and floated off into the realm of biased speculation."[22] Interestingly, the qualitative domain in itself is not free from tensions. There are criticisms between those who follow the lived experience

---

[20]   Mark J Cartledge, *Practical Theology: Charismatic and Empirical Perspectives,* (Cumbria: Paternoster, 2003), 77.

[21]   Norman K Denzin and Yvonna S Lincoln, 'Introduction: The Discipline and Practice of Qualitative Research', 1-46 in *The Landscape of Qualitative Research,* 2nd Edition. (Thousand Oaks: CA, Sage, 2003), 12.

[22]   Deborah K Padgett, *The Qualitative Research Experience,* 'Introduction: Finding a Middle Ground in Qualitative Research' 1-18, (Belmont, CA, Wadsworth/Thomson: 2004), 4.

or the performance turn. According to Weiss, there are evaluation theorists who claimed that it was impossible to combine qualitative and quantitative approaches responsibly within an evaluation.[23] Five ways in which qualitative research differ from quantitative are:[24]

- Uses of positivism and post-positivism
- Acceptance of postmodern sensibilities
- Capturing the individual's point of view
- Examining the constraints of everyday life
- Securing rich descriptions

Figure 3: Differences between Quantitative and Qualitative Approaches[25]

QUANTITATIVE	QUALITATIVE
Test hypothesis that the researcher begins with	Capture and discover meaning once the researcher becomes immersed in the data
Concepts are in the form of distinct variables	Concepts are in the form of themes, motifs, generalizations, taxonomies
Measures are systematically created before data collection and are standardized	Measures are created in an ad hoc manner and are often specific to the individual setting or researcher
Data are in the form of numbers from precise measurement	Data are in the form of words from documents, observations, transcripts
Theory is largely causal and is deductive	Theory can be causal or non-causal and is often inductive
Procedures are standard, and replication is assumed	Research procedures are particular, and replication is very rare
Analysis proceeds by using statistics, tables, or charts and discussing how what they show relates to hypotheses	Analysis proceeds by extracting themes or generalizations from evidence and organizing data to present a coherent, consistent picture

Research in theological education cannot achieve the expected results by randomly following some form of methodology and method. It reaches beyond into the task of doing theology. Perhaps the awareness that the theology researchers

---

23   CH Weiss, *Evaluation*, 2nd Edition, (Upper Saddle River, NJ: Prentice Hall, 1998), 268.

24   Norman K Denzin and Yvonna S Lincoln, 'Introduction: The Discipline and Practice of Qualitative Research', 1-46 in *The Landscape of Qualitative Research*, 2nd Edition, (Thousand Oaks: CA, Sage, 2003), 14-16.

25   W. Lawrence Neuman, *Social Research: Qualitative and Quantitative Approaches*, 2nd Edition, (Boston: Allyn & Bacon, 1994), 317.

mostly needs is that the knowledge derived from both the quantitative and qualitative types constitute only part of our understanding of the society and that they have to accomplish the higher task of theologizing. The transformational vision in learning has been explored and reinforced by experts in the formal education over many decades. The section below makes a pointer to the role of transformative engagement in *deeper learning,* which is the essential terrain in qualitative researching.

Enhancing Deeper Learning: Educational Indicators

This concise section on educational indicators is intending to motivate researchers to explore how these theories work for themselves and others. A consistent emphasis on holistic learning is identified are varying levels in the educational theories, which will serve to supplement the case for integrated qualitative research in theology. Benjamin Bloom's educational taxonomy introduced the conceptual framework for learning that grows from *remembering content* to *creating content*[26]. This design of instruction built content knowledge through the processes of remembering, understanding, applying, analysing, evaluating and creating. The pedagogical instrument in the design encompassed the cognitive, affective and psychomotor learning domains. So, learning is not static or fixed, it is progressive and transformative for the individual as application and further steps make it firmly ground-related.

Lee Shulman[27] developed a table of learning claiming to offer a more constructivist approach in learning and teaching with the corresponding features of:

- Engagement and Motivation
- Knowledge and understanding
- Performance and action
- Reflection and critique
- Judgment and design
- Commitment and identity

The accreditation handbook of the Association of Theology Schools observed the usefulness of Shulman's taxonomy in theological education thus, "While Benjamin Bloom's taxonomies are widely known and used by instructional designers and measurement specialists, the taxonomy developed by Shulman might be more useful to seminary faculty and administrators....for him, learning involves all of

---

[26] From the original Bloom's Taxonomy of Educational Objectives in 1956 that used nouns such as knowledge, comprehension, application, analysis, synthesis and evaluation, this revised version came in 2001, using verbs and with slight rearrangements.

[27] Lee Shulman, 'Making Differences: A Table of Learning', Article in Change, The Magazine of Higher Learning 34(6):36-44, November 2002.

one's being."[28] Shulman's concepts of engagement and the table of learning that do not situate in a hierarchy have been gaining more approval in the assessment of theological education.[29] This process of deep learning starts off with the most critical learning principle that is, *engagement*, as conceived in the critical pedagogies of engagement as McGee articulates, "Shulman believes that learning begins with engagement as conceived in Edgerton's work on 'pedagogies of engagement.' Engagement may indicate a variety of approaches to providing for learning in terms of being cognitively engaged (I understand and want to know more), physiologically engaged (I am paying attention), emotionally engaged (I have a vested interest), or strategically engaged (I am in 'in the action'). Evoking engagement in a learning object design is a challenge; each learner may have different ways they are engaged. Additionally, the learning experiences that are wrapped around, proceed, or follow a learning object interaction may affect the engagement of the learner."[30] Meaningful research endeavour will engage the student cognitively, physiologically, emotionally and strategically.

For research projects in theology to be transformative learning experiences, students need to engage in multiple dimensions of learning. Evoking engagement is perhaps one of the most difficult task in learning because that is the thickest wall that every researcher has to break all through in the process. Deeper Learning Principles (DLPs) point out the standards of a logical research practice that engages the learner who actively reflects, explores and creates knowledge. The symbiotic learning experiences in the DLP in the Carmean's[31] typology include the following:

- <u>Active</u> learning involves solving real-world problems; using judgment and exploration; situated in action; emphasis on practice and reinforcement; involvement in real-world

- Learning that is <u>social</u> provides opportunities for cognitive apprenticeship; reciprocity and cooperation among students; prompt feedback; encouragement of contact between student and faculty; emphasis on rich, timely feedback.

[28]   Handbook of Accreditation Section Eight, Association of Theology Schools 'A Guide for Evaluating Theological Learning.' 14-17. http://cf2015.bhcarroll.edu/files/session-2-toward-a-learning-century/assessment/assessment-handbook-section8-ats-harris.pdf accessed on 25 June, 2017.

[29]   Refer, Lee S Shulman and E R Kieslar, *Learning by Discovery: A Critical Appraisal,* (Chicago IL: Rand McNally, 1966) and Lee Shulman, *The Wisdom of Practice: Essays on Teaching, Learning and Learning to Teach,* Edited by Suzanne M Wilson, (San Francisco: Jossey-Bass, 2004).

[30]   Patricia McGee, 'Learning Objects: Bloom's Taxonomy and Deeper Learning Principles', Department of Interdisciplinary Studies & Curriculum and Instruction, The University of Texas at San Antonio, Abstract published online <http://educ3.utsa.edu/pmcgee/nlii/LOBloomsMcGee.doc> accessed 25 June 2017.

[31]   Carmean, C. Mapping the Learning Space. Referred from Patricia McGee, 'Learning Objects: Bloom's Taxonomy and Deeper Learning Principles' Paper at Department of Interdisciplinary Studies & Curriculum and Instruction, The University of Texas at San Antonio, USA. faculty.coehd.utsa.edu/pmcgee/nlii/LOBloomsMcGee.doc accessed on 20 April, 2017

- Contextualized learning builds on existing knowledge and is integrated into the learner's world; knowledge is demonstrated; deep foundation of factual knowledge; consideration of leaner preconceptions; focus on how the world works; facts and ideas in the context of a conceptual framework; concrete rather than abstract
- Engaged learning addresses diverse talents and ways of learning; high expectations; high-challenge, low-threat environments; intrinsic motivators and natural curiosities.
- Learning encourages ownership so that learners can organize knowledge in ways that facilitate retrieval and application; learner control of own learning; time on task; learner independence and choice; time for reflection; higher order thinking

Research in theology, as in any academic setting, requires extensive designs and applications to facilitate deeper learning, particularly with the aim of transformation of the persons and their social environment. Learning is not external, it is internal and, envisioning transformation beyond the immediate action into life-long impact.

Furthermore, the principles of adult learning theory or andragogy demonstrate potential insights that the qualitative research practices in theology can draw from. Knowles' four principles of adult learning provide certain indicators for the design of research in theology settings. They are:

- Adults need to be involved in the planning and evaluation of their learning
- Experience (including mistakes) provides the basis for the learning activities
- Adults are most interested in learning subjects that have immediate relevance and impact to their job or personal life
- Adult learning is problem-centred rather than content-oriented.

Knowles listed the following five assumptions on adult learners[32]:

- Self-concept: As a person matures his/her self-concept moves from one of being a dependent personality toward one of being a self-directed person
- Adult learner experience: As a person matures he/she accumulates a growing reservoir of experience that becomes an increasing resource for learning
- Readiness to learn: As a person matures his/her readiness to learn becomes oriented increasingly to the developmental task of his/her social roes
- Orientation to learning: As a person matures his/her time perspective changes from one of postponed application of knowledge to the immediacy

---

[32] Refer Malcolm Knowles, *The Adult Learner: A Neglected Species,* 3rd Edition, (Texas: Gulf Publishing, 1984), 12. Also, Malcolm Knowles, *Andragogy in Action* (San Francisco: Jossey Bass, 1984).

of application, and accordingly his/her orientation toward learning shifts from one of subject-centeredness to problem-centeredness.

- Motivation to learn: As a person matures the motivation to learn is internal.

How does theological study as an adult undertaking facilitates research and learning? We may need to think alongside the methodological procedures in Practical Theology. The enlightenment era's working on the hierarchy of academic disciplines had caused the fragmentation of learning and that is deeply engraved both in the systems and the minds. However, the discipline of practical theology seems to have a resolution to handle this persistent problem of compartmentalization by sound theological and pragmatic methodology. Various world views, denominations, departments, approaches, methodologies and human experiences interlace the task of theological research. Political, pastoral, psychological, philosophical, narrative-based, gender studies, empirical and Marxist focuses are interwoven in the theologian's task. Children, women, tribal communities, the disabled and the disadvantaged- all become real concerns for the researcher. The inquiry begins not from a hierarchy of academic disciplines, rather a genuine point of human experience, a need or a challenge. Its process of exploration is eclectic as Swinton and Mowat wrote about practical theology's role that "locates itself within the diversity of human spiritual and mundane experience, making its home in the complex web of relationships and experiences that form the fabric of all that we know."[33] As an academic discipline within theology, practical theology can inform our philosophy and practice of transformative qualitative research.

Shaping Research in the Methodology of Practical Theology

The critical interfaces between qualitative research and practical theology are expounded by Swinton and Mowat[34], who also introduced the model of practical theology as action research. Neither practical theology nor qualitative research follows a single standardized method; but they possess similar characteristics such as procedural diversity, focus on human social reality and the action-reflection-action process. Browning (1983 & 1991) identified an acute tension between theology and social sciences within Practical Theology due to the fact that the methods and approaches of the social sciences have frequently been an important dynamic within the process of practical theology inquiry. Without necessarily attempting to correlate the two, this section explores areas that are central to the learning methodology in practical theology.

---

[33]   John Swinton & Harriet Mowat, *Practical Theology and Qualitative Research*, 2nd Edition, (London: SCM, 2016), 3.

[34]   Swinton and Mowat, *Practical Theology and Qualitative Research,* 2016.

The discipline of Practical Theology assumes a wide-ranging audience in its frame of thought and contribution: Scholars, theology students, theological educators, mission leaders, pastors, believers, and people in the wider society- and learning is influenced by all of them. The researcher's realization of an audience comprised of consistencies beyond the theology scholars can change the entire momentum of inquiry. Miller-McLemore preferred a descriptive rather than prescriptive definition for practical theology and affirmed the multivalent nature of the discipline in terms of "four distinct enterprises with different audiences and objectives"[35] namely,

- A discipline among scholars
- An activity of faith among believers
- A method for studying theology in practice, and,
- A curricular area of sub-disciplines in the seminary.

Ogletree recognizes practical theology not simply as a branch but as the central intent of theology saying,

> Practical theology is not one of the branches of theology; the term practical rather characterizes the central intent of theology treated as a whole. Where distinctions are made among discrete theological tasks, it is better to speak of dimensions of practical theology, not of practical theology in opposition, let us say, to historical theology or philosophical theology. Theology is practical in the sense that it concerns, in all of its expressions, the most basic issues of human existence...Theology does have a theoretical side. Yet the theoretical does not stand in opposition to practical knowledge. It arises as a moment within practical theology itself, a moment in which, relatively speaking, we distance ourselves from the immediacies of experience.[36]

It is not only multiple audience but multiple tasks and analytical dimensions as well. A coherence definition for mentoring task in practical theology research follows the multi-dimensional task orientation in the discipline: Descriptive-empirical task (What is going on?), Interpretive task (Why this is going on?) Normative task (What ought to be going on?) and Pragmatic task (How might we respond?). Ogletree divided the learning task conceptually, referring to three dimensions[37] such as the Meaning dimension (Truth aspect), the Action dimension (Pragmatic/ Ministry aspect), and the Self dimension (Personal Formation aspect). Learning

---

[35] Bonnie Miller-McLemore, 'The Contributions of Practical Theology', in *The Wiley Blackwell Companion to Practical Theology*, Ed. Bonnie Miller-McLemore (Oxford, UK: Blackwell Publishing, 2012), Kindle Edition. 923.

[36] Thomas W Ogletree, 'Dimensions of Practical Theology: meaning, Action, Self' 83-101 in Don S Browning (ed) *Practical Theology: The Emerging Field in Theology, Church and World* (San Francisco: harper and Row, 1983), 85.

[37] Thomas W Ogletree, 'Dimensions of Practical Theology: Meaning, Action and Self' in *Practical Theology: The Emerging Field in Theology, Church and World*, 1983, 90-93.

happens by interweaving these methodological grids and researchers are equipped to test and affirm the transformative scope of their work for themselves. In similar tone, Brookfield and Hess identified the three pedagogical emphases in theological endeavour as: "a commitment to continuously researching the pedagogic contexts in which we work and to responding publicly to what we learn from the research, a deliberate attempt to treat learners as adults with the attitude of respectful attention to student's experiences this implies, and modeling a public, critically reflective engagement in spiritually grounded learning."[38] Above all these, we recognize that effective practice of qualitative theological research has to set standards to meet the ultimate objectives of theological education such as:

- Progression of holistic practices in teaching and learning
- Interdisciplinary explorations and formation of reflective thinking and practical theological wisdom
- Enrooting of *mission focus* at the core of theological education
- Authentic engagement of students in expression of views, dialogue, and participation in action
- Lessening of the long-debated gap between church and seminary
- Hands-on experience of the ground realities of the church and society

Towards this end, qualitative research in theology can draw a number of guiding principles from the discipline of practical theology for effective learning and research as depicted below.

Problem-Based: Researcher seeks answer to a question/problem that actually exists. The research problem in qualitative study is a real problem that is experienced, realized and explained in a given context. Inquiry starts from the problem and the researcher grapples with questions that are concrete, ensuring that the goal, process and results are all real and life-oriented. Thus genuine issues emerge, greater clarity about the methodology obtained and functional interventions sought. However, the study is not problem-centred for the theology researcher, but God-centered. Precisely, the context and the issue is the starting point, but the inferences are grounded and directed in God's perspective for human beings according to the scriptural revelation. Osmer's proposal of practical theological model of interpretation has four essential tasks: the descriptive-empirical ('what is going on?'); the interpretive task ('why is it going on?'); the normative task ('what ought to be going on?'); and, the pragmatic task ('how might we respond?')[39]

---

[38] Stephen D Brookfield and Mary E Hess, 'How can we Teach Authentically? Reflective Practice in the Dialogical Classroom' 1-18 in Mary E Hess and Stephen D Brookfield (eds), *Teaching Reflectively in Theological Contexts: Promises and Contradictions* (Florida: Krieger Publishing Company, 2008), 4.

[39] Richard R Osmer, *Practical Theology: An Introduction* (Grand Rapids, MI: Eerdmans, 2008).

Learner-Centered: Because the research problem arises from the student's own context, student is not a detached professional rather, an active participant in the process of study. Not a spectator of events in a community; rather the one affected by those events and committed to act in the context. This is a significant characteristic that integrates the researcher's experience effectively in the process of inquiry by design. The researcher has to explore and immerse in the experiences of the persons or communities in the study. Noticeably, narratives and parables are used in the methodology of practical theology not only as genres in research but as critical experiential learning points for self-reflection and theological wisdom. According to Anderson, "what makes theology practical is not he fitting of orthopedic devices to theoretical concepts in order to make them walk. Rather, theology occurs as a divine partner joins us on our walk, stimulating our reflection, and inspiring us to recognize the Living Word."[40] Learner learns to approach theoretical theology and practical challenges of the church in the world with the new insights of practical wisdom, critical mediation, culture-theology balanced hermeneutic and a deep concern for the world and the church.

Action-Oriented: What inspires the ardent practical theologian in the tiresome path of research is not the accumulation of abstract knowledge or the award of a degree; it is a sustainable practical contribution, grounded in theological wisdom. Practical theological research is about responsive undertakings where a situation or process that someone feels should be changed is studied.[41] Researcher as a practitioner holds that theory without practice is hollow and that this practice must have solid theoretical foundation. One of the guiding factors in the mentoring process is this action/mission orientation. That is why research mentors that employ the pedagogy of engagement in the process usually make deeper impact in terms of mission. This pedagogy of engagement is defined as, "…an experiential approach to education that invites faculty to meaningfully engage students in interpersonal relationships, rooted in the values of mutuality and dignity. By acknowledging an embodied, intersubjective, dialogical approach to education, faculty members are able to engage the varied hermeneutics that emerge out of the richness of diversity while confronting the underlying objective and objectifying tendencies of a persistently biased, power-laden culture."[42] Mission focus in practical theological research integrates the reflection of theory and practice, interdisciplinary learning and, language and narratives etc. and, the role of mentor in the process is crucial. Handling human

---

[40]   Ray S Anderson, *The Shape of Practical Theology: Empowering Ministry with Theological Praxis* (Illinois: Inter Varsity Press, 2001).

[41]   Gerben Heitink, Trans. By Reinder Bruinsma, *Practical Theology: History, Theory, Action Domains* (Michigan: William B Eerdmans, 1999), 225.

[42]   Roy E Barsness and Richard D Kim, 'A Pedagogy of Engagement for the Changing Character of the 21st Century Classroom' 89-106 in *Theological Education*, Vol.49, Number 2 (2015), 90.

problems, mediation and essential skill development are considered crucial tasks in practical theology.

Critically Reflective: Relegating the discipline of Practical Theology to a simplistic academic form of field study has been disadvantageous to the theological enterprise. This is primarily because such positions are built on flawed understandings regarding the methodology. The discipline indeed sets a critical reflective task in the learning methodology that embeds a competent theory-practice equilibrium. Apparently, it is our naive approach to field education that forms in us a mindset that *this thing is not that academic*! This flawed perception should be reviewed through the practice of qualitative theological research. Studebaker and Beach articulate, "The critical need is to help students make the art of theological reflection on Christian life and ministry a life-long practice. This discipline has often been relegated to field education, which lingers on the margins of the academy. The theological curriculum often treats field education as a second-class citizen... Field education should be integrated with the more academic side of the theological curriculum and not only run parallel to it."[43] We recognize that mentors have a great role to play in advancing the impact of qualitative study in academia. Even across the fields within theological education we need schemes and constructions to nurture critical reflection of theology and context. Hence, practical theology researcher is not the one gathering some easy-to-handle information from the field but critically engaging with life's realities cognitively, affectively and practically. Longkumer puts it this way, "Critical engagement is about engaging the whole mind, body and soul in learning and understanding, not mere theoretical and abstract content of factual information... It is also about critical analysis and reflection in the reality of the contemporary world because theological education is a praxis education context. It is action-reflection in the reality of people."[44]

Hermeneutically Balanced: The methodology of the practical theologian is hermeneutical from beginning to end. As stated by now, the researcher does not confine learning to field study or empirical explorations alone. Grounded hermeneutical undertakings such as contextual hermeneutic, biblical/theological hermeneutic and theory-practice hermeneutic underpin the entire learning process. The researcher has to be intentional in balancing the theological vision of knowing, doing and being. In other words, qualitative researcher in theology bridges the gaps hermeneutically in the historical, philosophical, cultural, geographical, missional and theological aspects in the context. We nonetheless recognize this for the researcher

---

[43]   Steven Studebaker and Lee Beach, 'Friend or Foe? The Role of the Scholar in Emerging Christianity' 43-56 in *Theological Education*, Vol. 48, Number 2 (2014), 53-54.

[44]   Limatula Longkumer, 'Theological Education as Critical Engagement' 115-125, in *Communion on the Move: Towards a Relevant Theological Education* (Bangalore: BTESSC, 2015),116.

as a difficult assignment that require multiple answers to conflicting issues from a wide variety of angles.

Biblically Grounded and Theologically Operational: Practical theologian's act has to get far beyond the duty of a social worker or activist precisely due to the revelatory, prophetic and eschatological mission involved. According to Wood, "theological education is a complex affair largely because theological inquiry is a complex affair… In the first place, theological inquiry involves several distinct academic disciplines, or families of disciplines".[45] He explained the other sort of complexity as the expectation to engage in the threefold operation that corresponds essentially to the structure of theological inquiry, which Martin Luther referred to as *oratio, meditatio* and *tentatio* meaning respectively, prayer, meditation and testing. Moment of attentive, receptive listening, moment of reflection and the moment of appropriation. The norm that guides the reflection and action is God's Word and it does not breed confusion in spite of the proliferation of human struggles. Aiming to achieve orthopraxy without this orthodoxy will just be mere drudgery.

Research by its very design, engages the student in actual experiences in ministry and thus makes learning not merely preparational, but operational as well. Biblically grounded research embeds a prompting to set out in mission with the outcome of the study, in spite of the challenges and demands. "If teachers do their work well, their students will come to appropriate at a deep level that the integration to which practical theology points calls or life-long learning and is finally an eschatological hope. They will take up their ministries with a readiness to struggle on an ongoing basis with these issues, continually deepening the level at which they reach out for wholeness and fullness of being."[46] Learning and research thus extend from the academic content to a theological mandate for the active engagement in mission.

Standing on the solid biblical-theological ground, the researcher consistently explores how to allow substantial space for interpretation, reflection and wisdom. Amidst the current worldviews that deny claims of absolute truth, the practical theologian takes the position that God's truth is absolute and that only can help the confused world to find authentic answers to their questions. The postmodern perspective holds that there is no such thing as a universally acceptable true account of a situation. Truth therefore is considered relative from person to person and context to context. As from context to context, the same issue may gather data that differ much in the social, religious, political, emotional and cognitive perspectives,

---

[45]   Charles M Wood, *An Invitation to Theological Study* (Pennsylvania: Trinity Press International, 1994), 6-7.

[46]   Thomas W Ogletree, 'Dimensions of Practical Theology: Meaning, Action and Self' 83-104 in *Practical Theology: The Emerging Field in Theology, Church and World*, Don S Browning (Ed) (San Francisco: Harper & Row, 1983), 100.

some researchers look for a workable and shared reality or a set of meanings that constitute a true account of a social reality. The concept of data saturation assumes that the vigorous collection of data from multiple sources using multiple methods processed through a very careful analysis and inference move towards a closer approximation of the human reality. Still some others take the stance to suspend every other claim until proven otherwise as a shared reality. While all these suggest various ways of looking at human problems and essential existential questions, the theology researcher analyse all of these on the truth of God revealed through Jesus Christ. God's eternal design in Jesus Christ about restoring the depraved world back to him contains the infinite and comprehensive wisdom that humans need, irrespective of the diversity of culture or the intensity of the problem. This foundation has to underpin the task of practical research and the researcher is the one who vigilantly uncovers this wisdom through genuine reflection and research.

Analytically Correlational: In theology scholarship, this characteristic is also referred to as *critically correlational*. Tracy used the expression *critical correlational*[47] to describe how various theological categories will function at the intersection of the various conversations[48]. In the complex task of combining situation and theological analyses, practical theologians "...seek the reintegration of experiences, but on a higher, more critical level of awareness and with a fuller mobilization of our powers of being. We seek above all a more mature understanding of the complexity of life, and hence, a determination to resist simplistic solutions that unify experiences only by truncating it, by closing out some of its crucial aspects."[49] In a more philosophical line, Heitink lists the multiple currents in operation within the field as: the normative-deductive current, hermeneutical-mediative current, empirical-analytical current, political-critical current and the pastoral-theological current.[50] Researcher in theology aims to formulate a design that correlate these dynamics meaningfully to the level that theology can answer to the critical questions of other disciplines regarding the hardest questions about reality and meaning. The researcher as the analytical thinker and practitioner attempts to make a theological-practical response to life's issues also by interdisciplinary or cross-disciplinary correlations. Holistic learning and mentoring practices facilitate attempt to integrate such correlations in research, opening up for the researcher the wider horizon of wisdom. "Studies in development psychology, sociology of religion, and political economy provide us

---

[47]   Aiming to maintain a dialogical method of critical correlation between the Christian tradition and the questions post by the postmodern worldviews, Tracy used the slightly modified version of the concept of critical correlation introduced by the protestant theologian Paul Tillich (1965).

[48]   David Tracy, *Blessed Rage for Order: The New Pluralism in Theology* (Chicago: Chicago University Press, 1975), 79.

[49]   Ogletree, 1983, 100.

[50]   Heitink, *Practical Theology: History, Theory, Action Domains* (Michigan: William B Eerdmans, 1999), 171-177.

with a new angle of vision on our quest for the appropriate enactment of Christian faith. They surface dynamics that constrain and channel our action possibilities. They suggest the sorts of skills and competencies likely to be requisite for effective action amidst those realities making up our social existence."[51] Researchers, in such environment of transformative engagement, fearlessly immerse in the inquiry by relevant correlations and develop better clarity about their theological convictions. Others normally sink in mediocrity, confusion and distraction with regard to the stated objectives of the study.

We have seen some of the indicators in practical theology that correspond with the theoretical guild of qualitative methodology and thus, serve as pointers to a holistic learning. "Training qualitative researchers require someone to train the mind, the eye, and the soul together."[52] Practical, qualitative approach, as discussed, is an established domain in social research that facilitates the coherent development of the learner in thinking, reflection, evaluation and application. For this *deep learning* to occur, a strategic design that sets in active engagement and critical reflection is crucial.

---

[51]   Ogletree, 1983, op cit, 93.
[52]   V J Jenesick, *Stretching Exercises for Qualitative Researchers*, 2nd Edition, (Thousand Oaks, CA: Sage, 2004), 2.

Reflection Box:
Whose voices are not heeded?

Student A & B submitted a paper, applauding the economic achievement made by a strategic farming scheme in the given village. They spent days visiting libraries and government offices and had gathered over thirty literature resources, copies of short documentaries and statistical data from the government- all highlighting what could be literally termed an economic paradigm. A & B got the theory right.

For the research in the final year, A & B decided to set out to live in this farm area for a few months. There, the farm fields showed them a radically different side of the story. They saw a community that suffered intense economic exploitation behind the so called economic development. The major portion of the daily income of these poor, lower class, and mostly illiterate people was being looted off by their landlords. The inhibited community suffered threats, false promises, lies, mental torture and physical abuse. The land owners would stop A & B from talking or making any association with the villagers saying, "Ask us, we will answer all your questions. These people are insane. Fools, they don't know anything." A & B developed an action research design aiming at improving the conditions of the people side by side with researching.

CONSIDER:

- Whose story is not heard?
- When does a story become a whole story?
- When we focus on one particular class in a community for data gathering how does it impact our view of the reality?
- How much of caution to be maintained in balancing theory and practice?
- When issues regarding development and justice are handled, how important is it to listen to many voices?
- How many academic disciplines A & B must excavate and how many practical challenges to face to transform this village community?
- Why the biblical mandate is crucial for students who are to reach out to the suffering world around them?

CHAPTER 2

PRIMARY GENRES IN QUALITATIVE APPROACH

SECTION CONTENTS:

- Phenomenology
- Ethnomethodology
- Ethnography
- Case Study
- Action Research
- Grounded Theory

Qualitative research, as discussed in the previous chapter, is a dynamic form of inquiry in social research. This chapter presents the basic genres or approaches in qualitative research. *Genre* simply means *a category that has a particular form.* An introductory reference line for further exploration and implementation on the primary genres are provided in sections below without attempting to make a comprehensive text.

The first four genres outlined here focus heavily on data gathering approaches, while *Action Research* has its added insight on practice engagement and improvement and *Grounded Theory* retains its commitment to its on-going process of analysis. Overall, the six genres presented in this chapter intend to help researchers to figure out the value of each and hence arrive at clear decisions on the approach to take in their particular topic.

Figure 4: Primary Qualitative Genres

GENRE	DESCRIPTION	TASK
Phenomenology	Method that makes sense of social realities exclusively from people's points of view	Understand how people use social interactions and interpretations to maintain an ongoing sense of their social realities
Ethnomethodology	Method people use in making sense of their world	Recognize how the commonsense social facts from individuals make sense of a reality
Ethnography	Method of people in making, articulating and maintaining a culture collectively	Reconstruct the history/ description of the culture
Case Study	Method of studying the detailed account and analysis of one or more cases	Observe closely and probe deeply into a given case of individual or community
Action Research	Method of researching with people in a given action-situation towards improved practice	Instigate improved understanding and wisdom and a more effective practice
Grounded Theory	Method of analysing knowledge that is grounded in the empirical data	Attempt to inductive analysis of grounded data towards the development or evaluation of a theory

Phenomenology

Philosophers Edmund Husserl[1] (1859-1938), Martin Heidegger[2] (1889-1976) and sociologist Alfred Schutz[3] (1899-1959) are key developers of this research approach. Phenomenology investigates social reality as grounded in people's experience and articulations by focusing on the constructs people rely on to make sense of their social environment, rather than individuals themselves. The researcher develops an order of intellectual constructs on different levels and simultaneously retains a coherent base of knowledge purely from the people's point of view. It starts from a perspective free of hypotheses and any pre-determined thoughts on outcomes.

The fundamental query in phenomenological approach is, 'what is the meaning, structure and essence of the lived experience of this particular phenomenon by an individual or a community?' In other words, it brings to fore people's experience, preferably cohesions across people rather than specifics of an individual. For example, studying believers' experience of an unhospitable pastor, the researcher explores the real life experiences of the believers towards gaining knowledge of their experiential environment. The phenomenon of unhospitable pastoral function can also help the researcher to make distinctions between the hospitable and unhospitable pastoral styles. The phenomenological methods seek to explore the meaning of individual lived experience, as Patton elaborates, "how they perceive it, describe it, feel about it, judge it, remember it, make sense of it and talk about it with others."[4]

This approach is rather descriptive in nature than explanatory in addressing how individuals experience a phenomenon and articulate it. The researcher gets into the lived experience of a phenomenon mainly through in-depth interviews to gather people's descriptions of their own experience. Research participants' oral or written self-reports and any aesthetic expressions such as poetry, art or narratives are useful sources. Unique expressions of the research participants are analysed to discover the *essence* to an experience and also to compare it with others who also have had that experience. Hence, a study on the experience of female Syrian refugees in other countries will explore their identity struggles, transitional hardships, feelings of rejection and realization of the need for courage as they describe the lived experience in their terms. Data analysis follows an emergent strategy that carefully trails the

---

[1]   Edmund Husserl, *Ideas Pertaining to a Pure Phenomenology and to a Phenomenological Philosophy*, Trans. By F Kersten, (Springer Science and Business Media: 1983). Also see, Dan Zahavi, *Husserl's Phenomenology*, (California: Standford University Press, 2003). Martin Heidegger, *The Basic Problem of Phenomenology*, Transl. by Albert Hofstardter, (Indiana: University Press, 1988).

[2]   Martin Heidegger, *The Basic Problem of Phenomenology*, Transl. by Albert Hofstardter, (Indiana: University Press, 1988).

[3]   Alfred Schutz, *Phenomenology of the Social World*, (Illinois: Northwestern University Press, 1967). Alfred Schutz, On Phenomenology and Social Relations (University of Chicago Press, 1970).

[4]   Michael Quinn Patton, *Qualitative Research and Evaluation Methods*, 3rd Edition, (Thousand Oaks, CA: Sage, 2002), 104.

nature of the data. For example, an evocative/artistic/poetical data will be analysed differently from the interview data.

The growing interest to study the experiential side of faith and religion has led this methodology to rapid acceptance in theological studies. It challenges the naïve positivist approach to spiritual experience and faith and emphasizes on praxis, theological reflection, action, interpretation of faith and the social dynamics of experiences of spirituality. The phenomenological approach is seen as theologically, philosophically and historically vital and is being explored more than ever today in studies of comparative religions and the empirical domains in theological research. The researchers in theology undertaking phenomenological studies are not merely accomplishing it sociologically but also in profound theological dialogues and reflections.

Scholars have been excavating the interrelationships between philosophic theology and phenomenology from Friedrich Schleiermacher in the nineteenth century who held that religion is best understood as a kind of sensory awareness of the infinitude of being and Rudolf Otto in the twentieth century who referred to the numinous, the awestruck feeling of the wholly other and now continuing with the many contemporary scholars who engage in explicating the theology-phenomenology interaction[5].

The researcher in dealing with the meaning of the several individuals of their lived experiences, identifies a shared experience and how it is collectively experienced, locates the universal nature of the experience and the individual's experience of the shared phenomena, and attempts to recognize the essence of the experience.

Methods of sampling, data collection and analysis are fluid, iterative, complex and multi-dimensional in exploring people's experience. For example, a homogenous, purposive sampling (among many options), may serve well in the study of social phenomena such as, the increasing level of suicidal tendency in a given community or, adolescent children leaving their churches in large numbers in a given context, where the researcher follows a one-on-one semi-structured or open-ended interview method as guided by the research question. Then a four-stage analysis of data is done where the researcher; (1) does the initial reading of the data multiple times, content analysis of recorded information and reflective note-taking of all that was observed and learned, questions and concepts emerging, (2) returns to the data to derive concise phrases grounded in the transcriptions for deeper conceptual understanding, (3) revisits the emergent themes and cluster ideas according to the patterns of interconnections or for what is termed as conceptual similarities and develops a

---

[5] See e.g., Patrick Masterson, *Approaching God: Between Phenomenology and Theology*, (London: Bloomsbury, 2013).

structure of the phenomenon projecting the converging concepts and relationships, and (4) finally, designs the table/figure depicting the refined structure of thoughts with major themes and sub-divisions, illustrated briefly with corresponding cases or actual quotes from the participants.

This is a methodology applauded for the scope to make voices heard and surface deep issues. Its epistemological paradigm that centres on individual experience and interpretation of a phenomenon allows the research to reach beyond conventional assumptions and theories to actual reality. And, it overlaps with other qualitative genres including ethnography and ethnomethodology that are explored in the following sections.

Ethnomethodology

Combining the phenomenology of Schutz and sociology of Talcott Parsons, it was Garfinkel[6] who first used the term in his *Studies in Ethnomethodology*. Garfinkel focused on the study of ordinary society, where individuals work hard to maintain consistency, order, and meaning in their lives. The term *ethnomethodology* simply meant *methods of people*. It refers to the way in which the members of a community make *common sense* of their society. These common-sense social facts from several individuals are considered reflexively accountable. Ethnomethodology is thus, used to understand and explain the social situation people live in. It is about how people use social interaction and interpretation to maintain an ongoing sense of their life's realities. Built on the theoretical underpinnings of phenomenology and linguistic philosophy, this approach addresses people's reasoning of the social world using methods such as participant observations, conversational analysis in natural settings and unstructured interviews. The approach was developed in the 1960s at the linguistic turn of philosophy where language and use of language gained immense priority in social inquiries and thus took conversational analysis as a central feature.

Ethnomethodology developed its form from symbolic interactionism that set an alternative to mainstream sociological approaches. It grew neither as particularly prominent nor as a crucially problematic method and has been criticized for its relatively low capacity for meaning constructions in that what it tells is mostly what is already known. Nevertheless, the way in which conversations in real life settings are taken as the object of research has made remarkable influence on the conventional assumptions in social research.

Researcher in the conversational analysis method tape/video record conversations for detailed analysis attending to how conversation was initiated,

---

[6]   Harold Garfinkel, *Studies in Ethnomethodology*, First Edition, (Malden, MA: Blackwell publishers, 1967).

how interruptions occurred, why they occurred, what were major turns in talk, what were emotional expressions, where were the long pauses, silence, anger and so on. Authentic conversations for example, hold unique characteristics in engaging, expressing, articulating, responding, correcting, and agreeing and such social interaction produces the data.

The goal of conversational analysis is mainly to examine how conversation is organized. The underlying assumption is that it is not the formal logic, but the practical reasoning that helps people to make sense of their social world and function in it. However, Maynard and Clayman[7] questioning the tendency to impose homogeneity in ethnomethodology, outlined several subgroups within ethnomethodology such as theory, phenomenology, cognition, conversation analysis, research in institutional settings, studies of science and applied research. In terms of methods, it uses a variety of ethnographic methods including ethnomethodological experiments, conversational analysis, non-participant observation techniques and documentary analysis.

Ethnomethodology attempts to make social science ordinary by not distinguishing between *doing science and engaging in life's other activities*. It directs a radical standpoint against the traditional sociology of the day. Ethnomethodology researchers regard their subject they are studying as the product of accountability, *accounts* referring to the social constructs and creations from social interactions in the past. In other words, *accounts* are ways in which members in a community signify, describe or explain the properties of a specific social situation. Have's discussion on ethnomethodology emphasizing local accountability, time, local and time-bound features of social reality, detailed features of the production of social order, indexicality, indexical expression and reflexivity establishes an extensive view of the process.[8]

Theoretically, the object of ethnomethodology is social order taken as the community members' concern and at the same time is a clearly perceptible and shared reality. Two central principles are indexicality and reflexivity. Indexicality is that there is no such thing as clear definition in language as meanings come in reference to other words and the context in which the person speaks. There are indexical expressions that the research has to take into account. A statement is indexical when it is dependent on the embedded situation for its meaning. Reflexivity maintains that our sense of order is a result of conversational process that is created while talking. In ethnomethodology, reflexivity is not used as self-reflection rather to describe the

---

[7]   Douglas W Maynard and Steven E Clayman, 'The Diversity of Ethnomethodology' 385-418 in *Annual Review of Sociology,* Vol. 17 1991.
[8]   Paul ten Have, *Understanding Qualitative Research and Ethnomethodology* (Thousand Oaks, C A: Sage, 2004), 17-25.

resolve of meaningful action in context. As Shaw says qualitative conversational processes are "iterative in which each step leads to the next with a need to repeat each step at a deeper, more integrated level until arriving at meaningful themes that reflect people's views regarding the topic. Discovering these themes is the point of research."[9] This genre, therefore, is insightful and transformative when employed with clear understanding and direction.

Ethnography

Ethno denotes people or *folk* and *graphy* means *describe something*. Derived from cultural anthropology and qualitative sociology in the nineteenth century, this approach seeks to study how human groups collectively build and maintain a culture. Ethnography is the name of "the attempt to reconstruct the history of culture."[10] It is defined "as a noun it means a description of a culture or a piece of culture and as a verb, doing ethnography, it means the collection of data that describe a culture."[11] In this approach, the researcher undertakes a detailed investigation of specific groups, societies and cultures. Ethnography is referred to as the hallmark of qualitative inquiry and "the earliest distinct tradition."[12] An ethnographer is the one who inscribes (graph) the culture (ethnos). Having *culture* as the central concept, data are gathered at micro-level from the actions and interactions within the social group in the form of organizations, micro communities or social movements or macro-level, from countries using multiple methods in data generation, which could take long-term contextual immersion from multiple angles. The researcher's primary query is, "What are the cultural characteristics of this group of people or of this cultural setting?"

In discovering the culture of a group, the ethnographer goes deeper into beliefs, values, language, norms, rituals, dress codes, practices, and celebrations for example. Ethnography takes the forms of ethnology, which is the comparative analysis of cultural groups and ethno-history, which is the study of the cultural past of a community. Mission researchers and anthropologists consider various concepts as crucial in ethnography such as ethnocentrism, which is the problem of judging others with one's own cultural values; going native, the situation when the researcher

---

[9]   R Daniel Shaw, 'Qualitative Social Science Methods in Research Design' 141-151 in Edgar J Elliston, *Introduction to Missiological Research Design* (Pasadena, CA: William Carey Library, 2011), 149.

[10]   A R Radcliffe-Brown, *Method in Social Anthropology* (Chicago: Chicago University Press, 1958), 25.

[11]   H Russell Bernard, *Research Methods in Anthropology* (Thousand Oaks, CA: Sage, 2004), 16-17.

[12]   Michael Quinn Patton, *Qualitative Research and Evaluation Methods,* 3rd Edition, (Thousand Oaks, CA: Sage, 2002), 81.

gets completely immersed in the research setting in a way that guarding against subjectivity is no longer possible. Fetterman's[13] list is extensive.

- **Culture:** The broadest concept in ethnography that consists of beliefs, values and behaviours of a cohesive people

- **Key informant/key actor:** the individual or group that closely interact with the ethnographer.

- **Emic terms:** the specialized terms of the insider perspective, used in a particular culture.

- **Etic terms:** the specialized words used in the outsider's perspective by social scientists.

- **Holism:** the study of the unit as a whole rather than the sum of its parts and essential correlations. Forces researcher to seek beyond the immediate scene or experience.

- **Contextualization:** placing grounded observations and interpretations in a larger context.

- **Non-judgmental Orientation:** prevent contamination of data and any inappropriate or unnecessary judgments.

- **Structure and Function:** structure is the social configuration of a group like kinship and, function, the social relationship within the group. Ethnographers make skeletal structure and thread of social system.

- **Symbol and Ritual:** symbols are expressions of powerful feelings or thoughts and rituals, the repeated patterns of symbolic behaviour.

- **Operationalism:** a focused concept that directs the ethnography, establishing specific relationships between facts and interpretations.

Ethnography follows the rich variety of participant observation, case studies and sense-making. To understand the culture from the native point of view, the researcher documents the routine lives of people, spends months and years with them, discovers guiding themes evolving in the process of observation, and makes sense of a culture from an outsider bias-free point of view. While living with the community, the ethnographer uses field methods such as personal interviews, autobiographic interviews, participant observation, questionnaires, folktales, reviewing existing documents and many more.

Data analysis is done through stages such as: assessing relevance of key themes, locating patterns of relationship, exploring unique cultural perspectives, designing

---

[13]   David M Fetterman, *Ethnography: Step by Step*, 2nd Edition, (Thousand Oaks, CA: Sage, 1998), 16-29. Refer also, Janice M Morse and Lyn Richards, *Readme First for a User's Guide to Qualitative Methods*, 3rd Edition, (Thousand Oaks, CA: Sage, 2002), 40-44.

diagrams and charts, and presenting the themes and interpretation through rich descriptions. One aim could be to make the culture of a community known to the outside world based on the data gathered from first hand and participant experience within the community. It is exploring the insider's life by becoming an insider. Ethnography claims a holistic approach in that it carries out data collection and analysis concurrently, oscillating between groups and persons. Lately, ethnographers are using methods that integrate qualitative and quantitative techniques and often grounded theory.

There are variants within ethnography such as realist ethnography, critical ethnography and case study. *Realist Ethnography* is the traditional anthropological model of studying a culture from a bias-free, third person's perspective of life in a community. The ethnographer mostly uses participants' words for interpretations but the approach maintains objectivity in data by guarding it is uncontaminated by researcher's predispositions, judgments and political standpoints. *Critical Ethnography* is politically driven for the empowerment and transformation of persons and communities. The researcher openly recognizes the bias with which the study is undertaken, challenges status quo and links the issues in the community with socio-political power structures. *Case study* helps the researcher to inquire on unique cases using multiple sources of data and locate the case within the cultural context of the inquiry.

The ethnographer has to identify a culture-sharing community, learn their cultural patterns, draw themes from the culture by investigating the shared patterns in beliefs, behaviours and values, describe the culture in emic and epic terms, interpret the patterns of relationship within the culture, reflexive description of ethnographer's personal impact of the cultural context.

The relevance of an ethnography is determined on the questions[14] of Substantive Contribution (Does the research make a substantial contribution to understanding a social context?); Aesthetic Merit (Does the study do well aesthetically?); Reflexivity (How deep is the ethnographer's self-awareness and reflective skills to interpret life in the community?); Impact (How does this report challenge an outsider to think and act?); and Expression of Reality (Does the report provides a realistic and credible account of the cultural reality?).

---

[14]   L Richardson, 'Evaluating Ethnography' in *Qualitative Inquiry* 6 (2), 2000, 253-255.

Case Study

Case study is a qualitative research approach that provides a detailed account and analysis of one or more cases, which can be a group, organization, person, activity, event or a process. As a genre case study is a search to know precisely the deeper elements or characteristics of a case. The inquiry is intensive in the whole unit. It uses personal documents, official documents, life history, and all available resources that help the researcher have an overall view of the matter. The researcher asks this fundamental question: "What are the characteristics of this single case or of these many cases?" A wide range of data collection techniques can be employed such as observation, interviews, documents and narrative techniques. According to Gerring,

> For anthropologists and sociologists, the key unit is often the social group (family, ethnic group, village, religious group etc.). For psychologists, it is usually the individual. For economists, it may be the individual, the firm or some larger agglomeration. For political scientists, the topic is often nation-states, regions, organizations, statues or elections.[15]

Cohen and Manion explain Case Study's distinction from other experimental approaches thus,

> Unlike the experimenter who manipulates variables to determine their causal significance or the surveyor who ask standardized questions of large, representative samples of individuals, the case study researcher typically observes the characteristics of an individual unit-a child, a clique, a class, a school or a community. The purpose of such observation is to probe deeply and to analyse intensively the multifarious phenomenon that constitute the life cycle of the unit with a view to establishing generalizations about the wider population to which that unit belongs.[16]

The case study approach is interdisciplinary in nature and allows a broad variety of explanations and concepts in handling the cases. The final report of a case study provides a rich and holistic description of the cases studied. Consistency across cases can be a concern to the researcher although generalization is not the primary objective. "Credibility is increased when the researcher can show that core concepts and themes consistently occur in a variety of cases and in different setting."[17]

Cases and case study methods are diverse. *Extreme case* method selects a case because of its extreme value on an independent or dependent variable of interest. Studies on domestic violence may choose extreme instances of physical abuse of

---

[15]   John Gerring, *Case Study Research: Principles and Practices* (Cambridge: University Press, 2007), 1

[16]   Louis Cohen and Lawrence Manion, *Research Methods in Education* (London: Routeledge, 1994), (Reprint 1995), 106-107.

[17]   Herbert J Rubin & Irene S Rubin, *Qualitative Interviewing: The Art of Hearing Data* (London: Sage 1995), 90.

children. The *deviant case* method selects the case/s that, by reference to some general understanding of a topic (either a specific theory or common sense), demonstrate a surprising value. Case Study may be classified into further divisions that include:

- Intrinsic case study has interest only in understanding the particulars of the single, unusual case.

- Illustrative case study uses one or two cases to make an unknown phenomenon or issue known

- Instrumental case study uses a case to gain more insights into one issue or theme. It attempts to understand something more general than the case.

- Multiple/Collective case study addresses multiple cases in a single research study to provide insights into one issue/theme.

- Cumulative case studies aggregate information from several sources in several places and times

- Exploratory case study is normally used to pilot a large-scale research project. It is a condensed attempt to bring to light the need and authenticity of further inquiry.

- Historical case study aims to investigate the development of a particular phenomenon over time.

The case study approach ensures focus, often used to illustrate problems (teenage school drop-outs), or indicate good practices (social service organization systematically rehabilitating drug addicts). Survey model case studies and a few numbers of in-depth case studies are all possible. Social researchers may choose to study many cases superficially or select a few cases to study intensively. "Sometimes, in-depth knowledge of an individual example is more helpful than fleeting knowledge about a larger number of examples. We gain better understanding of the whole by focusing on a key part."[18] George and Bennett write the fundamental understanding of *case study* might mean:

> (a) that the method is qualitative (b) that the research is holistic, thick (a more or less comprehensive examination of a phenomenon), (c) that it utilizes a particular type of evidence (e.g., ethnographic, clinical, non-experimental, non-survey-based, participant observation, process-tracing, historical, textual or field research) (d) that its methods of evidence gathering is naturalistic (a "real life context") (e) that the topic is diffuse (case and context are difficult to distinguish) (f) that it employs triangulation ("multiple sources of evidence") (g) that the research investigates the properties of

---

[18]   John Gerring, *Case Study Research: Principles and Practices* (Cambridge: University Press, 2007), 1.

a single observation, or (h) that the research investigates the properties of a single phenomenon, instance or example.[19]

Experts have discussed the advantages and disadvantages of the Case Study method[20] illustrated in Figure 5.

Figure 5: Advantages and Disadvantages of Case Study

Advantages	Disadvantages
• Data drawn from people's experiences and practices are seen to be strong in reality • Case Studies allow for generalizations from a specific instances to a more general issue • Allows researcher to show the complexity of social life • Can provide a data source for which further analysis can be made. • May become a subset of a broader action research project • Data can be more persuasive and more accessible	• The very complexity of cases can make analysis difficult • Generalization may raise questions of credibility • False sense of confidence • Difficulties in collecting historical data • False generalizations • Cost and time factors • Possibility of error • Sometimes unorganized/unsystematic

Case Study is driven by deep insight. An early document by Waller explained it well, "The product of a good case study is insight, and insight is "the unknown quantity which has eluded students of scientific method. That is why the really great men of sociology had no "method". They had a method: it was the search for insight. They went "by guess and by God", but they found out things."[21] The researcher in case study is essentially an artist with great insight.

---

[19] Alexander L George and Andrew Bennett, *Case Studies and Theory Development* (Cambridge: MA: MIT Press, 2005), 17. George and Bennett define a 'Case' as an instance of a class of events. Refer also, John Gerring, *Case Study Research: Principles and Practices* (Cambridge: University Press, 2007), 17.

[20] Loraine Blaxter, Christina Hughes and Malcom Tight. *How to Research*, 2nd Edition, (Buckingham: Open University Press, 2001), 73.

[21] Willard Waller, 'Insight and Scientific Method', *American Journal of Sociology* 40:3 (November) 285-297, 1934, 296-297.

Action Research

The literature uses the term *action research* in many ways. It is referred to as "a term, process, enquiry, approach, flexible spiral process and as cyclic. It has a practical, problem-solving emphasis."[22] This is not a research on people, but with them and the researcher develops knowledge and understanding as part of practice. The researcher as the one who seeks to improve understanding of his/her practice, needs to maintain good group skills and knowledge of how to work as a facilitator while being a researcher.

> Action research begins with a process of communication and agreement between people who want to change something together ... [this group] then moves through four stages of planning, acting, observing and reflecting. This process may happen several times before everyone is happy that the changes have been implemented in the best possible way.[23]

Action research is used widely in educational and organizational research but can be employed in any research that is problem-solving oriented or practice-improvement oriented.

Action research aims to improve the subsequent practices in the given setting rather than producing theoretical knowledge of a situation. Improvement of practice reflects in the process of inquiry and the function of the case concurrently. Huang succinctly explains that unlike the conventional social science, the purpose of action research is "not primarily or solely to understand social arrangements, but also to effect desired change as a path to generating knowledge and empowering stakeholders. We may therefore say that action research represents a transformative orientation to knowledge creation in that action researchers seek to take knowledge production beyond the gate-keeping of professional knowledge makers."[24] Denscombe's action research model[25] consists of five elements: professional practice, critical reflection (identify problem or evaluate changes), research (systematic and rigorous enquiry), strategic planning (translate findings into action plan) and action (instigate change).

There are criticisms of action research that is conducted on the researcher's own field of practice. Participants are colleagues; they work within a system and therefore the ethical standards for credibility need to be enhanced. Moreover, the researcher must see the difference between doing their work and conducting the research. It is a flexible spiral process that accommodates research and development simultaneously

---

[22]   Patrick J M Costello, *Action Research*, (London: Continuum, 2003), 5.

[23]   Catherine Dawson, *Practical Research Methods* (New Delhi: UBSPD, 2002), 17.

[24]   Hilary Bradbury Huang, 'What is good action research? Why the resurgent interest?' 93-109 in *Action Research*, Vol. 8 (1), 2010, 93. Sage Publications DOI: 101177/1476750310362435

[25]   Martyn Denscombe, *The Good Research Guide for Small Scale Social Research Projects,* (Buckingham: Open University Press, 1998), 60.

in the process of "systematic reflection, enquiry and action carried out by individuals about their own professional practice"[26] Denscombe suggests that action researchers must make sure that official permissions are obtained, confidentiality maintained and, the identities of the participants protected. This is primarily because their practices and the changes envisioned can hardly be put in place without some knock-on effect for others who operate close-by in organizational terms.[27]

Participatory action research (PAR) serves improved capacity and participation of researchers to achieve practical outcomes of change and growth. PAR is also used as an acronym to explain the process:

- **P**lanning a change
- **A**cting and observing the process and consequences of change
- **R**eflecting on these processes and consequences and then, re-planning, acting and observing, reflecting and so on. (emphasis added)[28]

Since those affected by a problem are actively participating with meaningful observations, opinions, questions, analysis and initiations, both the research process and the participants' situation improve. While the focus of action research is on improving the practice and not the accumulation of theoretical knowledge, participatory action research develops a local theory that guides the application of learning in actual life. Action research simultaneously applies the insights while participatory action research waits for a more reflected-on, concrete local wisdom to take form before it is applied. However, these two are similar in the characteristics of active participation, open-ended purposes for improvement and deeper level of devotion on the part of the participants for problem-solving or practice-improving aims.

PAR aims at emancipation of the voiceless persons and communities from whom all forms of developmental actions should begin. It starts as a practical response to the crisis that a community faces and hence calls for active and full collaboration between the researcher and the participants. The researcher and the participants fully engage in an act of posing the pertinent questions and exploring methodical procedures to handle them. The cycle of research-reflection-action continues towards the emancipation of the community and possibly many more communities in its acquaintance.

---

[26]   P Frost, 'Principles of the Action Research Cycle' in R. Richie, A Pollard, P Frost and T Eaude (eds) *Action Research: A Guide for Teachers. Burning Issues in Primary Education*, Issue No. 3, (Birmingham: National Primary Trust, 2002), 25.

[27]   Martyn Denscombe, *Ground Rules for Good Research: A Ten Point Guide for Social Researchers*, (Buckingham: Open University Press, 2002), 63.

[28]   Stephen Kemmis and Robin McTaggart, 'Participatory Action Research', 567-607 in N K Denzin and Y S Lincoln Eds., *Handbook of Qualitative Research*, 2nd Edition, (Thousand Oaks, CA: Sage, 2000), 595.

Members in the community are active agents all through the process including, design of the study, implementation of action, communication of results, and further planning. Research informs the reflection of the community and these reflections deeply impact further steps in research. Members in the community investigated have significant roles in the validation of the data. Prior to embarking on research, the researcher has to consider factors such as time, resources and effort for such a transformative undertaking in a community.

Both Action Research and PAR are post-positivist approaches but with their own unique philosophies. While learning is chiefly the part of the researcher in action research, it is a collaborative activity of participants and the researcher in PAR. Action researcher facilitates change in a community while action is the shared process taken by the researcher and the participants in PAR. There is no expert in the participatory; participants take crucial role with the researcher in providing data on problems, methods and the entire process of development and change. The approach tends to be more holistic due to its working with the participants, while action research will be relatively subjective for the role of researcher and possible other experts in the process. While action researchers achieve improved capacity and wisdom, PARs demonstrate creativity in groundbreaking procedures in transforming structural assumptions.

Grounded Theory

Grounded Theory[29] is a major approach in qualitative research that sets a reasonable challenge to scholars who criticized qualitative methodology for not being scientific. It rapidly gained wider acceptance. It refers to the development of an inductive theory that is "grounded" directly in the empirical reality. The process of Grounded Theory is essentially analytical. The researcher reads and re-reads the corpus of field notes, to derive categories, properties and concepts that are immersed in the data and their patterns of relationships. The emergence of the theory grounded in the data is the central task. Although primarily inductive, the generation of data at times also follows deductive thinking.

Grounded Theory has special features. Various levels of data processing simultaneously happen with data gathering although comprehensive coding starts with the entire data at hand. The ability to perceive variables and relationships is termed as *theoretical sensitivity* and is affected by a number of things including one's reading of the literature and use of techniques designed to enhance sensitivity. Theoretical sensitivity is about being sensitive of what data is important in

---

[29] Barney G Glaser & Anslem L Strauss, *The Discovery of Grounded Theory: Strategies for Qualitative Research* (New York: Aldine Publishing Company, 1967). A. Strauss & J Corbin, *Basics of Qualitative Research: Grounded Theory, Procedures and Techniques* (Newbury Park, CA: Sage Publications, 1990).

developing the theory. Grounded Theory does not require pre-research literature review. In a view to facilitate maximum theoretical sensitivity, this feature guards the researcher from being impacted by borrowed concepts. Theorists may embark the review of literature while coding the memos. This method generally views taping and transcribing the data as counterproductive as the researcher might hurry to delimit the data by what is on the written notes and jump to conclusions. Talks on the theory under construction are not encouraged for the fear that it would drain the researcher of motivational energy.

Grounded Theory method aims to: Formulate functional hypotheses based on conceptual ideas and allow emergence of theories; sometimes test or elaborate upon previously generated theories; verify hypotheses that are generated by constantly comparing conceptualized data on different levels of abstraction, and these comparisons contain deductive steps; and discover the main concerns of the participants and how they continually try to resolve it. The on-going questions are "What's going on?" and "What is the main problem of the participants?" or "How are they trying to solve it?" General elements in the Grounded Theory research design are:[30]

- Question formulating
- Theoretical sampling
- Interview transcribing and contact summary
- Data chinking and data naming (Coding)
- Developing conceptual categories
- Constant comparison
- Analytic memoing
- Growing theories

Grounded Theory's data is never limited to formal methods of interviews or questionnaires. Anything that helps the researcher to have a rounded understanding of the problem and the generation of the theory is valid data. Grounded Theory holds that everything the researcher encounters in the research context is theoretically sensitive to be analysed. Field notes can come from informal interviews, lectures, seminars, expert group meetings, newspaper articles, internet mail lists, even television shows, conversations with friends, etc. Handling the corpus of qualitative data in the form of field notes, code notes and theoretical notes, the researcher writes brief notes to oneself that are called memos. Memoing, which is theorizing of

---

[30]   Anslem Strauss and Juliet Corbin, *Basics of Qualitative Research: Grounded Theory Procedures and Techniques*, 2ⁿᵈ Edition, (Newbury Park, CA: Sage, 1998); Kathy Charmaz, *Constructing Grounded Theory* (Thousand Oaks: Sage, 2006); John W Creswell, *Research Design: Qualitative, Quantitative and Mixed Approaches* (Thousand Oaks, CA: Sage, 2009), 13, 229.

the gathered information from field notes, allows the interconnections of concepts towards the emergence of a theory. From the thorough comparison of the field data and the memos derive the theoretical and substantive codes. Theoretical coding helps the researcher to find interconnections and meanings within scattered ideas that will be developed into working hypotheses for the building of a theory.

Theoretical memoing is central to the Grounded Theory methodology, where the researcher theorizes the substantive codes of concepts and their patterns of relationship. The approach allows sorting memos, naming concepts, specifying links, and writing memo-on-memos to carefully generate theory. Creativity embedded in memoing helps the researcher to immerse in the data, familiarize with every single aspect of it, and allow realistic concepts to emerge. In the Grounded Theory approach, codings and the gradual reduction of data take place iteratively. Coding is a form of content analysis where the researcher identifies the underlying themes from the large body of data. In coding, the data is divided and simultaneously reduced into units of analysis. Multiple coding protocol is used where statements in the data represent more than one concept category. After the conceptual categories are reduced into a core set of categories, a narrative will be developed to explain the properties and dimensions of the categories, and the circumstances under which they are connected. This explanation of the phenomena under investigation is what is termed as theory in Grounded Theory methodology.

Glaser and Strauss introduced four key stages in formulating Grounded Theory: Comparing incidents applicable to each category, Integrating categories and their properties, Delimiting the theory and Writing theory. Regarding the strength of such a development Glaser and Strauss said, "When the researcher is convinced that his analytical framework forms a systematic substantive theory, that it is a reasonably accurate statement of the matters studied, and that it is couched in a form that others going into the same field could use- then he can publish his results with confidence."[31]

Data analysis is mainly done through six types of coding in Grounded Theory.[32] Data is split into smaller segments in the first cycle of analysis by using the *vivo coding, process (action) coding* and *open (initial) coding.* In the second cycle of analysis, comparison of codes, emergence of patterns, reorganizing data into major categories are done through focus coding, axial coding and selective (theoretical) coding. Vivo coding finds the exact words or specific phrases of the participants and puts them in inverted commas so that they stand out in the notes. In process coding, the researcher marks the action words or phrases, indicating an ongoing action as the

[31] Barney G Glaser and Anslem L Strauss, *The Discovery of Grounded Theory: Strategies for Qualitative Research* (Aldine Transaction, Inc, 1967), 113.

[32] Johnny Saldana, *The Coding Manual for Qualitative Researchers,* 2nd Edition, (London: Sage, 2013), 51-101.

response to a situation. Open coding is reading transcripts line-by-line and breaking the data into distinct parts based on the identified major concepts. This is concerned with identifying, naming, categorizing and describing phenomena found in the text. Essentially, each line, sentence, and paragraph is read in search of the answer to the repeated question "What is this about? What is being referenced here?"

In focused coding, the researcher identifies the most frequently used codes to formulate the significant data categories as key divisions and sub-divisions in hierarchical format. Axial coding is the strategic process of reassembling the data that was earlier split at the open coding. In this process, the researcher organizes the concepts and makes them more abstract and relate codes to one another on the basis of their categories and properties, using a combination of inductive and deductive thinking.

In selective coding, the researcher carefully formulates the core category that covers all other codes and concepts under its theoretical explanation. This is the process of focusing on the main ideas, developing the story, and finalizing the Grounded Theory. One category is selected as the core with the purpose to develop the single theory line to which everything else is connected in a certain order.[33]

Grounded Theory is tested on the questions such as: Is the theory realistic and clear? Does the theory correspond to real-world data? Is the theory generalizable to settings other than the context of the study? Can the theory be applied to the same context to produce same results? The Grounded Theory develops with what is termed as the *theoretical saturation*, which occurs when theory reaches its best validation level that no new concepts could emerge from the data. Strauss and Corbin lists four standards of validation[34] for Grounded Data as:

- The analysis should fit the phenomenon under investigation; theory has to derive from diverse data and be adherent to the common reality of the area
- It should provide understanding and be understandable
- Because the data is comprehensive it should provide generality, in that the theory includes extensive variation and is abstract enough to be applicable to a wide variety of contexts; and,
- It should provide control, in the sense of stating the conditions under which the theory applies and describing a reasonable basis for action.

Qualitative researchers sometimes tend to go superficial about obvious data rather than immersing in the data. A well undertaken research, however, will have the researcher immersed in the data and moving steadily from the familiar to the

---

[33]   Saldana, *The Coding Manual for Qualitative Researchers*, 2013, 213-225.

[34]   Anslem Strauss and Juliet Corbin, *Basics of Qualitative Research: Grounded Theory Procedures and Techniques*, First Edition, (Newbury Park, CA: Sage, 1990), 295-310.

unknown details. The researcher explores what is behind the master narratives, a new story, a different experience. This is life impacting and hence able to serve as a credible link between the academy and the world.

Amazing Puzzle with Students!
'10 minutes… Find Tips'

Explore Qualitative Research Ideas in the Book of Acts

- Phenomenology: The Pentecost event (Acts 2); Peter's miraculous escape from prison (Acts 12)
- Ethnomethodology: Paul's defense before King Agrippa (Acts 26)
- Ethnography: Malta Islanders (Acts 28)
- Case Study: Healing of crippled beggar (Acts 3 &4)
- Action Research: Choosing of the seven to serve (Acts 6) Improved performance
- Grounded Theory: Jerusalem Council (Acts 15)

  And, there are more in relation to our research discussion spread out everywhere!

- Practical Theology and Grounded Theological Wisdom: Paul's Athenian speech (Acts 17)
- Narrative Analysis: Paul's trials before Felix and Festus (Acts 24 & 25)
- Interpretation: The Word (Ethiopian Eunuch) and the vision (Peter)
- Transformative learning: Combines knowledge, practice, reflection, conviction, courage (Acts' accounts of Peter)
- Community: Holistic nature (Acts 2:42-47)
- Mentoring: Aquila and Priscilla to Apollos (Acts 18)

IMPACT: It's all THERE! The Bible

CHALLENGE: Study the book of Nehemiah this same way

Reflection Box:

Explore your World, Think Out of the Box!

Mathew P John's doctoral research at Fuller Theological Seminary aimed to develop a theoretical framework in anthropological research for considering cinema as a 'datum of culture.' He used the Elements Trilogy, an Indo-Canadian film series; *Fire* (1991), *Earth* (1998), *Water* (2005), as a case study to derive a methodology for observing and interpreting ethnographic information embedded in the diegetic world of film. The ethnographic data generated from the films through a process of 'Virtual Participant Observation' were compared and contrasted with actual data collected from the field to test the authenticity of the filmmaker's re-presentation of culture. His field research involved Participant Observation, Focus Groups and Ethnographic Interviews conducted in India, the context of the films. He was also privileged to conduct an interview with Deepa Mehta, the writer/director of the Trilogy.

In order to develop a methodology for a cultural exegesis of film, John proposed to integrate auteur criticism and context criticism, two methodologies borrowed from the discipline of film studies, with 'Virtual Participant Observation.' In the end he interlaced this methodology with prominent methods in the field of theological criticism of film to propose a method for doing a 'religious reading' of film. It was argued that both the cultural perceptions of God (religion) and God's revelation to culture (theology) in a given context could be explored through films.

CHAPTER 3

THINKING *ETHICS* IN QUALITATIVE RESEARCH

SECTION CONTENTS:

Credibility of the Qualitative Data

Credibility, Consistency and Confidentiality

Credibility Safeguards in Qualitative Research

Biases of the Researcher

Rights of the Research Participants

Institution's Guidelines and Researcher's Personal Ethics

Ethics in Qualitative Research

Social research happens in a social environment and therefore, has perceptible ethical features and repercussions. For the qualitative researcher who is seen as a *bricoleur*, ethical practice is an ongoing pursuit. This is particular because a *bricoleur* is defined as a "Jack of all trades or a kind of professional do-it-yourself person."[1] Denzin and Lincoln referred to this term used by French anthropologist Claude Levi-Struass to describe the researcher as the multi-tasker, who can sort through many sources of information to come up with a new formulation, what they term as *bricolage*. The qualitative genres are characteristically multifaceted designs as they "embrace and try to make sense of the "messiness" of everyday life."[2]

Marshall and Rossman define the methodology as "a broad approach to the study of social phenomena...various genres as naturalistic, interpretive and increasingly

---

[1]   C Levi-Strauss, *The Savage Mind,* 2nd Edition, (Chicago: University of Chicago Press, 1966), 17.

[2]   Catherine A Hansman, 'Navigators on the Research Path: Teaching and Mentoring Student Qualitative Researchers' Chapter 3, 41-66 in *Research Methods: Concepts, Methods, Tools and Applications* (Hershey, PA: IGI Global, Informative Resources Management Association, 2015), 43.

critical and they typically draw on multiple methods of inquiry."[3] By reason of these innate characteristics, there are several possibilities for being deceptive or dishonest in the process of qualitative research as to make us think that doing an ethically sound study is nearly impossible. Social research experts, however, affirm that "while ethics and good science sometimes conflict, it must also be pointed out that often they do not."[4] We see that it is by the researcher's constant vigilance in addressing the potential areas of compromise that we resolve the ethical concerns substantially. Obviously, this ethical vision needs to undergird the theology student's indispensable commitments to honesty and genuineness.

Credibility of the Qualitative Data

Reliability and validity are words for truth, known to be the essential characteristics of quantitative data analysis. While reliability suggests that the same data would have been collected each time in repeated observations of the same phenomenon, validity refers to the extent to which an empirical measure adequately reflects the real meaning of the concept under consideration. Generally, the researcher's methods are expected to be reliable and the results of the study, valid. In research, *objectivity* in data analysis and *generalizability* of findings are terms rooted in the quantitative philosophy. As generally claimed, implementing these indicators in their absolute scientific references might be more distracting rather than clarifying the data process in qualitative studies. It is held that "most indicators of validity and reliability do not fit qualitative research. Instead, researchers judge the credibility of qualitative work by its *transparency, consistency-coherence, and communicability;* they design the interviewing to achieve these standards."[5] Ethical awareness and application, being central to any relevant research practice, demand our notional consideration.

Qualitative research methodology is often criticized for its non-quantified data that do not guarantee the replication of the properties in the social world in similar studies. Termed as soft science and minor approach, qualitative methodology is mostly disparaged for its selective use of supportive examples in analysis by completely neglecting the unclear or negative cases. The book *Naturalistic Inquiry*[6] opened serious explorations on the question of reliability of the research data. Evoking challenging questions on aspects such as; the trustworthiness of the data, the process of analysis and the claims made on social realities, the authors introduced alternative terms such as credibility, confirmability, dependability, and

---

[3]   Catherine Marshall and Gretchen B Rossman, *Designing Qualitative Research*, 5th Edition, (Thousand Oaks, CA: Sage, 2011), 3.

[4]   R F Guy, C E Edgley, I Arafat and D E Allen, *Social Research Methods: Puzzles and Solutions* (Boston: Allyn and Bacon, 1987), 32.

[5]   Herbert J Rubin and Irene S Rubin, *Qualitative Interviewing: The Art of Hearing the Data* (London: Sage, 1995), 85.

[6]   Yvonna S Lincoln and Egon G Guba, *Naturalistic Inquiry* (Beverly Hills, CA: Sage, 1985).

transferability that would better reflect the procedures in the qualitative research domain. The following is a brief discussion of three of the concepts to guide further explorations on the trustworthiness of the qualitative data.

Credibility, Consistency and Confidentiality

Credibility of a study speaks more in line with the *reliability* theme previously mentioned and it refers to trustworthiness of the data and the results. Terms such as *trustworthiness, soundness, authenticity, genuineness, dependability* are used synonymously with *credibility*. This, in fact, is grounded on the motivation and authenticity of the researcher herself/himself and is epitomized at every stage of the work. In this section we seek to explore on this theme, reflecting its characteristics on transparency[7], coherence[8] and many other.

Figure 6: Dimensions of Ethical Trustworthiness in Research

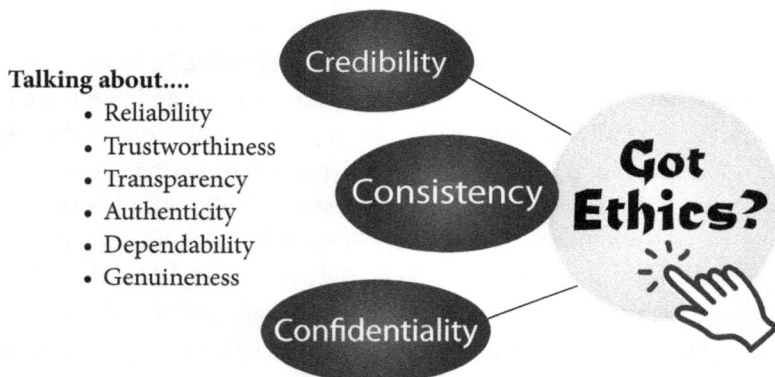

Talking about....
- Reliability
- Trustworthiness
- Transparency
- Authenticity
- Dependability
- Genuineness

Credibility

Consistency

Confidentiality

Got Ethics?

Padgett reasons that the lack of these features occurs in research, "partly from ethnographic traditions in which field research was shrouded in mystery, but it also stems from the flexible, nonlinear nature of qualitative research."[9] Manipulations, gaps, inconsistencies and all forms of deception in data generation and processing do not characterize good research practice. Making the case for the conceptual cogence of qualitative data, Padgett says,

---

[7]   *Transparency* in the context of research refers to operating in a way that it is easy for the readers to see how research decisions, data gathering and processing and generalizations are done.

[8]   *Coherence* refers to the logical, unified and cogent nature of the qualitative study. In detail, it denotes the fit between the objectives, the conceptual views adopted, background review of literature, the role of the researcher in the study, the procedures of qualitative data gathering, analysis, interpretation and the presentation of the findings.

[9]   Deborah K Padgett, *The Qualitative Research Experience*, 'Introduction: Finding a Middle Ground in Qualitative Research' 1-18, (Belmont, CA: Wadsworth/Thomson: 2004), 4.

Quantitative data are collected in bits, stored in bytes, and interpreted via statistical analyses where hypotheses are tested by aggregating (and re-aggregating) the data. Qualitative knowledge is based not on decontextualized bits of information, but on weaving back and forth between local context and conceptualization. Only humans are sentient beings who can connect the dots.[10]

We may contend here, however, that by added rigour that is "open to interstitial meaning, to see both the overarching contours and the hidden crevices"[11] the credibility of the data can be enhanced.

Qualitative data come to the researcher with dissimilar descriptions in the verbal accounts of people. It becomes the task of the researcher to enhance the coherence of the data through social research techniques such as triangulation, further data immersion and cross checking and many more. In all of this, *imagination of the researcher*[12] plays its role, and it can be subject to ethical test. Although imaginative process is embedded in qualitative approach, how the researcher safeguards the data from subjective treatment is crucial. Much of the process of data being unknown to others usually engenders a certain amount of ambiguity. Another concern arises when the research attempts end up producing one-sided or diverse information. The way data is managed in this situation has serious ethical implications. For example, when interview notes are varied,

> the researcher may have to pick between versions, weighing the quality of evidence, the nature of the interviewees' memory, and evidence of slant to sort out which version is more credible. Alternatively, the researcher may decide to present the two different versions because they help explain the nature of the conflict and are strongly held and believed by the interviewees.[13]

Part of the task of the researcher is to explain how inconsistencies in the process were resolved because, research reports with gaps and contractions are not acceptable in academia. In addressing the variations, researchers seek for more detailed responses from the participants or raise a few more questions on the seeming gap, until the data turns out to be transparent and dependable. The final report of a good research will have evidences that the keen researcher has checked out ideas that appeared to be inconsistent.

> In qualitative research the goal is not to eliminate inconsistencies, but to make sure you understand why they occur. When people present different versions of the same

---

[10] Padgett, 2004, 4.

[11] Padgett, 2004, 4.

[12] *Imagination* is the creative cognitive capacity that shapes the form and content of qualitative research. Researcher, while inquiring on a social reality, is expected to acquire and shape the imaginative processes within the given socio-cultural setting.

[13] Rubin & Rubin, 1995, 85.

event you either have to offer evidence why you accept one version or the other, or show why in these circumstances people can hold contradictory understandings. If you find inconsistencies of themes across cases, you either modify the emerging theory, or limit how far your findings extend.[14]

One of the main aspects in enhancing coherence in the research is to offer explanations to seeming inconsistencies or contradictions. In doing this, the researcher is ensuring that any possible gap in the work is prudently recognized or addressed.

Qualitative researchers sometimes mediate topics that necessitate a high level of confidentiality. In this case, research participants are assured that their responses will be kept confidential, which means, the researchers will not associate the names of the participants with the data anywhere in the report. In other cases, the researcher guarantees anonymity, which is that the researcher himself/herself cannot identify participants with their responses, and hence is able to handle data with maximum impartiality. Research ethical committees in academia usually publish their own guidelines in this. One document asserts the requirement thus,

> Generally, researchers must process data acquired about personal matters confiden-
> tially. Personal data must normally be de-identified, while publication and dissemi-
> nation of the research material must normally be anonymized. In certain situations,
> researchers must nonetheless balance confidentiality and the obligation to notify.[15]

Responses are anonymous when research participants drop their response sheets in a box in a common place or send it to the researcher without revealing their identity (or the location) or using an electronic anonymous survey procedure. Researchers sometimes ask for printed or ticked document so that recognition by calligraphic (hand writing) identification is withheld. Babbie summarizes these safeguards thus[16], "Confidentiality is guaranteed when the researcher can identify a given person's responses but promises not to do so publicly" and "Anonymity is guaranteed in a research project when neither the researcher not the readers of the findings can identify a given response with a given respondent." Finally, the call is to determinedly guard the research process from all forms of deception.

---

[14]   Rubin & Rubin, 1995, 85.

[15]   The Norvegian National Research Ethics Committee, Guidelines for Research Ethics in the Social Sciences, Humanities, Law and Theology, 4th Edition, June 2016, 17. https://www.etikkom.no/globalassets/documents/english-publications/60127_fek_guidelines_nesh_digital_corr.pdf accessed on 25 April 2017. https://www.etikkom.no/globalassets/.../60127_fek_guidelines_nesh_digital_corr.pdf

[16]   Earl Babbie, *The Practice of Social Research,* 10th Edition, (Belmont, CA: Wardsworth/Thomson, 2004), 65-66.

Credibility Safeguards in Qualitative Research

Practice of deception in qualitative research ranges from outright lying by way of embarking on a research with wrong motivation, providing faulty information to the participants, and the use of confederates as part of the sample, and so on. Deception is sometimes obvious; otherwise, subtle. Deliberate deception either by projection or omission and all forms of misrepresentations on the part of the researcher are forbidden in the ethical codes of social science research. Clifford Christians emphasizes, "Even paternalistic arguments for possible deception of criminals, children in elementary schools, or the mentally incapacitated are no longer credible."[17] Disproving any form of deception in research affirms Soble, "If the knowledge to be gained from deceptive experiments" is clearly valuable to society, it is "only a minor defect that persons must be deceived in the process."[18]

Research participants also may tend to use certain illusive methods in the process as they realize the purpose of the study. This ethical dilemma occurs to the qualitative researcher when the participants choose to play to the purpose of the study or try to subvert it. Credibility of the research is at stake in either situation. Since the qualitative process is grounded in human affairs in which the researcher gets actively involved, effective methodologies need to be in place to counter the issues around inaccuracy and dishonesty. Some are given in Figure 7.

Figure 7: Credibility Safeguards for Qualitative Data

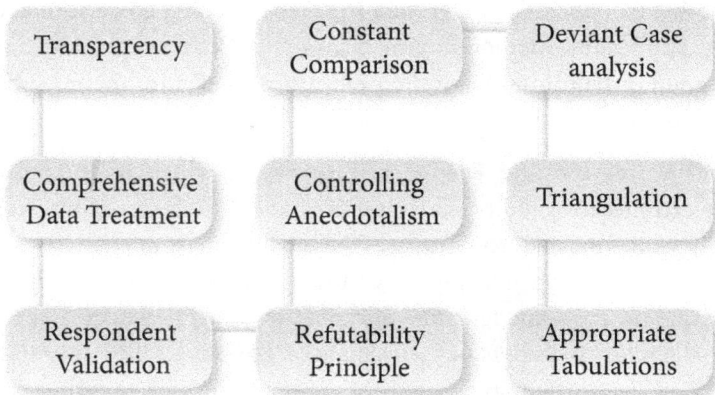

Transparency	Constant Comparison	Deviant Case analysis
Comprehensive Data Treatment	Controlling Anecdotalism	Triangulation
Respondent Validation	Refutability Principle	Appropriate Tabulations

Transparency: As mentioned elsewhere, transparency is maintained when the reader is able to see through the details of the processes in research. The researcher keeps

---

[17] Clifford G Christians, 'Ethics and Politics of Qualitative Research', 208-244, Chapter 5 in *The Landscape of Qualitative Research: Theories and Issues*, 2nd Edition, Norman K Denzin and Yvonna S Lincoln (eds) (Thousand Oaks: Sage, 2003), 217.

[18] A Soble, 'Deception in Social Science Research: Is Informed Consent Possible?' *Hastings Center Report*, 40-46. October 1978, 40.

transparent the biases, limitations, conscientiousness, strengths and weaknesses in the qualitative study. Traditionally, the system is at fault in which much of the original data and the research process is kept inaccessible to the curious reader. Imaginative fancy is controlled "when the original interviews are publically available and quotes from the interviews are used in the report to support each major conclusion."[19]

An essential competence of the mentor in qualitative study is the courage to verify the original data, and, the rigour to assess how the researcher has processed the information gathered. Manipulation of data may happen in multiple ways such as, reporting information that was not given by the participants or interpreting and presenting the data in ways that the respondents never intended. Conscious errors and misinterpretations of data are unjustifiable practices at all stages of qualitative study. In the case of any gap that surfaces, the researcher's job is not to conceal but to explain the matter or at least acknowledge it by raising relevant observations and questions. Also following the "on record" and "off record" principle in data gathering will help produce a reliable and transparent report.

Comprehensive Data Treatment: This is about the researcher's conscious attempt to control the biased, subjective selection of cases in arriving at the findings. Every part of the data needs to be inspected repeatedly until the generalization applies to every single element of it. Corroboration of data analysis in qualitative methodology relies greatly on this practice. The comprehensive data treatment makes qualitative generalization as authentic as a statistical correlation because it explains the research problem coherently rather than through sweeping correlational claims on antecedents and results. Methodological techniques used in a qualitative study may be judged good or bad in terms of their effectiveness as a technique and based on their consequences on the participants and the society at large.

Respondent Validation and Feedback: The way in which traditional, positivist research determines the validity of an inquiry is based on the use of well-established, scientifically authenticated techniques. The qualitative route, in its own right, employs methods like participant validation to allow the professional mode to operate beyond the hard-and fast rules of validation. Qualitative researchers in order to advance the trustworthiness of their database, go back to their respondents with the transcribed data or tentative report of analysis and seek to refine them in the light of their further feedback. Carried out with intention and rigour, this can assist the task of enhancing the overall fidelity of the study, otherwise, it only confirms the respondents' expressions or the researcher's preliminary observations. For instance, in a case study on re-shaping of indigenous liturgy in the light of traditional folklores,

---

[19]   Herbert J Rubin and Irene S Rubin, *Qualitative Interviewing: The Art of Hearing the Data* (London: Sage, 1995), 87.

the qualitative researcher may use in-depth personal interviews with the elderly in the given tribe. The researcher going back and forth to the respondents for validation and further feedback on the data advances the credibility of the study.

Constant Comparison: The researcher does not classify responses into pre-defined groups but rather, attempts to find another case through which the initial set of data categories or provisional hypothesis may be tested. This method is normally used in the development of Grounded Theory.[20] From the free and spontaneous responses given by the participants, the researcher carefully identifies salient patterns of relationships and meanings. Units and incidents from the data are constantly compared and as a result, the categories undergo changes in their definition and content. Patterns of relationship are developed between categories as comparison continues and the focal concepts and their properties are refined. In shared research endeavours, a method employed in advancing objectivity by two sets of data are compared by two researchers simultaneously to see if categories developed are comparable.

Constant comparison is sometimes referred to the practice of comparing new data with that of the previous studies. This can go on and thus cause researcher's prolonged engagement in the research task at times depending on the nature of the focus-of-inquiry. For example, we consider a study on the phenomenon of missionaries changing their minds while serving in a distant country. The researcher goes deep into data from the focus of inquiry, develop conceptual categories, constantly compare incidents (or meanings), and discover patterns of relationship among these groupings and their contents. Unlike collecting a few broad answers, this guides the researcher deep into the issues in developing a candid understanding of the situation.

Refutability Principle: Silverman's five interrelated ways for critically weighing the cogency of the qualitative data are: the refutability principle, the constant comparative method, comprehensive data treatment, deviant case analysis and using appropriate tabulations.[21] The principle of refutability refers to the attempt of searching for disconfirming evidences during the research. This enhances the soundness of the study with its indicators of the researcher's sensitivity to the gaps and contradictions. For instance, setting a case against non-church going Christianity, the researcher deliberately searches for a group whose single option would be the secret practice of their faith. The researcher then explores how the larger community of faith extends

---

[20]   Barney G Glasser, 'The Constant Comparative Method of Qualitative Analysis in Social Problems', Vol. 12, No. 4, Spring 1965, 436-445. Later in Chapter 5 in B G Glaser and A L Strauss, *The Discovery of Grounded Theory: Strategies for Qualitative Research* (New York: Aldine De Gruyter, 1967).

[21]   David Silverman, *Doing Qualitative Research: A Practical Handbook* (Thousand Oaks, CA: Sage, 2000), 177-78.

support to them in discipleship and steady growth while still upholding the validity of the argument for a church-based faith practice.

Controlling Anecdotalism: Anecdotal issue is raised on the research report when it includes selected exemplary cases of an incident or behaviour that are culled out from the field notes and avoid the others. This tendency of presenting selected examples of a social reality without taking effort to address the contradictory or unclear examples of the same phenomenon has been identified as a potential flaw in the qualitative process. Anecdotalism makes it hard to determine the representativeness of the claims made in the study. Bryman explained the problem succinctly,

> There is a tendency towards an anecdotal approach to the use of data in relation to conclusions or explanations in qualitative research. Brief conversations, snippets from unstructured interviews…are used to provide evidence of a particular contention. These are grounds for disquiet in that the representativeness or generality of these fragments are rarely addressed.[22]

For example, in a study affirming church's supportive attitude to women's ministry development in a rather conservative context, the researcher selectively reports the cases of outstanding women ministers, while consciously avoids others who represent a contradictory/different reality. If the projected participants are exceptional cases of women who find their way in ministry in the midst of various forms of resistance from the church, it adds to the misrepresentation of data. Hence, for the proposition of church-enabled ministry development of women, the anecdotal approach conceals part of the social reality. In summary, the devious projection of favourable cases and the avoidance of negative cases are viewed unethical in the conduct of qualitative study.

Deviant Case Analysis: *Deviant case* is the aspect in the data that appear to contradict (or be less supportive) patterns or explanations emerging from the data analysis. The deviant case safeguard in qualitative study suggests that the researcher actively searches for and addresses deviant cases, which are also known as discrepant or negative cases. Rational treatment of deviant cases makes the research valid since the analysis includes all the data and the primary analysis themes are tested against the outstanding *exemplary cases*. We take for instance a qualitative researcher who was determinedly contending the practice of domestic child labour, recognizes during the data collection that in the cases of some children, the story proved just the reverse. The domestic labour situation provided some children with the safest place and excellent opportunities for education.

---

[22]   Alan Bryman, *Quantity and Quality in Social Research* (London: Unwin Hyman, 1988), 77.

Triangulation: This is the method of using more than one method to collect data on the same topic. A powerful way of ensuring credibility of data is by cross verification from different ways of looking at the data or varied claims on the study. However, simply using different datasets cannot guarantee credibility. A rather significant step would be to decide how to enhance the constancy of the data by approaching the problem from the most efficient angles or data resources.

In a study on the increasing school-drop out of teenage children in a given place, the researcher may use triangulation of methods such as personal interviews with teens, questionnaires to parents and focus groups with school administrators/teachers. There are many other methods such as case studies of drop-out teens, content analysis of recent literature, telephone/face-to-face conversations with governmental departments associated with education or child welfare or visits to Christian non-governmental organizations. The decision is not exactly regarding the number of methods but the reliability of the methodology in helping the researcher gather relevant information.

Appropriate Tabulations: An essential ethical property in qualitative research is ensuring accuracy of the data. Deliberate omissions, deceptive additions, uninformed use of contrivances, fabrication of information, use of duplicitous sources are particular forms of data mismanagement. Counting the frequency of responses by itself does not always authenticate evidences. Tabulation method in qualitative research is a much debated issue since the methods of tabulation often remain undisclosed to others. Most often the problem arises when the qualitative researcher fails to follow a theoretical rationale in tabulation or state it clearly. Readers' access to the field notes or the original transcripts can also be a legitimacy control in qualitative research. In this, the reader enjoys the privilege of reaching beyond the depictions and interpretations of the researcher in judging the actual perspectives of the research participants. Tabulation check is therefore an important component in the cogency of data analysis.

Biases of the Researcher

There are multiple ways in which researcher's bias, also known as the insider-bias, impact the way in which qualitative data is generated. If not intentionally addressed, these biases will be evident in the review of literature, the criteria in sampling and the methods in data gathering. Qualitative data is said to be produced not *by* someone but *with* someone and consequently the data can be influenced by the cultural context and the personal skills and approaches of the researcher. Two ways in which *researcher-bias* normally appears in the study are: the subjective, one-sided approaches in the conduct of research that would impede the credibility of the findings; and, the narrow personal standpoints/views with which the study is directed. Debates on insider bias are to continue as a prime focus in qualitative undertakings.

Figure 8: Basic Types of Researcher - Biases

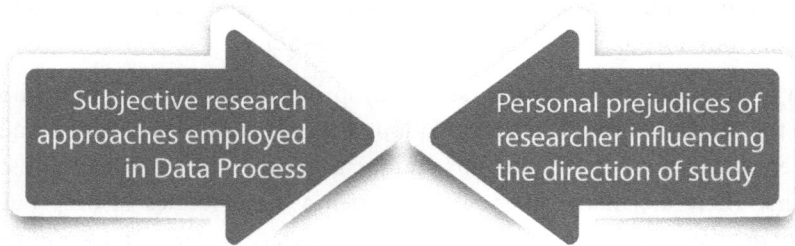

Subjective research approaches employed in Data Process

Personal prejudices of researcher influencing the direction of study

Indeed, scholarship suggests the integration of the reflexes of *researcher's self* as fundamental to the qualitative research approach. Strong arguments were set forth in early 1990s especially in the feminist studies for the disclosure of the cultural self of the researcher in the research, against the conventional criticisms on *researcher's subjectivity* in the positivist approach. It was contended that the self or its deep rooted biases have significant impact in the process particularly in the reflections, imaginations and judgments made during data generation and interpretation. As a matter of fact, every decision made by the researcher is someway influenced by the doctrinal, contextual, cultural, personal, spiritual, ideological and academic formations of the person. Yet, questions remain as to: How much of researcher's bias impacts the study? Does substantial revelation of researcher's *self* in research serve for the better or for worse in terms of the trustworthiness of the research? What measures are to be taken to guard the data process from unprincipled subjectivity?

Qualitative research being a deeper inquiry into human experiences and perceptions, researchers who adhere to this approach believe that it is not possible to control or eradicate the disclosure of the cultural self in the endeavour or, that there is no need to do so. Rather, for them, it can actually guide the inquiry with better focus and credibility. Yet there are several queries that a researcher encounters while handling issues regarding sensitivity and objectivity hand-in-hand.

Sensitivity is a central quality in the data process of qualitative research. Strauss and Corbin speak of sensitivity as "the ability to respond to the subtle nuances of, and cues to, meanings in the data" while objectivity is "the ability to achieve a certain degree of distance from the research materials and to represent them fairly...."[23]

---

[23]   A Strauss and J Corbin, *Basics of Qualitative Research,* 2nd Edition, (Newbury Park, CA: Sage, 1988), 42-43.

Padgett's study[24] proposed that we do not necessarily need to eliminate our personal beliefs and biases, but instead need to be aware of their impact on the research. Ongoing examination of the researcher's biases in qualitative research would indicate constant vigilance in the way he/she handles the data and this obviously enhances the level of understanding one's own self and the phenomenon/people in the study.

An essential area of awareness for the qualitative researcher is about how best to draw the divides between the high level of trust and friendliness with the participants. We know that in-depth study of humans with rich data on their experiences, perceptions, feelings, and attitudes is possible only with trustable relational rapport. But the researcher should realize that there is more to this rapport (than the personal aspect) in research. Mason reminds the researcher not to overlook the professional and formal purpose in qualitative data gathering.[25] The researcher has to proceed with consistent awareness of issues regarding sensitivity in the process and keep employing effective measures to address it.

The researcher's values play an important role in the shape and direction the study takes. Famous sociologist Weber believed that even the conclusions and implications drawn will be largely grounded in the moral and political values of the researcher. While the statistical, positivist approach enforces objectivism in which the researcher takes a value-free or value-neutral stance, the qualitative research generally employs normativism, which operates subjectively to particular world views.

In theology, where fundamental faith convictions are retained, the researcher's credibility of procedures and findings demand deeper attention. The researcher addresses personal questions like: What are theological assumptions at the backdrop of the study? How do my spiritual, social and political values impact the processes? Is the merging of faith-wise subjectivity and social research subjectivity acceptable in scholarship? Are there areas that would demand relevant disclaimers for the readers with regard to beliefs, practice or the conduct of research? How, when and where to do so?

Researcher bias has numerous other effects on the study. Biased sampling, or the selection of research participants, will produce wrong results. For instance, the researcher's preoccupation with certain categories of participants on the basis of class, caste, gender, religion or politics, will have serious impact on the data gathering, analysis and findings. The process of data analysis and the way in which inferences are drawn must be guarded from potential researcher biases.

---

[24]   Deborah K Padgette, *Qualitative Methods in Social Work Research: Challenges and Rewards* (Thousand Oaks: CA: Sage), 1998.

[25]   Jennifer Mason, *Qualitative Researching* (Thousand Oaks, CA: Sage, 1996), 166.

Conducting social research in the researcher's second language is an area that is often neglected in the research talks. Inquirer must be able to see the possible setbacks in using a second language in data tools and data gathering. The question is, 'Will the use of vernacular provide a more authentic or a different set of data?' Another area that brings to fore the researcher-bias is the unsubstantiated generalizations made in the research report. All of these point to the need to scrutiny if any area is shaded directly or indirectly by the biases of the researcher. Following section adds more responsibilities for the researcher-the rights of the participants need to be protected.

Rights of the Research Participants

The *participants' rights* which the researcher needs to act upon consistently, is a central consideration in the design of qualitative study. Participants are not mere resources of data but the ones that live the reality and therefore, have the right to know the data procedures and results. A few important areas identified are given in Figure 9.

Figure 9: Participant's Rights in Qualitative Research

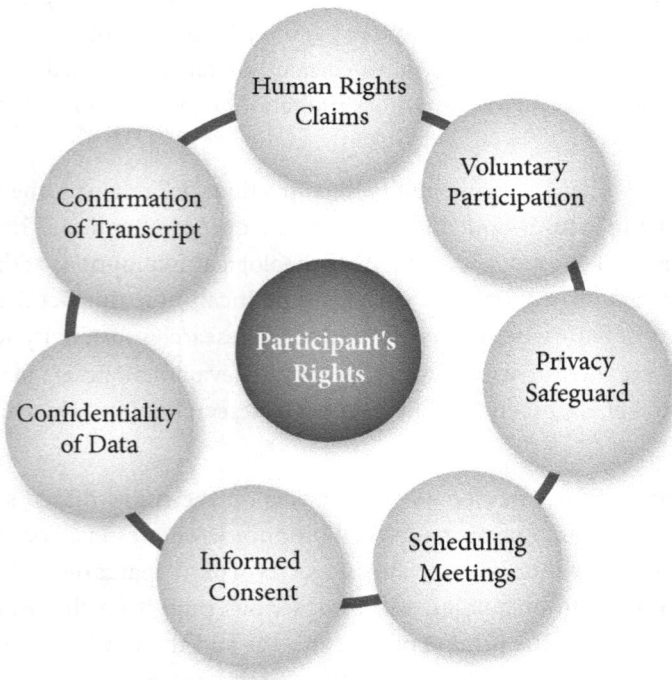

The *Human Rights* Aspect: In an age that characterizes itself by discourses on human rights, researchers need to ensure that participants' rights are not in any way violated in the process of inquiry. Respect for persons is intrinsic to human research irrespective of the context of the study. "Respect for persons captures the notion that we do not use the people who participate in our studies as a means to an end (often our own) and that we do respect their privacy, their anonymity, and their right to participate-or not-which is freely consented to."[26] By the very nature, qualitative data gathers large amounts of data on the personal and public lives of people. In the processes of data collection, analysis and interpretation, there are several key ethical concerns including the rights of the research participant. Any kind of manipulation of the participants, for instance, making them respond in a particular way to enhance the anticipated results in the study, is an outright disciplinary offence. Participants have their say regarding the disclosure of their identity in the research report. Nations and institutions have specific policies in research regarding vulnerable populations that consist of minors, the differently abled, mentally incapacitated, frail elders, pregnant women, lower caste groups, prisoners, tribal communities, etc.

Voluntary Participation: The researcher should not expect or compel anyone to provide information but rather seek permission from the research participants for data gathering. Individuals have the right to speak or be quiet; protect or reveal information. According to basic structured questionnaires include response options such as 'no comment', 'none of these', 'I don't know'. Participants also have the right to know the purpose and procedures of research while offering their consent to provide information. Observing participants without their knowledge obviously raises questions regarding voluntary participation. While, governments and police forces exercise controlled autonomy to do this as part of their formal, legal procedures, it evokes crucial ethical implications for the qualitative researcher. Likewise, the use of hidden cameras or other recording devices aiming to reach the secret layers of social reality hold similar apprehensions.

Privacy Safeguard: On private or personal matters, some participants fervently provide the data, while others do not. How the researcher handles inquiry in this situation involves ethical decisions. The researchers are to accord due importance to the legal rights of vulnerable categories like street children, sex workers, HIV/AIDS victims, child labourers, victims of domestic violence, people with special needs, criminals, and so on. As data gathering progresses, what happens inside of the researcher as a person is important in terms of the direction taken in data analysis. Experts in qualitative domain warn us that in studies that involve deeply relational or emotional content, researchers must maintain their ethical boundaries by constant

---

[26]   Catherine Marshall & Gretchen B Rossman, *Designing Qualitative Research* (5th Edition) (Thousand Oaks, CA: Sage, 2011), 47.

evaluation of their thinking and behaviour.[27] Sharing personal experiences is an accepted and natural practice in qualitative process. However, this might, in the initial times of developing rapport with the participants, lead to ethical quandaries as they enhance the personal trust and feelings in the participants for the researcher. The researchers, especially in contexts where close relational communications take place like in an interview, need to effectively balance trust building and professional commitment to scholarship.

Privacy safeguard in interviews has been a much deliberated topic in particular. The researcher may be held back during an interview while asking about sensitive relational issues, failures, guilt feelings and so on. The only way out in such situations is to structure the data generation tool and the order of questions in a non-threatening, hearer-friendly format. In that Rubin and Rubin write, the researcher

> shows a little knowledge of the issue so that the conversational partners do not feel that they are 'washing dirty linen'.... . Another alternatively gentle way of persisting at getting sensitive material is to 'throw out the rabbit', which involves a series of non-threatening questions that allude to sensitive subject matter without directly asking about it. Another method is to raise some other delicate issue him- or herself as a way of breaking the ice.[28]

Interview ethics in general requires that the interviewee is given an environment to feel at ease, he/she can exercise due amount of control as a participant in the process of data collection, intimidating patterns are avoided in the conversation and any form of recording is done only with the wilful permission of the participant. In all of this, the researcher needs to guard the process from undue intrusions. "Avoiding undue intrusion means thinking through carefully why research is needed and whether all the planned data collection strategies are needed. Good qualitative research means in-depth probing and investigation, but this needs to be proportionate."[29]

Privacy protocol is crucial in research with particular reference to the ever-increasing intrusion of media and the human rights protests in research. Perhaps defining what *public* and *private* are, makes the difference in the research approach. We know that even when the research is carried out in an educational institution with the permission of the administration, there might be areas that still need to be clarified and protected. Ethical etiquettes in qualitative study call to safeguard

---

[27]   K Lerum, 'Subjects of Desire: Academic Armor, Intimate Ethnography and the Production of Critical Knowledge' *Qualitative Inquiry,* 7(4), 466-483, 2001.

[28]   H J Rubin and I S Rubin, *Qualitative Interviewing: The Art of Hearing Data* (London: Sage, 1995), 219-221.

[29]   Stephen Webster, Jane Lewis and Ashley Brown, 'Ethical Considerations in Qualitative Research' Chapter 4 in *Qualitative Research Practice: A Guide for Social Science Students and Researchers* (2nd Edition), Jane Ritchie, Jane Lewis, Carol McNaughton Nicholls and Rachel Ormston (eds), (Thousand Oaks, CA: Sage, 2014), 108.

the identities of the research participants and of the at-risk venues/institutions from being exposed to the public. It is only with anonymity that the researcher can disclose the personal data gathered from the participants. Anonymity and confidentiality are related terms; yet they are not the same. Anonymity refers to the wish of a respondent not to be identified in the research report. Confidentiality refers to the range of people who might have access to the data. Ensuring anonymity, researchers use fictional names or letters or numbers to specify research participants. In some cases, their field notes and transcripts do not contain the identification details of the participants.

Using pseudonyms does not always guarantee privacy safeguard. C. Christians puts it thus, "Despite the signature status of privacy protection, watertight confidentiality has proved to be impossible. Pseudonyms and disguised locations are often recognized by insiders."[30] The rich and detailed qualitative data requires to be analysed in a more holistic manner than transferring information into statistics. Mason admits, "The confidentiality and privacy of those who have some personal involvement with the research may be more difficult to maintain than where, for example, data are turned into statistical trends, patterns and correlations."[31] This issue sustains in various forms in the research context.

Scheduling Meetings: The researcher has to value his/her respondents' rights of privacy, availability and willingness to be part of the study. Unreasonable demands on the participants are not the pattern of efficient qualitative practice. Fixing appointment for interviews is now a standard practice in research even in cultures that would not necessarily require any such formalities. However, if the research setting that is strongly community-oriented operates better without appointments and laborious scheduling that will reduce the complexity inherent to data gathering. We notice today that institutions are ever more conscious in establishing strict regulations for the conduct of research and interviews in their settings. Unlike the past, for instance, researchers cannot simply walk in to interview children at the schools. Privacy rules and security laws are in place for constituencies that are characterized as vulnerable population. These are of course vital considerations for the researcher even while selecting the topic for study.

Informed Consent: The term informed consent refers to the agreement of the respondents to participate voluntarily in the research process, being aware of the nature of the research and their role in it. Clarifying the intentions of the researcher to the research participants prior to the conduct of research can resolve much of the

---

[30] Clifford G Christians, 'Ethics and Politics of Qualitative Research', 208-244, Chapter 5 in *The Landscape of Qualitative Research: Theories and Issues* (2nd Edition), Norman K Denzin and Yvonna S Lincoln (eds) (Thousand Oaks: Sage, 2003), 217.

[31] Jennifer Mason, *Qualitative Researching* (Thousand Oaks, CA: Sage, 1996), 166.

possible stress and anxiety in interaction. In this, the researcher first of all has to determine the purpose of the study, its socio-political and religious impact, and what exactly is expected of the participants and what are the not-so-obvious matters they should be aware of. It requires an attentive judgment on the part of the researcher on the amount of information and introduction to be given to the informants in preparation for the data collection. On investigator's right in social scientific research and the legal concerns Reynolds commented,

> The legal definition of informed consent causes two problems for research. First, there is the assumption that the participant's knowledge of the research will not affect the research phenomenon itself.... The second lies in the assumption that informed consent should be required for all research, even if the data are collected in public or there are no direct effects on the participants.[32]

What should the researcher inform the participants? According to Soble, "... subjects must be told the duration, methods, possible risks, and the purpose or aim of the experiment."[33] Nonetheless, informed consent is not about merely notifying something.

> The Mill and Weber tradition insists that research subjects have the right to be informed about the nature and consequences of experiments in which they are involved. Proper respect for human freedom generally includes two necessary conditions. Subjects must agree voluntarily to participate- that is, without physical or psychological coercion. In addition, their agreement must be based on full and open information.[34]

Participants can ask to know the benefits that might accrue to them by participation. There are ongoing debates in this. Opining that a strict application of codes may restrain and restrict a great deal of innocuous and unproblematic research, Punch suggests the codes of ethics in research to serve as a guideline prior to fieldwork, but not intrude on full participation.[35] Punch says, "In much of the fieldwork there seems to be no way around the predicament that informed consent-divulging one's identity and research purpose to all and sundry-will kill many a project stone dead."[36] However, negligence in gaining the informed consent can drive the researcher into unnecessary dilemmas including legal restraints. Perhaps there are a few helpful questions the researchers should ask themselves: What, where, when and

---

[32]   Paul Davidson Reynolds, *Ethics and Social Science Research*, (New Jersey: Prentice Hall, 1982), 115.

[33]   Alan Soble, 'Deception in Social Science Research: Is Informed Consent Possible?' *Hastings Center Report*, 40-46. October 1978, 40.

[34]   Clifford G Christians, 'Ethics and Politics of Qualitative Research', 208-244, Chapter 5 in *The Landscape of Qualitative Research: Theories and Issues* (2nd Edition), Norman K Denzin and Yvonna S Lincoln (eds) (Thousand Oaks: Sage, 2003), 217.

[35]   Maurice Punch, 'Politics and Ethics in Qualitative Research' 83-97 in *Handbook of Qualitative Research*, N K Denzin and Y S Lincoln (Eds) Thousand Oaks: CA, Sage, 1994), 90.

[36]   Punch, 1994, 90.

how compromises occur in the process? Who are my research participants? What are their special characteristics? What preparatory information should be provided for the informed consent and how well I need to do this? What are possible risks including the very minor aspects for the participants and how to minimize these?

Confirmation of Transcript: In the case of researcher transcribing the conversation, a re-check with the respondents for the final approval of the document is an ethical essential. We, however, do not expect this activity to enhance credibility of the research by default, rather to confirm the transparency of the recorded data. Probes in confidential topics and their analysis and reporting involve several ethical concerns. Any form of falsehood, hiding or distortion of relevant information in the process of data collection or interpretation is unacceptable in qualitative study and therefore, a cross-check advances the authenticity of the transcript and thus impact the overall quality of the data.

Research approaches have their own intrinsic ethical strengths and limitations and therefore, we choose ethical scrutiny that is appropriate to the methodology employed. Mason posits that the qualitative researchers cannot be satisfied with the standardized or codified answers to ethical and political dilemmas. For her it is because, "…ethical and political issues arise or take shape contextually throughout the research process, and need to be dealt with in ways which are informed or situated rather than formal or abstract."[37] Nonetheless, we realize that there are learning contexts that need primary orientation in the process and its central values. From there, an authentic awareness on the ethics of qualitative researching stems forth. Answers to most ethical dilemmas in qualitative research come from awareness of *ethics guidance*, Ryen argues,[38] coupled with ongoing reflection, previous research information and where possible, discussion with colleagues and research supervisors. Ultimately, we envision a form of theological research practice that will stand high in authenticity amidst methodological criticisms and the scrutiny of the academic etiquette.

Institution's Guidelines and Researcher's Personal Ethics

Adherence to the institution's policies and guidelines is a key determinant in the successful process of research and thesis writing. Listed below are a few basic ethical commitments for the student to take into account.

True Documents of Credentials: The academic documents submitted at the time of admission/registration should be certified as true and the motivations leading to

---

[37] Jennifer Mason, *Qualitative Researching* (Thousand Oaks, CA: Sage, 1996), 167.
[38] A Ryen, 'Ethics and Qualitative Research' 416-438 in D Silverman (ed) *Qualitative Research,* 3rd Edition, (London: Sage, 2011), 416.

the study, sincere. In treading the path to an authentic future in ministry, whether serving the church, the society, or academia, this is pivotal.

Institution's Policies: The researcher's thorough understanding about the research guidelines, procedures and potential problems on the way is another dimension of ethical safeguard. Figuring these out prior to joining a program can guard researchers to avoid any errors at a later stage. In the formal academic setting of a seminary or university, the researcher's acquaintance with the institution's policies and requirements on the legal/justice issues is a relevant ethical consideration for the novice. However, there are qualitative researchers (experienced professors or field missionaries) whose primary aim is the personal accomplishment of a study or publishing a report of a specialized inquiry, rather than securing a degree. For them obviously the time frame and work style will be flexible.

Official Permissions: Another area within the institution's ethical commitment is obtaining necessary permissions for the study project. Human subject research (HSR) and associated legal bearings are taking on complex procedures over the past few decades. Theological institutions are insisting that their researchers obtain official permissions from the relevant organizations, sponsors, participants and sometimes, the civil governing body before the actual conduct of the inquiry. Ideally, copies of such consent documents should be handed in to the academic committee as a prerequisite for the approved initiation of the research. When a project contains critical organizational evaluations or matters of certain private nature, these formal authorizations safeguard both the legal standing of the institution and the academic pursuits of the researcher. The researcher should set appropriate ethical safeguards so that the name of the theological institution or church is not dragged into undesirable public debates.

Official Documents: There are situations when various types of document-misappropriations happen during the higher education/research pursuits, including the illegitimate use of official resources for personal gains. Utmost ethical courtesy is required when mentors/faculty allow freedom to the researchers as their colleagues, for instance, to access offices or formal papers. Any form of misuse or manipulation is a disciplinary offence and moreover, violation of the principle of honesty.

Sponsoring Body: the researcher's ethical commitments extend to the sponsoring/funding body. When organizations, churches, or other agencies fund a project, the researcher normally signs an agreement. Deliberate breaches to the agreement occurs by way of; wilful delays that result in prolonged stay in the place of research (sometime long enough to secure citizenship or a permanent resident status in another country), not returning to serve in the country of origin (in spite of the mutual agreement clauses to serve in the socio-religious context of the inquiry), misuse of financial resources and mismanagement of time by getting overly involved in other jobs and so on. The researchers prolonging their assigned period of study for vested personal interests also hinders the educational prospects for other potential researchers.

Disciplined Conduct: The researcher should carry out the task realizing that the institution has the right to prevent the researcher in cases of unethical procedures for example, ongoing negligence in the study, plagiarism, manipulations/attacks of any kind on a supervisor and so on. Good research is accomplished only with proper measures of accountability in place. Part of the responsibility of the researcher is to guard the study as well as the report from all forms of falsehood, lying, apparent contradictions and any type of distortion of facts. Respecting the individual space of research mentor, fellow researchers, and the research participants also needs to be prudently handled. In spite of the freedom given in conversations, friendship and trust, the researcher has certain professional boundaries to uphold, not allowing any of the corrupt relational dynamics to develop.

Plagiarism

An outright breach of academic integrity, *plagiarism* is defined as presenting someone's ideas as one's own, and incorporating the ideas of the author with or without proper consent or not fully acknowledging the source. Published works, manuscripts, research reports, electronic sources, illustrations, graphs, and charts fall under the term *source*. Plagiarism is described as irresponsible, intentional or unintentional.[39] *Irresponsibility* is when the writer avoids putting the quote in quotation marks or providing incorrect reference information. Plagiarism is charged as *intentional* whenever the researcher turns in someone's idea as his/her own or copying sentences or ideas without giving due credit to the original source. *Unintentional* plagiarism accusations are assigned to occasions where the writer appeared to have followed a flawed method in writing particularly due to unawareness. In other words, this is a type of plagiarizing that results from the disregard for conventional academic patterns, for example, by not fully citing what is termed as "common knowledge" or by not "quoting" or indenting the information provided. Sometimes when wrong references are provided alongside the words or ideas of others, they too are classified as unintentional, based on the pattern followed. When scrutinized against academic regulations, all except the *unintentional* are classified as disciplinary offence in academia.

Discussion on cyber and library ethics is progressing in academic circles. Many find the technological highway easier than the discomforts of hours spent in the

---

[39]   https://www.ox.ac.uk/students/academic/guidance/skills/plagiarism?wssl=1 accessed on April, 24, 2017 The University of Oxford document 'Plagiarism'.

library, reading, referring and taking notes. Technology, unfortunately, has made things easy for the writers to *cut 'n paste*. More than regulations imposed, the researcher's personal ethic has to operate here, while global academia's battling against this peril continues. The technocratic world offers students freedom to do things in a much easier and more convenient ways. The amazing cyber world is accessible to anyone who has a computer and internet facility. Free online conferencing software is getting widely and effectively used for group discussions with visual interactions. With the World Wide Web's information explosion comes many more challenges around the concerns of plagiarism.

Plagiarism is classified as an offensive intellectual theft and deception that prevents efficient personal learning and development as it is presenting ideas of others as one's own for some personal or academic advantage. The researchers are required to guard their report by not giving the slightest chance to the supervisor or examiner to find evidences of plagiarism. Once researchers are indicted of it in a formal institution, legal procedures are followed to the extent that they lose the current degree for which the research was done. Sometimes this might result in serious disciplinary actions (outside of academia, e.g., in churches, missions or religious organizations) by which the researcher loses associated privileges, titles and even honours from former degrees. The researchers must remind themselves of the world's leaders who lost their dream positions on charges of plagiarism in doctoral theses. In the pursuit of higher education in theology, we reiterate that academics without character will not take us to any sustainable heights. Academic writings that happen in theology schools are not insusceptible from the concerns of plagiarism. Often it is just that we seem to be lacking intentional and cohesive academic procedures to address it.

Forms of Plagiarism

Verbatim (word for word) use of text: Use of exact words without proper acknowledgement is an outright instance of plagiarism. Quotes from other sources should be in inverted commas or indentation along with the complete reference. Readers/examiners must be helped to distinguish effortlessly between the quoted words/sentences and the ones written by the researcher.

Paraphrasing: This occurs in many ways such as closely resembling the structure of the original sentences, or making slight alternations in the order of words or the way of presenting. The original sources of the paraphrased sentences also need to be acknowledged fully.

Collusion: In the case of group works or collaborative writing endeavours, the writer must clearly associate each sentence/section with its actual contributor. Presenting it all pretentiously as one's own writing is a plagiarism indicator. Failure to acknowledge any form of research or writing assistance is plagiarism.

Cut 'n Paste from the Internet: Information derived from internet sources need to be fully referenced with the author's name, title of the paper, the URL reference and the accessed date and time. The examiner/reader should be able to access the source without difficulty, using the references provided.

Auto-plagiarism: Partial or full submission of one's own previous papers or research reports again for assessment comes under the category of auto-plagiarism. If this is with works that are submitted to the same institution concurrently for two requirements, or the same institution for two different courses/times, or between different seminaries/universities, it is an academic offence.

Inaccurate Citation: Accurate citation is academic ethics for primary, secondary and tertiary sources. In the main text, footnote or endnote, the writer has to provide full reference in the style prescribed by the institution. Leaving any information ambiguous will raise the issue of plagiarism. The full name of the author/s, indication of editor/s, title of the article/book, actual page numbers if it is an article or chapter in a book, place and name of publisher, year of publishing and exact page number of the quote are basic items required. When information is derived from secondary source, both sources (secondary source and the mention of the primary source in it) need to be acknowledged fully.

Researchers need to practice using quotation marks or block quotes when exact words or sentences of an author are used. Both these cases allow no modification in the quote. A new word added in the original quote has to be placed in square brackets and any omissions from the quote, with ellipses. Quotes in more than three lines are to be made block quotes. The researcher must credit the sources upfront even if only ideas are referred to.

Plagiarism has no place in authentic research and thesis writing since it hinders the development of the student's own thinking and expression and obstructs the transformative and total learning process.

Factors underlying the tendency to plagiarize include: the behavioural tendency of researchers to hurry in the last minute; mentors who show much disinterest in the research; subject becomes heavily theoretical; pressure to turn in literature review or chapters of the thesis while other course work needs to be handed in; unlimited opportunity conferred by the information technology to copy-paste; and limitations in language and expression of the researcher to list a few of the many factors.

Great researchers keep asking critical questions of themselves all through the process of inquiry. At the close of this chapter on research ethics, we ask ourselves a few reflective questions at random: How do the tenets of spontaneity and imagination help or hinder the ethical soundness of the qualitative study? Why is it crucial for the theology researcher to have a central theological matrix in the study, rather than presenting it as merely a sociological undertaking? Why is it difficult to identify one's own biases (personal, missiological, contextual, doctrinal or any other) and handle them effectively during the research? How could the theological academy ensure that the researchers are trained to do their work with highest ethical etiquette?

Reflection Box:

Do not panic when evidence contradicts…

Student B rushed to the mentor's office in the middle of the hectic days of data collection with a rather confused face, "I'm sorry … think I've got my assumption wrong." Her exhaustive effort to discover the evils of domestic child labour is now at stake as two of her selected cases had proved otherwise. Those two kids enjoyed greater security in the homes where they worked. She found them safe, joyful and even allowed to attend school. In panic, her initial instinct was to hide these evidences and look for more cases that will support her thinking. In fact, all other cases represented the unconceivable measures of abuse and child right violations going on.

CONSIDER:

What did the mentor say?

- I appreciate your honesty. Without you sharing this, I would have never known the reality. So, remember, a qualitative researcher is never afraid to speak the truth!
- Deviant cases do not disprove your research; rather they prove the credibility of your qualitative inquiry.
- Qualitative researcher is not signed on to present a total number of supportive evidences to make generalizations on a social reality. The unbiased study of the complex human experiences and perspectives gives you surprises all along!
- The important step now is to probe perceptively deeper and interpret these special cases for your readers. Let them gain the whole view of things!

CHAPTER 4

THE THEORETICAL MILIEU AND THE LITERATURE REVIEW

SECTION CONTENTS:

- Setting the Theoretical Framework for Research
- Purpose and Function of Literature Review in Research
- Primary, Secondary and Tertiary Sources

Setting the Theoretical Framework for Research

One of the curiosities for the reader is about the way in which the qualitative researcher develops the theoretical framework and the literature in the scheme. *Theoretical framework* is not referring to any one existing theory, rather the foundational structure of the research. It can be explained as,

> Theories in social research are formulated to explain, predict, and understand phenomena and, in many cases, to challenge and extend existing knowledge within the limits of critical bounding assumptions. The theoretical framework is the structure that can hold or support a theory of a research study. The theoretical framework introduces and describes the theory that explains why the research problem under study exists.[1]

Theories (a set of concepts that defines the research problem) are made from concepts (specific ideas derived from the problem) and concepts take their form from models (conventional formats describing the problem). Thus from common models of experiences we formulate concepts and a set of relevant concepts builds a theory that provides the logical structure to the research. Apparently, this theoretical frame does not stand on its own, rather it holds every aspect of the study closely,

---

[1]   Gabriel Abend, 'The Meaning of Theory', *Sociological Theory* 26, 173-199 (June 2008), 173. Refer also, Richard A Swanson, *Theory Building in Applied Disciplines* (San Francisco, CA: Berrett Coehler Publishers, 2013).

in particular, the research question, objectives of the study and the review of the literature. It has concepts identified and defined on evidences from the review of the literature. The research question emerges from a social situation that has multiple models and concepts already in operation. The researcher identifies the interconnectedness of these concepts through the lens of the research problem and undertakes a comprehensive review of literature and hence, develops the theoretical framework.

A widespread misconception among novice researchers is that the qualitative research does not need a theoretical frame. Silverman says,

> Some people become qualitative researchers for rather negative reasons. Perhaps they are not very good at statistics and so are not tempted by quantitative research. Or perhaps they have not shone at library work and so are not tempted to write a purely theoretical dissertation.[2]

Those who relegate qualitative theological research into a naïve field task also assume no theoretical grounding for this form of research undertaking. Doing research without a theoretical frame, nevertheless, is like building the house without a structure. Without theoretical matrix, the study will suffer the dearth of a guiding structure, and resultantly, its authenticity, meaning and impact. Jenesick affirms that the qualitative researchers should have 'open but not empty minds'.[3]

There are researchers in the qualitative domain, who presume that the procedure can take any turn any time as they claim *originality*, saying, 'no research has been undertaken on the issue so far'. They tend to proceed without a tentative theory frame, consequently producing research reports that are not deep, authentic, transformative or connected to the existing world of knowledge. The contention might be that the qualitative researcher functions on flexibility and creativity. However, the proposal here is that the qualitative study operates in a cohesive conceptual frame that is rooted in the research problem and constructed in view of the possible theoretical momentum it assumes to take. This is deeper than incorporating a theory in the study for its own sake. We also recognize, on the other hand, that research will not benefit from a rigid theoretical frame that obstructs the creative approach in qualitative inquiry.

Researchers ask instantaneously, how then to formulate a theoretical frame? As mentioned previously, since a readily available theoretical frame may not fit with one's research direction, the researcher needs to be innovative. The social researcher,

---

[2]   David Silverman, *Doing Qualitative Research* (London: Sage, 2000), 75.
[3]   V Janesick, 'The Choreography of Qualitative Research Design: Minuets, Improvisations and Crystallization', 379-399, in N Denzin and Y Lincoln (eds), *Handbook of Qualitative Research*, (2ⁿᵈ Edition), (Thousand Oaks, CA: Sage, 2000), 384.

for his/her own academic advantage, has to think through the conceptual grounds of the research problem and develop a theoretical matrix to address it. Apparently, it takes preliminary research to get to this stage. Faculty mentors use a variety of methods to help the researcher come to a focus. In fact, much of it is done by raising critical questions at the choices that the researcher has already made in the thesis proposal. The researchers, in the beginning, tend to be vague about what they are doing.

Mind-mapping is one helpful task here. When a brand new idea sparks off in your mind, you may draw the idea with all its corresponding points like a trunk of a tree with its branches, or using any other form of diagrams. New subsidiary ideas should be linked to its own main idea and those that should radiate from the centre or a particular end, should be drawn likewise. Thus the researcher obtains clarity about the research process and is able to formulate a communicable theoretical framework that directs and controls the inquiry.

The theoretical matrix is not copied from the available literature, rather, it is constructed by the researcher who analyses the research question and the conceptual path in the data process towards arriving at a cohesive conclusion. Identifying and stating the theoretical assumptions and analytic patterns of the researcher serves as a great roadmap. Towards formulating the theoretical frame, researchers may use resources such as methodologies introduced in previous course works, relevant theoretical designs employed in other research undertakings, and consultations with cross-disciplinary experts in academic disciplines. In other words, researcher's working ideas and intuitions can be assessed against theories used in previous research, emergent theories in the real time and the underlying issues in the topic. Also, exploring theories and their workings across academic disciplines in the context of a research question are very informative. The researcher thinks through the many theories available while proceeding to designing the theoretical frame for the inquiry. Grant and Osanloo[4] outline several theory categories, a few of which are given below for initial reflections.

- Behavioural theories
- Queer theories
- Systems theories
- Trait theories
- Transformational/Relational theories

4   Cynthia Grant and Azadeh Osanloo, Understanding, Selecting and Integrating a Theoretical Framework in Dissertation Research: Creating a Blueprint for your "House" 12-26 in *Administrative Issues Journal: Connecting Education, Practice and Research* Vol 4, Issue 2, 2014, 14-15. DOI:10.5929/2014.4.2.9 accessed May 18, 2017. http://jolle.coe.uga.edu/wp-content/uploads/2015/02/89596_manuscript-file_249104.pdf

- Situational theories
- Developmental theories
- Feminist theories
- Gender theories
- Functionalist theories
- Marxist theories
- Change theories
- Identity formation theories
- Cognitive theories
- Transactional/management theories
- Intersubjectivity theories and so on

Each of the above theory fields has multiple divisions and sub-divisions for the researcher to unearth. For example, *Developmental Theories* are referred significantly across the fields of learning and administration. Illustrating psychological theories of human development, there are divisions such as cognitive development, faith development, emotional development, physical development, mental development in addition to the numerous varieties of stage-development theories. For the social researcher, a foundational understanding of theories related to his/her inquiry is a vital step in the making of a theoretical frame. However, it is not just the knowledge of theory but rather, the interrelations of the research question, objectives, data design, and theory that provides the dynamic matrix for the qualitative study. Uncritical use of a theory therefore, only invalidates the inquiry. Silverman presented[5] three unreliable approaches in theoretical development:

- 'simplistic inductivism', in which researchers immerse themselves in the research setting, hoping that constructs and ideas will emerge through in-depth exposure
- 'kitchen sinkers' whose minds are cluttered by all kinds of unordered and unstructured ideas
- 'grand theorists' who are too uncritically attached to a theory and need to be reminded of the role of new data in their study

Good research has a philosophical underpinning. This frame of logic could be sociological, historical, philosophical, theological, or hermeneutical or all of these or the combination of a few. Research approach needs to be built on a functional philosophical stance and that forms an important feature in the direction of the inquiry. The data process and the outcomes are determined largely on this. The philosophical assumptions used in handling the research problem are crucial components in the

---

⁵ David Silverman, *Doing Qualitative Research*, 3ʳᵈ Edition, (London: Sage, 2010), 84-88.

formulation of the theoretical frame. In fact, the very use of the term *methodology* should denote the theoretical frame of a logical continuum starting with ontology and epistemology.[6] From the beginning of the inquiry, a researcher has to *think* about his/her ways of *thinking*. Consider a few core philosophical assumptions that regulate the style of thinking. Which of these **philosophical assumptions** is taken on in the inquiry as the theoretical frame is being designed?

- Ontology: The science of being. It deals with the nature and characteristics of the phenomenon being studied. The perspective of the social world where the nature of being is the philosophical focus. Ontology refers to the fundamental nature of the world and what it means to exist in that world. Question is: What is?

- Epistemology: The branch of philosophy that deals with the sources of knowledge. It is the study of knowledge; of grounds on which we claim to know something about the world. e.g., positivist epistemology suggests that the truth claims in the research are based upon the broader tenets of natural sciences. Question: How do we know? Generally recognized sources of knowledge are:
  1. Intuitive knowing (faith, intuition and such generally accepted knowledge)
  2. Authoritative (new information received from books, experts, authority sources)
  3. Logical (knowledge that derives from active reasoning between the two above)
  4. Empirical (knowledge based on observation/experience/experimentation)

- Phenomenology: The science of phenomena as distinct from that of the nature of being. It is the study of experience. It is about how people view their experience uniquely. Question: How do we experience?

- Axiology: the science that adds value to the inquiry; recognizes the value-laden nature of information gathered. Question: What values reinforce the inquiry?

- Logic: It is about valid reasoning. A critical additional question for the theology researcher is, for example; Does the Bible assume a crucial role in our reasoning? Question: How do we reason?

- Ethics: The science of right or wrong. Question: How should we act or live? Again, what is the norm?

---

6 Paul Oliver, *Writing Your Thesis* (London: Sage Publications, 2008), 23-24.

The ***interpretive assumptions*** on which the researcher works out the process are also taken into account in designing the theoretical frame. The qualitative inquirer is not choosing some data gathering methods at random. There are coherent interpretive frameworks that underpin the research design, the literature review and the entire path of argument. Creswell's[7] extensive outline presented below has pointers for reflection on the interpretive assumptions of the researcher. These interpretive frameworks are social science theories or social justice theories that include mainly Positivism, Constructivism, Hermeneutics, Cultural Studies Model and Post-Colonialism and a broader category of frameworks such as:

- Post-positivism: Follows scientific approach but is not confined strictly to cause and effect logic; it believes that all cause and effect is a possibility to occur or not.
- Social Constructivism: Participants make subjective interpretations of the social reality they live in. Knowledge is seen as what people construct.
- Transformative frameworks: Base on the view that knowledge has power to transform relationships and societies and therefore suggest a transformative action agenda in inquiry. Knowledge is seen as not merely abstract.
- Post-modern perspectives: Build on deconstructionism, anti-foundationalism, multiple meanings and perspectives. Knowledge claims are counted as conditional to the changes in thinking as the world goes.
- Pragmatism: Focuses on the results and consequences of the study. What works is the way it takes. It does not restrict to any philosophical or scientific theory rather offers freedom to choose what works in the given time.
- Feminist Theories: Address issues relating to gender domination and related issues in patriarchal settings. Seeks collaborative relationships, consciousness-raising and transformative thinking.
- Critical Theory and Critical Race Theory: Empowers humans to transcend the boarders set by the society in the name of class, race, colour, and gender. Calls dialogues and acclaims participants' own power to interpret the meaning of social reality;
- Queer Theory: Deals with the complex interpretations of human identity as to how identities are constructed, how they develop and transform the society. Theories of identity as fixed or normal are challenged.
- Disability Theory: Addresses the issues of disability and meanings of inclusion of the disabled in social forums.[8]

---

[7]   John W Creswell, *Qualitative Inquiry and Research Design: Choosing Among Five Approaches* (Thousand Oaks, CA: Sage, 2013).

[8]   Adapted from John W Creswell, *Qualitative Inquiry and Research Design: Choosing Among Five Approaches* (Thousand Oaks, CA: Sage, 2013), 23-33.

The researcher should also take into account the **reasoning methods** that guide the project. Is there a particular reasoning method from the social research that reinforces the study? A few types are:

- Inductive reasoning: Generating theory. Reasoning and research that moves from specific observations to general, the theory. Grounded Theory is an inductive method that is based on a specific epistemology or philosophy of knowledge.
- Deductive reasoning: Testing a theory or a hypothesis. It is about reasoning and research that tests or confirms certain propositions. It moves from general to specific data.
- Dialectical reasoning: The method that interrogates or examines competing ideas, perspectives, practices or paradigms; mostly takes sociological or philosophical forms; discourses to establish truth through reasoned arguments.
- Causal Reasoning: The method by which one makes an argument to establish a cause and result relationship, normally a correlation task.

The **Biblical methodological assumptions** mark a vital turn in theological research. The way in which the researcher approaches the Bible influences the direction of the theological study. In the formulation of the theoretical frame by a theology researcher, the hermeneutical and exegetical principles that guide the study have an important say. Hermeneutics concern the philosophy and science that guide the process of interpretation, particularly, the interpretation of communication. Exegesis is the actual task or process of interpretation. For the qualitative researcher, the hermeneutical lens determines the theological cue forward. Also, it is important to note that concerning the matter of religion and research, the theological assumptions that guide the pre-modernists and the post-modernists are different. We now consider a few varieties of exegetical approaches in theology studies:

- The historical-critical methods: e.g., textual, source, form, redaction, socio-historical, traditional-literary criticisms
- The historical-traditional methods: Canonical methods, Jewish-Christian hermeneutical methods
- The literary analysis methods: Narrative, semiotic and rhetorical methods
- The contextual methods: Feminist methods, Liberationist methods
- The human sciences methods: Psychological methods, anthropological methods, sociological methods

Another aspect that informs the theoretical frame is the **contextual assumptions** by which the study is led. Take for example, the contextual theology of Bevans, who outlines six models of contextual theology[9] that correspond to the impact between gospel and culture. Such constructs guide the researcher to evaluate the thinking patterns, weigh the pros and cons of the models, and make decisions on the exegetical path to take in the study. Comprehensive criticism on theoretical constructs is an advanced way of intellectual interaction.

- The translation model: Gospel made understandable to the culture.
- The anthropological model: Starting from the good in the culture and allow the gospel to work in and through it.
- The praxis model: Practice first; then reflection and modified practice; focusing on orthopraxy.
- The synthetic model: Holds the three above in balance.
- The transcendental model: Focus on individual knowledge of the truth; revelation seen private and personal.
- The counter-cultural model: Gospel challenging the culture: culture is approached with an amount of suspicion.[10]

The **theological reflection methods** of researchers are significantly varied. The researchers usually have their own ways to make sense of their theological vision in the inquiry. The interpretive paradigms discussed earlier in this chapter are at work in this. One of the vital dimensions in theology research is gaining awareness of the theological reflection method patterned in the study. The seven types of theological reflection in practical theology[11] by Graham, Walton and Ward are reflection methods to be considered throughout the process of the study.

- The Living Human Document - 'Theology by Heart'
- Constructive narrative theology - 'Speaking in Parables'
- Canonical narrative theology - 'Telling God's Story'
- Corporate theological reflection - 'Writing the Body of Christ'
- Correlation - 'Speaking of God in Public'
- Praxis - 'Theology in Action'
- Local Theologies - 'Theology in the vernacular'[12]

In view of all these, we ask, what is the theoretical structure being assumed or perceived in the study? How are concepts and processes intertwined? What is the frame that holds the many schemes and activities undertaken to systematically handle the research problem? Through systematic analysis of these several dimensions, the

---

[9]   Stephen B Bevans, *Models of Contextual Theology*, (New York, Maryknoll: ORBIS, 2004), 37-138.

[10]   Adapted from Bevans, *Models of Contextual Theology*, 2004, 37-138.

[11]   Elaine Graham, Heather Walton and Frances Ward (eds), *Theological Reflection Methods*, (London: SCM, 2005).

[12]   Graham, Walton and Ward (Eds), *Theological Reflection Methods* (London: SCM, 2005).

researcher first of all gains clarity about the process and simultaneously becomes able to design the theoretical framework. This framework strengthens and authenticates the qualitative researcher's task in many ways as suggested in the following points.

Function of a Theoretical Frame in Qualitative Research

- A good theoretical frame will demonstrate how the researcher views the research question as well the learning process philosophically, epistemologically, analytically, contextually and theologically.
- The diagrammatic design of the theoretical frame makes the conceptual interconnections and assumptions explicit.
- A functional theoretical frame enhances the literature review and helps it to maintain a clear focus.
- It sets the research question in place.
- It surfaces any unnoticed gaps between concepts and theories and thus gives the study a steadier direction.
- It enhances the methodological quality of the study, and withstands sharp criticisms on qualitative methodology for being less-theoretical.
- It helps the researcher to develop the research question, literature review and the data procedures logically.
- It assists the disintegrated concepts regarding the problem of study to discover operative interconnections.

In summary, a theoretical frame is a collection of interrelated concepts like a theory that is designed to guide the path of research or to show the basic conceptual frame that underpins the research task, yet, not a well-worked out, final form of theory. It guides the study to show us what to evaluate and analyse. It is the study of existing concepts and theories as to how these have changed over time, what new models are emergent and how these will be weighed in data analysis. Merriam[13] proposes it as the researcher's lens with which he/she views the world. If the lens is concerned over various forms of injustice, the researcher will identify patterns of oppressive and harmful structures. Theoretical frames offer a logical structure of connected concepts, displayed in some graphic form to show the theoretical correlations of the study. They are not, however, a simplistic display of ideas but are patterns of relationships between concepts and their ontological and epistemological paradigms or the forms of potential theories.

While establishing the significance of having a theoretical frame, we also realize that not all research reports will have their theoretical frames *made explicit*.

---

[13]   Sharan B Merriam, *Qualitative Research and Case Study Applications in Education* (San Francisco, CA: Jossey Bass, 1997).

Nonetheless, the way it can add value and direction to the researcher, research and the readers endorses the case of the framework's explicit inclusion somewhere in the study, say e.g., as a section in the literature review as certain researchers would prefer. With a well-aligned theoretical frame preferably shown in a diagram, the researcher obtains better confidence in the outcome of the study. Complex designs present many depictions of interconnections in the same diagram. The researchers make diagrams to illustrate their overall task or various stages in the inquiry. See Figure 10. a simple design that communicates the path of a Grounded Theory inquiry on the *impact of cultural forces on women's theological training and ministry in typically patriarchal contexts*. Remember, the same idea can be depicted in many other ways, and, definitely, in more articulate ways, portraying the multiple tasks involved and their underpinnings.

Figure 10: A Simple Theoretical Frame Model on Grounded Theory

Topic E.g. : Theological Education and Ministry of Women in Patriarchal Cultures

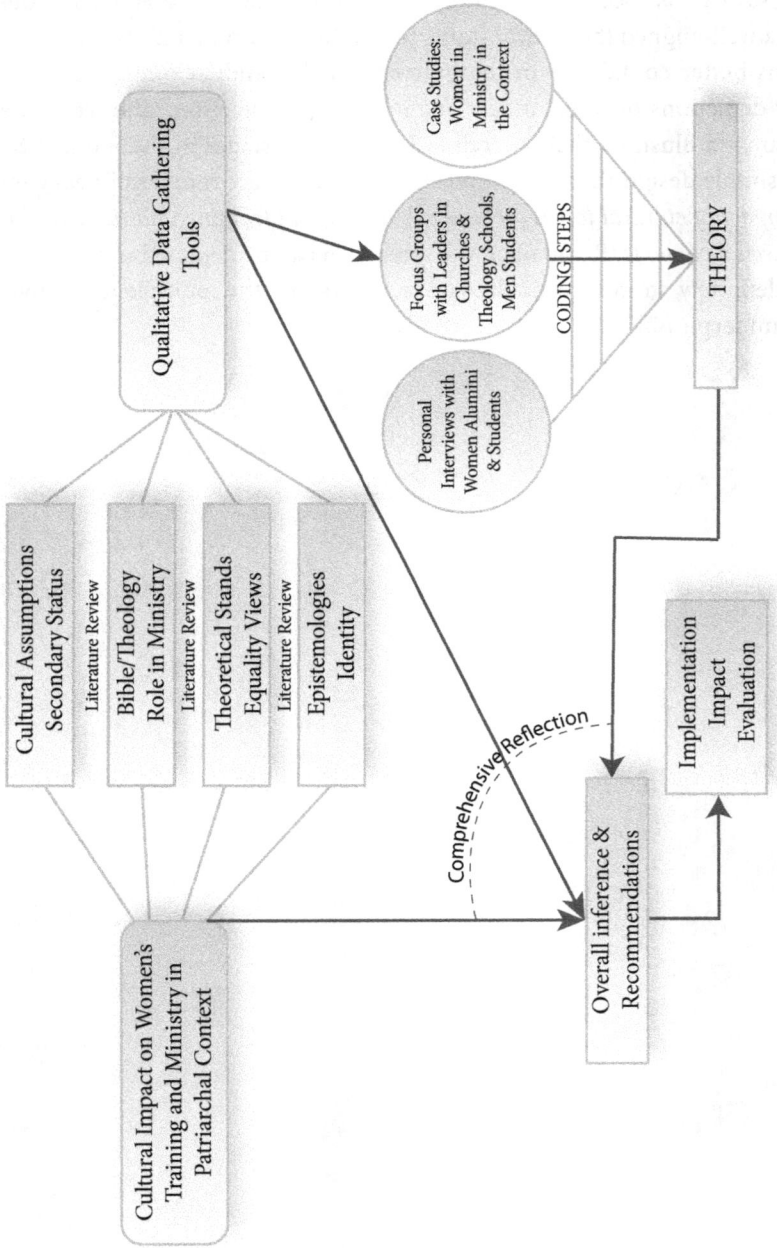

Inquiry

Visual depictions are highly useful not only for the researcher, but also for the reader. The researchers sometimes use theoretical frames to demonstrate their data analysis scheme. Let us see how the diagram below articulates the procedure followed in analysing a cultural situation. Remember, thinkers can use this model to reflect on cultural change in leadership, mission movements, educational philosophies and many other areas.

Figure 11: A Dialectical Hermeneutical Frame Work Model

Cultural Analysis- A Dialectical Hermeneutical Model

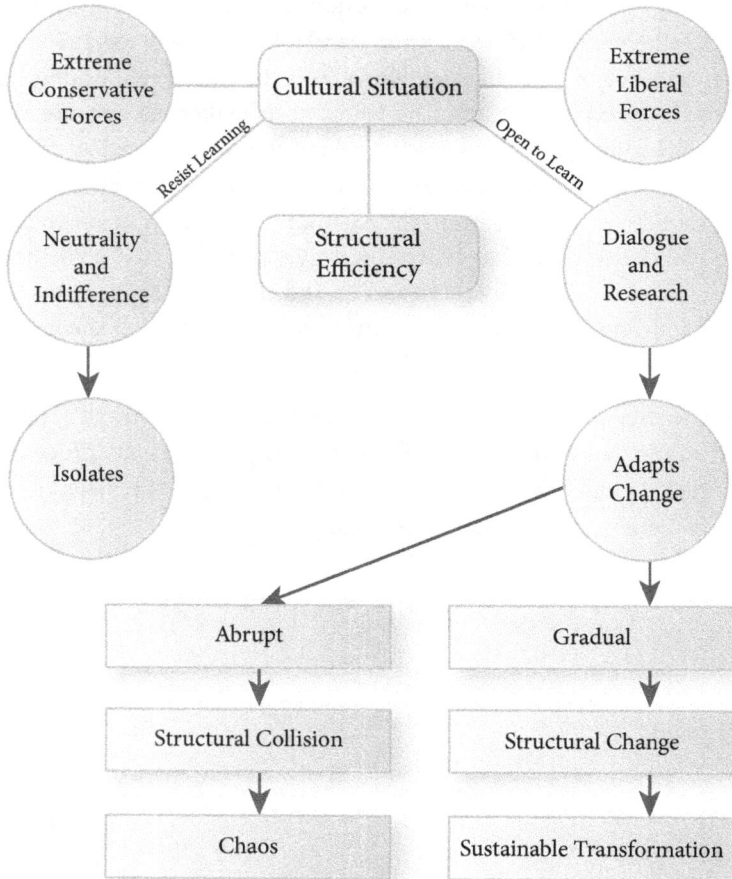

Purpose and Function of Literature Review in Research

Mapping between Theoretical Frame and the Literature Review

Theoretical frame provides the conceptual mapping to make effective interconnections between the research problem and the literature review and the development of the central argument. The pictorial depiction of interconnection of concepts, theories and the exiting themes in literature provides the structure for the entire process of research. Bryman suggests that the qualitative researcher employs an "oscillation between testing emergent theories and collecting data."[1] Hence, the review of literature might start with the statement and elaboration of the research problem and a general design of the review. The section that presents the theoretical frame will also define theory, key theorists, history and relevance of theory, gaps developed in theory, emergence of new theories, along with the conceptual underpinnings as discussed in the previous section. The framework makes explicit the theoretical and philosophical underpinnings and specifies the key theoretical principles to be applied to the study, organized around conceptual themes and sub-headings. Identification of conflicts and gaps in the existing literature are also explained. This logical mapping between the topic, research question, objectives, methodologies, literature, previous research, data procedures and the impact is specifically helpful in designing a strong literature base for the study. Thus, a good theoretical frame serves also to the enhancement of the literature review.

Relating to the previously mentioned topic of cultural impact on women's theological training and ministry, the following diagram presents procedures for a coherent review of literature. This visual depiction clarifies the areas of focus and their interconnections in developing the background theory.

---

[1]   Alan Bryman, *Social Research Methods,* 4th Edition, Chapter 3 'Research Designs' (Oxford: Oxford University Press, 2012:387).

Figure 12: Theoretical Frame: A Literature Review Model
Defining Literature Review

Topic Eg.: Theological Education and Ministry of Women in Patriarchal Context

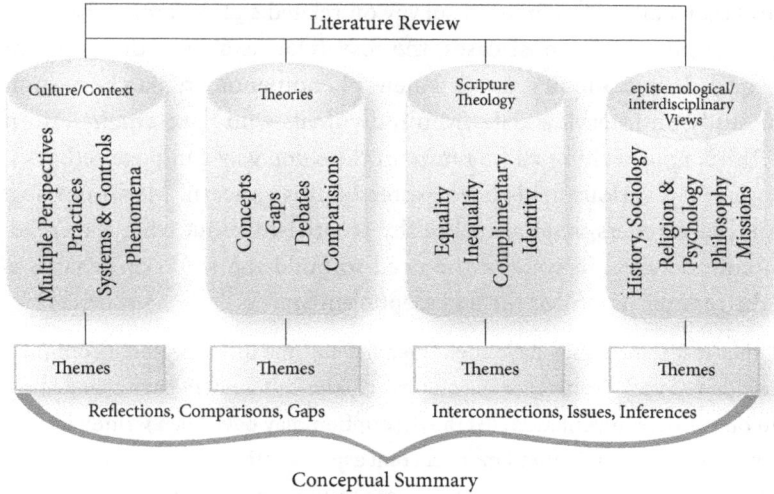

Literature Review is the detailed report of a research on the existing literature in the field of study, defined as "...a systematic, explicit, and reproducible method for identifying, evaluating and interpreting the existing body of recorded work produced by researchers, scholars, and practitioners."[1] The reviewing of scholarly literature is an on-going task for the researcher and there are two major reviews: first, the *preliminary literature review* or the *pre-review survey* that helps the researcher see if the research question is rightly placed in the existing knowledge, and, second, the *formal extensive literature review* presented in the research report that lays the foundational theoretical frame for the qualitative field inquiry. The pre-review survey can assist the researcher with the initial task of determining the key areas to cover in the review. In the initial phase of the study, researchers do extensive surveys of the periodical indices, dissertation abstracts, scholarly journals, bibliographies in recent publications, computerized data bases, selection on the library stacks, media and any relevant sources that provide information on the topic under consideration. Wide ranging sources like classics, texts, journals, theses, newspaper reports, thematic research magazines and official Government reports are reviewed.

Reviewing literature, however, involves various concerns. First, as information proliferates at a rapid rate, researchers need guidance in terms of where to find authentic resources and how to decide what to take and what to leave. Second, there

---

[1]   Arlene Fink, *Conducting Research Literature Reviews: From Paper to Internet* (Thousand Oaks, CA: Sage, 1998), 3.

are many learning contexts around the world where researchers still suffer the lack of availability or accessibility to literature. However, this does not invalidate the prominence of literature review in a research. In such cases, the researcher analyses the research problem and objectives of the study to determine the key contents in the inquiry and then conducts a focused survey on related subject areas where literature is available. Eventually, in most cases, the researcher is able to develop a relevant literature grid. When inquiry is on a new phenomenon, researchers sometimes base their study on interview data from individuals who have crucial information to share. Third, approaching all literature in the same way can pose setbacks to the study. Inquirers in various fields have expressed this concern. McKinney suggested that cultural researchers maintain a healthy scepticism about what they read about the given cultural area, in spite of the need to build the study on what is already written. The reasons identified for this scepticism are:

> (1) Other researchers may have spent insufficient time in the research communities to have delved very deeply into the culture, (2) the culture may have changed resulting in out-of-date information, (3) the description may have been written in the ethnographic present that ignored more current aspects of the culture, (4) the researcher may have been mistaken, (5) the researcher's results may have been coloured by his/her theoretical position so that what actually occurred in that culture was obscured, or, (6) the researcher had an inadequate grasp of the local language or worked only through the trade language.[2]

This cautions researchers in general about how they approach the literature. However, comprehensive discussion of the above mentioned challenges in the report will strengthen the research design as a whole.

The writing of the review report is another important consideration for the researcher. It is not about hoarding information from multiple sources. What matters is how the researcher read, understood, analysed, interpreted, recorded and reported the information. The analysis of literature should show evidences of relevant knowledge about the author, the time of publication, anticipated audience, the socio-religious/political context, central standpoint, critical biases, underlying philosophical assumptions, what the literature says, what it does not say, presentation of arguments and so on. The researcher is also advised ***not*** to use references to:

- "Impress your readers with the scope of your reading
- Litter your writing with names and quotations
- Replace the need for you to express your own thoughts

---

[2] Carol V McKinney, *Globe-Trotting in Sandals: A Field Guide to Cultural Research* (Texas, SIL International, 2000), 24.

- Misrepresent their authors"[3]

While analysing literature, the researcher is not presenting the abstract propositions of authors, but rather looks at each of the proposition against what other experts have said. In fact, scholars suggest that the process of literature analysis has the following key features [4] at work:

1.   Concepts: are abstract or general ideas, which are important for how we think about particular subjects or issues.

2.   Theories: are suppositions which explain, or seek to explain, something.

3.   Explanations: are statements which make something intelligible, about why things are the way they are.

4.   Understanding: is our perception of the meaning of something, in this case the subject area, the issues and/or the research questions under consideration.

Review of the literature has specific purposes and characteristics. The aim is not merely to make a chapter in a research report, rather, it is to build the study on the existing knowledge. Popularly, the researcher starts with the basic knowledge of facts regarding the problem of inquiry and moves from there to scholarly opinions, relevant official statistics, previous writings/theses, on-going debates, and existing and emergent theories. "If no one takes notice of previous work the wheel keeps getting re-invented. It is time-consuming, unethical, costly and not in the spirit of scientific work."[5] Key insights for data gathering derive from the literature review. Moreover, beyond summarizing related ideas and arguments on the research topic, the review lays a solid conceptual and theoretical foundation for subsequent processes in the study. Theological assumptions that are part of the theory frame may also constitute a cohesive section of the review or run throughout the review depending on the type of study. Literature Review is clearly organized in sections under headings and sub-headings, closing with a summary on how various elements in the theoretical frame logically connect to the rest of the process. A good review report will present issues, causes, concepts and consequences of the topic of inquiry with clear distinctions and maintain balance between sections, not doing too much for some and too little for the others.

Function of the Literature Review in a Research

Researching and reviewing the precedent literature has numerous advantages and is indispensable to the process of research. A solid review helps to:

---

[3]   Loraine Blaxter, Christina Hughes, Malcolm Tight, *How to Research*, 2nd Edition, (Philadelphia: Open University Press, 2001), 127.

[4]   Blaxter, Hughes and Tight, *How to Research,* 2001, 205.

[5]   Hennie R Boeije, *Analysis in Qualitative Research* (London: Sage, 2010), 21.

- Assess if the proposed topic is worth researching.
- Establish reasons for the relevance of the research undertaking.
- Qualify researcher's proposed theory or hypothesis.
- Discuss researcher's knowledge of the study by presenting key terms, ideas, theories, seminal research outcomes.
- Identify the major dimensions and debates in the subject area and hence develop clear premises for the research.
- Identify variables that are most crucial to the inquiry and glean ideas to develop questions for data gathering.
- Get familiar with the classics in the subject area, key contributors, research reports, theories and theorists.
- Focus the research problem and the question in appropriate context.
- See how concepts and practices are related or separated.
- Provide the reader with an up-to-date account of the issues relevant to the topic
- Specify the parameters and frontiers in the qualitative inquiry on the given topic.
- Get familiar with the principal contributors in their field of interest and hence develop the skills to make intellectual interactions with their concepts and perspectives.
- Make judicious decisions to avoid repetitions of similar studies; Guard from re-inventing the wheel and direct minds to newer dimensions in thinking.
- Formulate the conceptual and theoretical context in which the topic for research can situate.
- Discuss relevant research carried out on the same topic or similar topics.
- Knit together the theoretical, theological, historical and contextual data in the study through checks of consistency, evaluations on gaps, etc.
- Locate significant areas to be explored in further research.

Helpful Tips for the Review of Literature

1. *Do the preliminary survey of literature earnestly:* This pre-research survey provides an overall understanding of the research topic and enables the researcher to make significant decisions for the rest of the inquiry process

2. *Realize that the reviewing of literature can be confusing in the beginning:* This is not a well-defined, stress-free process. The researcher has to solve many issues along the way and explore newer questions and answers while carrying

out extensive reading and reflecting until a steady structure for the research emerges.

3. *Decide on what to take and what to leave:* All resources found in the library are not similarly worthwhile. The researcher handling the massive amount of published material, therefore, should determine 'what to search for', 'what not to focus on', 'how to record the information', and, 'how to integrate the frame of thought for the thesis'.

4. *Consider various approaches to literature reviewing:* There are a number of preferences e.g., go by classics in the field of inquiry, or by key theorists/debates in the subject area, or historical developments in thinking and writing (divided by time) or, content analysis from a broad reading on key areas on the topic. Content analysis is commonly used to derive an objective description of the manifest content of the material available. The choice is to be made on the purpose and direction of the study.

5. *Keep in mind the theological grid and the integrated matrix while reviewing:* A good review will encompass all areas pertinent to the research question. Thus, for the theology researcher, the theological reinforcement is vital. In the theological grid, the researcher shows typical competencies for theological reflection and exemplifies how good theology runs meaningful conversation with other disciplines. A crucial feature is the explanation of how the knowledge of God is corresponding to human realities. This theological matrix of theoretical, biblical, interdisciplinary, and contextual scholarship makes the review report most functional.

6. *Wait for the conceptual frame for research to emerge:* Initial struggle in formulating the conceptual frame is normal in the review process. The researcher has to continue reading on the diverse focuses in the subject area, step away from areas that are not-so-crucial, reflect on relevant theories and debates, and keep engaging in the literature until a purposeful theoretical pattern emerges.

7. *Develop verbal-visual designs during the course of the review:* As the potential theoretical frame emerges, the researcher has to write it down in the form of an outline or make a pictorial design of ideas and see the sequences or correlations to present ideas. This initial plan will be subject to revisions as the reading develops, but it can guard the researcher from getting lost in the unremitting, irrelevant reading.

8. *Handle the large chunks of information wisely:* One of the important decisions is on how to approach the massive amount of information in libraries and on the internet. The researcher has to keep making decisions on this, based on personal capabilities, data organization habits, and the time available for

the review. People are very different in their style of reading, taking notes, writing, thinking and evaluating. What works best for the researcher is what is essentially to be counted.

9. *Identify the best personal pattern for note-taking:* Laptops, netbooks, and smart phones with advanced facilities have replaced the traditional style of papers, files, notebooks, and note cards. However, the decision depends largely on what makes the task easy, what keeps the materials clear, safe and ready for later analysis. Cornell note-taking system or similar patterns of taking notes allows to record information or quotes with the researcher's reflections, questions and ideas beside it. This is taking notes in a way that provokes and records deeper thinking.

10. *Develop essential skills in research:* Researchers are not equally skilled in reading, reflecting and writing. For some, thoughts are clear, but organizing them in writing is simply hard. Those who have good writing skills may not process ideas efficiently. The researcher has to consistently work on these skills to ensure that the literature review has achieved an integrated whole.

11. *Show evidences of comprehensive research in the existing body of knowledge:* Refer various sources of literature in the report appropriately, including books, journals, encyclopaedias, dictionaries, reports, memos, minutes, diary records, personal letters, classic literature, contemporary writings, literary reviews, methodological reviews, theses, newspapers and other popular media.

12. *Develop a clear, communicative style in presentation of the literature review:* As writing develops, the researcher has to check through the sections, sub-sections, links between each part for consistency and most importantly so with the theoretical frame that is taking shape.

Common Concerns in Reviewing the Literature Review Report

- **Tendency to focus overly on convenient zones in the review:** For example, in a study on the pastoral care implications for caregivers of the terminally ill, the researcher may conveniently neglect the psychological or theological foundations while focusing exclusively on terminal illness that has plenteous resources. Literature review is not a matter of convenience, but of exclusive and strategic researching for the layers of knowledge on the topic of inquiry.

- **Unavailability of written documents:** In a study exploring the history of Christian missionary endeavours and the resultant loss of cultural Identity of a given community, the researcher may not have direct documents to consult with. Ideally in such situations, the researcher has the responsibility to consider producing literature sources that are necessary in the context.

The researcher should also engage in gathering literature from related communities as possible, verbal and non-verbal data, and research projects/ publications in similar notion in order to advance the conceptual foundation in the existing knowledge. For instance, the researcher may explore on cultural identity as a vital anthropological concept, in-depth biblical exegesis on the question of cultural identity, historical and sociological evidences of similar phenomena from other countries/contexts and the timeless gospel-culture debate in missiology to enhance integrate thinking. The whole idea of identity has its own significance in sociology, psychology, education, philosophy and religion. Advanced review will accomplish a comprehensive reference on all these dimensions.

- **Researcher's own constraints in exploring wide-range of literature sources:** Researchers can easily get stuck with a handful of texts. Indexes, abstracts and bibliographies concordances provide substantial aids in the review. Along with the classics and academic journals, the researcher can use theses, articles in newspapers, scholarly magazines, and official documents to integrate the topic under consideration. Unpublished articles, dissertations, seminar papers, reports of dialogues and summaries of strategic consultations are worthwhile resources. In developing the theological matrix, concordances, encyclopaedia, lexicons and handbooks serve as significant guideposts.

- **Multiple ways/options for presenting the review report:** The presentation of literature report trails largely on the pattern followed in reading, note-taking and laying-out the sections. If the researcher produces simplistic summaries of authors with no integrated review of thoughts or theories, the presentation will lack the vital contents for the theoretical frame. Literature review has to have effective links between the contextual background, the focal conceptual frame and the data theory. A basic task of the researcher is determining the lay-out of the literature review.

- **On-going revision of the literature review:** Typically, the researcher selects the topic for study after a thorough, preliminary review of literature. Modification and confirmation of the topic is done on the basis of critical analysis of the literature. The revision and development of the review continues through the entire process of inquiry. The frame of literature is so crucial that it serves as the base, the guiding force, and focus-building element in the inquiry.

- **Use of primary, secondary and tertiary sources:** Research project needs to be built firmly on primary sources (original, key sources) of literature. Excessive dependence on the secondary (second hand sources processing information) and tertiary resources (sources built on the secondary data) can downgrade the overall quality of the work. However, factors like the nature and objective of the writing impact this decision. For instance, a scholarly research design, by default, would require the use of classics and primary sources in the field of inquiry.

The following section provides basic information regarding different sources of reference.

Primary, Secondary and Tertiary Sources

Primary sources are those that consist of original works on the subject under study or sources that consist of data gathered at first hand by the researcher. They take the researcher to the people, places and ideas to the original setting of the topic or maximum closer to it. Primary religious scriptures, autobiographies, the Researcher's own first hand exposure in a given context, verbatim responses of people are considered as primary sources. Original works of literature, personal interviews, diaries, letters, original art works, photographs, speeches are all primary sources of information. Primary sources draw the researcher as close as possible to original ideas, events, and empirical research. Such sources may include creative works, first hand or contemporary accounts of events, and the publication of the results of empirical observations or research.

Secondary sources are works done about the original body of knowledge or the primary sources.

These sources analyse review, or summarize information in the primary resources or other secondary resources. Sources presenting facts or descriptions about events are considered secondary unless they are based on direct participation or observation. Moreover, secondary sources often rely on other secondary sources and standard disciplinary methods to reach results, and they provide the principle sources of analysis about primary sources. When a topic is explored in research for the first time, the researcher uses his/her own empirical data as the primary source and useful materials related to the subject area as secondary source for the purpose of interpretation. Monographs, biographies, journal articles, dissertations, indexes, abstracts and bibliographies are considered secondary sources of information. The researcher aims for an exhaustive preliminary study to make an extensive list of primary and secondary sources and determine the difference in employing them in interpretation and analysis. "In most studies researchers will use both kinds of materials-consulting primary sources to gather materials which they consider relevant, and consulting secondary sources to see, among other things, how other researchers have interpreted the same materials."[6] Any material prepared using secondary sources in situations with little access to primary sources are known as the *tertiary sources*. These provide overviews of topics by synthesizing information gathered from other resources. Tertiary resources often provide data in a convenient form or provide information with context by which to interpret it. Summaries or condensed versions of materials are presented, usually with references back to the primary and/or secondary sources. They can be a good place to look up facts or get a general overview of a subject, but they rarely contain original material. Talking in terms of the social and humanities disciplines, dictionaries, encyclopaedias and handbooks fall in this category.

Distinctions between these sources are ambiguous and overlaps are possible. For instance, bibliographies and textbooks could be categorized into secondary or tertiary sources based on the definition given in the given inquiry. However, the decision is made on the time of the production of the source and the result it achieved.

---

[6] Hunter P Mabry, *A Manual for Researchers and Writers*, (Bangalore: BTE-SSC, 1999), 48.

Figure 13: Types of Data Sources in Literature

	Primary	Secondary	Tertiary
Meaning and task	First hand sources from the time of events; represent original information or empirical data; not reworked by evaluations or interpretations	Sources that interpret or evaluate information from primary or other secondary sources; it communicates existing knowledge, issues, interpretations and evaluations on the topic; review, analyse or summarize primary information	Synthesize or repackage information from other sources; provide overviews of topics; summaries or condensed versions of information from primary and secondary sources
Source examples	Personal letters, correspondences, eye witnesses, statistics, government documents, first hand surveys, original literature, autobiographies, memoirs, diaries, photographs, artefacts, audio-video recordings, newspaper cuttings from the actual event-time, original official documents, organizational records, oral histories, interviews, internet communications, patents, speeches etc	Monographs, indexes, abstracts, biographies, commentaries, literature review in theses, critiques of original literature, articles in magazines and newspapers, reviews of books/ articles, text books, essays etc.	Dictionaries, handbooks, encyclopaedias, directories, manuals, textbooks, chronologies, bibliographies, facts books, almanacs, anyone-edit website information etc.

During the course of literature review, the Researcher consults with these sources in large numbers, yet, uses careful discretion regarding the relevance of the information provided and the value of the resource in handling the topic under study. As a general principle, a review has to ensure: a comprehensive positioning of primary sources, cautious use of secondary sources and preferably, limited references as much as possible, of the tertiary. There must be a portrayal of an integrated picture of the issue under review, culminating with a statement of the amount of available information and current debates and moreover, the need of the current research. The review report in a theological study must show evidences of the knowledge available in literature, theories, theological-biblical matrices, major discussions on the topic, concerns in the context of the researcher's ministry, and a meaningful correlation with other academic disciplines. More clearly, the review interweaves contemporary discourses with relevant researches, theories and the theological constructs and biblical foundations of the matter of inquiry. Downgrading of the revelatory scriptural frame in the literature foundation can create a critical conceptual gap in theological research. Shallow reflections and indiscriminate summaries in the literature review serve to the disadvantage of the inquiry. For academic researcher, literature review is not simply gathering information on the topic, but, mining for wisdom in the existing body of knowledge and providing a sound basis and direction to the qualitative inquiry.

Reflection Box:

Climbing up the Ladder of Literature

Student Y was wondering about the series of persecutions against Christians breaking out suddenly in two of her neighbourhoods. Vicious acts spread around in a variety of forms, so she wanted to research it.

CONSIDER her self-talks (ST) while surveying the literature:

- ST 1: Oh … there are multiple types of sources like newspapers, texts, other theses, religious leaders' public statements, government laws and policies, statements recorded in the police station and so on. Differentiating the unprejudiced versions from those that are politically and religiously coloured is going to be tough.

- ST 2: … the data indeed look absolutely multi-featured. Presenting them in separate bits would only make an awful piece for reading. Perhaps I should interact with the material in some other way. Could I do sections on: critiques, debates, key themes/concepts, key authors, comparisons, analytical induction from manifold sources, historical content analysis, Why not try writing the literature review imagining the role similar to that of a facilitator in a focus group, who hears voices from several angles and then give it a shape?

- ST 3: Still … that won't be enough. Now I'm concerned about the multiple perspectives in which the data appear, e.g., persecution from the position of: socio-political history, local church history, worldwide church history, fundamentalist religious philosophies, missiological interpretations and pastoral ministry dimensions and many more. I'd probably need a thorough preliminary survey of materials, to see the direction clearly. Of course, I can look at the topic of persecution from religion, mission, theology, history, biblical studies, history, pastoral ministry and counselling or a combination of a few.

- ST 4: Hmm … now the actual issue is locating my point of interest. So, will start primarily from the local historical accounts of persecution and not from the religious, psychological, socio-political or missiological points of view. One of the first inferences was the occurrence of persecution break out in the district on every tenth year. Interesting!

- ST 5: Which technical path to follow? An archival research? (from early documents or evidences of previous events of persecution?), historical analysis? (exploring historical developments, patterns, prospects, challenges etc.), historical comparison (compare histories of persecution in the place or between two areas in the land, consider different times of the socio, political, religious changes). Again, should I go about it synchronically (concerned with original, static time) or diachronically (studying phases separated by time)?

And, the self-talk goes on and on until student Y captures the right focus not only for the literature review, but the entire direction of the inquiry.

CONSIDER: These self-talks are not born of desperation, but of cleverness and precision.

CHAPTER 5

QUALITATIVE RESEARCH DESIGN

SECTION CONTENTS:

- Research Proposal
- Types of Qualitative Inquiry
- Participant Selection in Research

Formulating and Presenting the Research Proposal

A research proposal is a document that lays out the key elements and features of the inquiry, which help the researcher to elucidate the entire procedure. Research requirements might differ from program to program in spite of their procedural commonalities. Compared to the master's level, a doctoral research proposal will require a more substantial analysis of the topic and an advanced review of literature. Masters programs normally have taught components while doctoral research is largely an independent undertaking of the researcher in which he/she affords more complex methodological procedures. Theological institutions are making serious attempts to incorporate practicums or field study projects right from the basic programs. These research designs have various emphases.

Undergraduate level practicum takes the student to the community to fearlessly embark on a survey or a simple interview task and submit the report in the assigned format. The purpose is to enable the student to connect with the society and to value people's experiences and views and hence, develop confidence in addressing the real problems in the world. This can be quite insightful to a student who comes to the theology school from a rather narrow vision about the world, the church and the mission.

Practicums in the graduate programs will have to afford a little more depth. Students have to develop a plan for the field study and get it assessed and formally approved by the concerned faculty. This is expected to be a miniature project that contains the necessary elements of a formal research proposal. Students identify a relevant issue from their society or church, develop a field study plan and specify the theological reflection trajectory. The aim of this basic research practice is to release students from overly depending on a teacher's knowledge and to enable them to think for themselves. Whenever this happens, it marks the beginning of transformative learning.

Post-graduate research programs require skills in situation analysis, reflective competencies in theology, and expertise in research methodology. The proposal presumes greater clarity in purpose, procedure and outcome. Ideally, the post-graduate researcher has to systematically develop the research design through the taught courses that get him/her acquainted with multiple perspectives, thinking frameworks and methodologies. Therefore, the design and integration of courses in the post-graduate programs are prerequisite for persuasive research proposals. A fragmented curriculum will reflect itself in the students' thinking skills and research competencies. Research proposals that come out of such learning environments will be shallow and imaginary, rather than a genuine, responsive undertaking. Post-graduate programs expect the student to master the subject and gain advanced and coherent knowledge. An extensive research proposal has to be prepared, presented and approved for a research report written in about 25,000-30,000 words.

A doctoral research in philosophy provides original contribution to knowledge, and the report is written in about 100,000 words. The researcher formulates a well advanced proposal for inquiry and gets to deeper philosophical, epistemological, ontological and methodological analysis of the issue under consideration. The research sets rigorous rationale, addresses more complicated issues, handles complex data and uses sophisticated concepts and theories. It normally takes a while for the researcher to get to the stage of a proposal defense. The actual process of inquiry takes subsequent years and ends with a final defense before the assigned academic panel. The researchers who seek admission and scholarships in the doctoral programs apply with a comprehensive research proposal. Academic disciplines have their own standards set for the design. McKinney outlines the contents of a typical anthropological research proposal seeking scholarship thus:

> A research proposal typically includes a statement of the problem, literature review, hypothesis or hypotheses to be tested, field methods to be used, statement of the relevance of the proposed research, proposed budget including any equipment needed, a time table, references cited, and relevant appendices to the proposed project, as

well as your curriculum vita (CV) that includes references who can be called upon to evaluate you and your chances of succeeding in any research project.[1]

Notably, practitioners in ministry are doing very helpful research in their own context of service, recognizing the need for field-based, on-going evaluation. Although these research endeavours are not aimed at a degree, results of the inquiries are published, which become significant contribution to knowledge in that particular context. For academic degrees or for ministry enhancement, a research proposal needs to have its essential components ensuring the right direction. A practitioner may not make a lengthy written document of research proposal, yet, still benefit hugely by having this mind map for logical coherence and functional clarity. The following section elaborates the components of a research proposal, providing an overall view of what it takes to begin good research. The researchers should be following the specific guidelines of the academic board of the school. This chapter, however, provides general information as to help qualitative researchers to think in that direction.

Elements in the Research Proposal

- Relevant subject area
- Preliminary review of literature with references
- Specific title for the research
- Statement of the research problem
- Elaboration of the Research Problem
- Rationale or Hypothesis according to the type of inquiry
  - » Working Definitions of key terms
  - » Objectives of the research
  - » Key research question
  - » Research methodology
  - » Scope and Limitations of the Research
  - » Time Plan for the research
  - » Document prepared in the style and format required by the school/ university

The **Purpose of the Proposal Document** is to set out clearly the intention of research, methods and outcomes anticipated. All features of the research are presented succinctly with convincing claims on the need and significance of the undertaking. Methodological limitations, ethical concerns, preliminary list of references and

---

[1] Carol V McKinney, *Globe-Trotting in Sandals: A Field Guide to Cultural Research* (Texas: SIL International, 2000), 24.

detailed time plan are significant elements in the proposal. Proposal writers have to convince the academic panel of the purpose, rigour and relevance of the proposed research, well-substantiated by the literature. The Human Subject Research (HSR) proposals sometimes have the informed consent forms attached to the proposal document. The researchers should explore the need for ethical sensitivity as well as the several complexities relating to the informed consent form[2].

Relevant Subject Area: An extensive preliminary reading is essential to locate the study in the existing body of knowledge. Availability of resources and positioning of key debates in the subject area need to be estimated. The first point of consideration therefore, is the *topic*, which is the subject area of research. Selection of the topic is done in correspondence with the academic requirements of the department, the ministerial commitment of the researcher, and most importantly, the theological and sociological relevance of the subject. Coherent embedding of the theory-practice interaction and time allocated for the inquiry are guiding factors for the researcher. Qualitative research topics assume epistemological and ontological tasks of conceptualizing the social phenomena. As ontological perspectives take a wide range of possibilities made up of attitudes, customs, individual views, texts, language, behaviour, events, social relations, rules, cultures, religions, problems and many more, the researcher explores the following questions:

- How well does my research area correspond with the academic discipline of my choice?
- How relevant is the research topic theologically and sociologically?
- What are estimative conceptual and practical puzzles in this type of a qualitative study?
- Who are the prospective beneficiaries of the study and how feasible are my research methods?
- Am I committed to this cause beyond its immediate academic prospects?

The researcher uses these questions to gain clarity of purpose regarding the subject area. Research is excavation. It is mining with a purpose and therefore, those who settle on easy answers and a risk-free path will make too little of a contribution. The researcher needs to address mediocre academic tendencies seriously. Genuine research is done only on a topic that has aroused one's intellectual and practical curiosity and not on what is already known. The checklist below can help the researcher to critically assess the feasibility of the subject area.

---

[2] Refer e.g., K Bhattacharya, 'Consenting to the Consent Form: What are the Fixed and Fluid Understandings between the Researcher and the Researched?' *Qualitative Inquiry*, 13(8), 2007, 1095-1115; and, H R Milner, 'Race, Culture and Researcher Positionality: Working through Dangers Seen, Unseen and Unforeseen'. *Educational Researcher*, 36(7), 2007, 388-400.

1. Why should the church, mission and academia find this project significant?

2. In what ways does this subject area challenge my cognitive and missional assumptions?

3. What is my prospective theoretical framework for the research? Does it make sense to someone?

4. Do I have resource materials and expert guidance to develop a background study on this topic?

5. Are there formal permissions needed for the conduct of this research?

6. Is the allocated time adequate for the various steps imagined in the inquiry?

7. Will I have access to the research participants and their context? Will people share openly about the issues addressed?

8. Do I have finances for the study?

9. What are skills necessary for conducting this qualitative research?

10. What are foreseeable probable challenges along the way?

Review of the Literature: The summary of a preliminary review of literature provides the background theory that supports the structure of the research proposal. Proposal is built on the solid foundation of a review of existing literature in the field of study, with relevant input from theology, classics in the field, official statistics, contextual literature, key texts and theories, research reports, and historical data. The purpose and process of the review is elaborated in the latter part of Chapter 4. This review encompasses the contextual, theoretical, philosophical, sociological and biblical-theological matrix of the study that forms the baseline for the overall research frame.

A research proposal, however, presents a preliminary literature review, to help the reader to evaluate the reinforcements of the study from existing literature. Proposal writers must write their review comprehensively, outlining key dimensions of thought that underpin the research problem. Differentiating the primary sources of data (first-hand empirical data, primary resources in the field, original writings of a person etc.) and secondary sources (data culled from original contributions) helps the reader in tracking the development of the topic. Theology researchers spend considerable time reviewing the biblical-theological literature as the hinge in the process of interpreting the social reality. Proposal writers do reviewing in different ways such as reviewing of key texts, central themes, major debates, or major theories, depending on how the researcher develops the theoretical frame. In certain studies, historical review is crucial. For others, church traditions, ongoing debates in pastoral contexts, theological themes, and missiological theories from previous studies contribute significantly. Creating this historical-theological-pastoral-missiological-contextual milieu is central to the review process. Sections divided with headings and sub-headings provide a quick glance of the conceptual development. The review of literature in the research proposal document needs to conclude with a section of preliminary bibliography, indicating the familiarity of the researcher with the scholarly, seminal and relevant resources in the selected field of inquiry.

Title: *Title* is the specific heading; its primary characteristics are clarity and precision. Delineating the area of investigation and its relevance, it wins the attention of readers and appreciation of experts. Unusual and hard vocabularies should be avoided, yet it is not to be written in simplistic terms. The principle is, *use the fewest words that make the most comprehensive description of the research*. Rather than a generic articulation of a situation, the title must present to the reader the pertinent issue. For the theology researcher, the title cannot sound simply philosophical or sociological; it has to have the theological or ministerial component. The researcher must look for the crucial sub-layer in the issue in a specific geographical or cultural setting in order to reach the crux of the phenomenon. *Faith Development Crises of Youth* could be revised to *Youth of IT sub-culture in city X*. Following are helpful considerations in the formulation of title for the study.

1. The researcher has to process thinking further from the general subject area to the single issue of focus in the inquiry

2. Abstract it into specific terms and add flesh to it stating the methodological task, outcome, geographical focus or anything that the reader must know in the first place. Constructions that are too broad and too narrow will eliminate motivation.

3. The title is not a grammatically complete sentence but a precise and interesting caption. The writer has to explore the construction of research titles.

4. Search for the crucial focus in the inquiry that should be part of the title e.g., attitudes, customs, perspectives, texts, language, behaviour, events, social relations, rules, cultures, religions, problems. State it to provide a clear guidepost to the reader.

5. Make the title epitomize the specific task undertaken e.g., evaluating, critiquing, comparing, exploring, describing, assessing, contrasting, analysing, developing models or constructing theories.

6. If the title reads clumsy and lengthy, consider the option of a sub-title that mentions the context of the study, the learning task or the outcome of the project. Always highlight the key focus of research in the main title.

7. In summary, it must have all the key words eliciting the central tasks in the research. This is important to ensure that the thesis will be placed in the right category on the library racks.

Thesis Statement: The title is followed by the statement of the research problem, also known as the *thesis statement*, written preferably in a single sentence. This anchors the research plan and controls the direction of the inquiry. For some researchers, formulation of the thesis statement is the hardest part in writing. In a sense, the title is restated in the thesis statement in a modified form that highlights the central claim and the expected outcome of the study. It presents the issue in greater depth and relevance. For instance, from the *Impact of Television Programs on Pre-teens*, the researcher develops a more concrete statement like, *Television programs X & Y are leading to psychological crises during adolescence, and causing increased measures of delinquency among pre-teens.* Remember, this statement can be further refined for clear focus. This type of a construction needs to be a single, succinct, direct sentence in which the researcher reveals the summary of his/her major claim in the study.

The thesis statement defines the study. It is the cornerstone for the entire construction of research and will be substantiated through the process. A simple step is to formulate the key research question and write the answer as the thesis statement that also reflects the researcher's claim and expectation about the inquiry. Statements are invalid when constructed too broad or too narrow. *Famines affect children* is too vague a statement. *Because of famine, children suffered illness, lost their education, separated from their homes, got into wrong social networks* is a too specific statement. So the researcher may work around something in between e.g., *The X famine that strikes place Y for six months a year has detrimental effects on holistic child development, affecting the survival of the Z tribal community.*

A Thesis Statement is not:

- A question
- A vague topic
- An incomplete sentence
- A fact statement

It is the statement on the primary claim and purpose of the inquiry with the succinct definition of the process. *Understanding Converts from the Lower Castes in Country X* reads as a mere, vague topic. A thesis statement is neither saying 'I will study about the converts' nor asking, 'What is the experience of these converts?' But stating the insight with some of the key aspects of its definition for instance, *Understanding the challenges faced by converts from the lower caste communities in country X is only possible through an ethnomethodological approach underpinned with a socio-political, economical and ecclesial analyses.*

There are several ways to write a thesis statement. Major types are: Informative, Argumentative, Multi-part, Unified and Hybrid statements.

Informative thesis statement guides the reader to a conclusion through the claims made about the inquiry. *Argumentative thesis statement* contains a claim and a statement on why that claim is authentic. A *multi-part thesis statement* consists of a list of sub-definitions of the topic that show the direction of the study (e.g., *Low self-esteem in the adolescents in community Y is reflected in their behaviours, habits, and responses hence providing the youth minister with indicators for strategic ministry development in the twenty-first century*). A *unified thesis statement* simply focus on a simple cohesive statement from which multiple layers of directions can be developed (e.g., *Strategic youth ministry among the Y community requires a critical investigation on the experiences and expressions of the low self-esteem among the youth*). A *Hybrid thesis statement* will use the multi-part claims in formulating a unified direction and hence develop a comprehensive statement for the inquiry (e.g., *An in-depth psycho-social analysis of various symptoms of low self-esteem among the youth of Y community should form the baseline for a responsive pastoral intervention in this century*).

A thesis statement frame develops when the researcher ponders over questions such as: what does this topic require me to do? What should I claim to be doing about this topic? The proposal writer has to ask these questions constantly and attempt to write down several statements until a coherent and concise sentence is made. Check points for the statement can be questions such as:

- Does this sentence adequately highlight the one and the main direction of the research?
- Is this a realistic, focused and clear statement of the original claim on the inquiry as I conceived it?
- Will someone challenge my statement outright by placing a different statement?
- Will the process of inquiry competently fulfil the procedure proposed in this statement?
- Does this statement demarcate a transformative step in thinking and practice?

Elaboration of the thesis statement/problem statement: Thesis statements need to be substantiated with evidences. Therefore, the researcher adds this section of elaboration of the statement, preferably a comprehensive paragraph that contains supportive arguments/ideas, statistical evidences, expert quotes and so on. This paragraph or section aims to base the thesis statement on persuasive evidence. Insights drawn from the preliminary review of literature helps to formulate this paragraph, stressing statistical relevance, historical push, recent research, theological-ministerial dilemma, specific contextual cases, or exceptionally challenging quotes. The researchers follow distinctive methods in designing this cohesive piece of information in the proposal but they do so with the single purpose of authenticating the prevalence of the problem and need for research. This section seeks to explain reasons for the topic to merit academic and practical significance in the general corpus of knowledge. Particular mention of the primary beneficiaries of the research and the anticipated outcomes serve as great motivators to the reader.

Hypothesis/Rationale of the Research: Hypothesis is a formal statement that can be proved or disproved in the inquiry, mostly used in quantitative research that make predictions on the interrelationships of variables. The essential characteristic of a workable hypothesis is observability and testability. Qualitative researchers use the term *hypothesis* or *proposition* mainly with reference to the research question or the reason for inquiry and, not necessarily an hypothesis to be tested. Nevertheless, it is helpful to recognize the basic distinctions. "The traditional approach, often referred to as quantitative research leads to hypothesis testing research, whereas the qualitative approach leads to hypothesis-generating research."[3] When a hypothesis testing research is claimed in qualitative approach, it will follow a qualitative procedure and logic in the task of testing an assumption and/or developing a theory. Some ethnologists and ethnographers use hypothesis differently, for example, in the process of theory-to field research-to hypothesis- to action. Hypothesis testing research uses statistical methods to investigate the relationship between the dependent and independent variables of a phenomenon. But there are situations when we are unaware of formulating a hypothesis because of our own unfamiliarity with the dependent and independent variables in that setting. Such situations allow us to study subjective experiences directly through qualitative inductive methods where that task is "questioning rather than measuring and generating hypotheses using theoretical coding."[4]

Rationale is a parallel term qualitative researchers use in the research proposal, denoting a reason or set of reasons for the inquiry rather than testing out an assumption. Rationale typically signifies the contextual, personal, theoretical, or any of such assumptions or reasons that prompt the inquiry. It is a sub-proposal within the research proposal with specific focus on the reasons, significance and objectives stated concisely, enabling the research to be set in the context of existing evidences

---

[3]   Carl F Auerbach and Louise B Silverstein, *Qualitative Data: An Introduction to Coding and Analysis* (New York: New York University Press, 2003), 4.

[4]   Auerbach and Silverstein, *Qualitative Data,* 2003, 4.

and practical applications. As mentioned above, testing of hypothesis tends to operate using a positivistic epistemology, while designs involving the development of a theory tend to be within an interpretative epistemology. Certain research topics start with assumptions, claims or guiding questions between key variables in the research, stated in a value-neutral method. Depending on the approach, the researcher formulates the statement of hypothesis or rationale.

Working Definitions: Definitions are an important part of a research proposal. The researchers speak in terms of conceptualization and operationalization.

> Once you have a well-defined purpose and a clear description of the kinds of outcomes you want to achieve, you can proceed to the next step in the design of your study-conceptualization. We often talk pretty casually about social science concepts such as prejudice, alienation, religiosity, and liberalism, but it's necessary to clarify what we mean by these concepts in order to draw meaningful conclusions about them.[5]

The step of operationalization is explained thus, "if you have specified the concepts to be studied and chosen a research method, the next step is operationalization, or deciding on your measurement techniques. The meaning of variables in a study is determined in part by how they are measured."[6] Conceptual definitions are abstractions, articulated in words that facilitate understanding, while, "operational definitions consist of a set of instructions on how to measure a variable that has been conceptually defined."[7] A working definition signifies how the term is meant and used in the study and it is perceived by the researcher. It clarifies cultural connotations, theological perspectives, doctrinal qualifications and theoretical constructs. More importantly, this section guides the researcher in achieving clarity about the terms, meanings and their interconnections in the inquiry. Technical terms and specialized words are defined in terms of their unique meanings in the research. Alongside the development of working definitions of terms, the Researcher consistently starts analysis of concepts through dictionary meanings, traditional interpretations, theological framings, and personal definitions. Working definitions may sound inferior or superior to other definitions but it helps the researcher to clarify meanings and directions for the data process. Qualitative study makes the elements in a working definition subject to empirical examination and therefore, while defining the terms, the researcher considers the parts that assist in analysing the concept or experience.

---

[5]   Earl Babbie, *The Practice of Social Research,* 10th Edition, (Australia: Thomson/Wardsworth, 2004), 109.

[6]   Babbie, *The Practice of Social Research,* 2004), 110.

[7]   H Russell Bernard, *Research Methods in Anthropology: Qualitative and Quantitative Approaches,* 4th Edition, (New York: Rowman and Littlefield Publishers, 2006), 37-38.

Any term that employs a specialized meaning in the study is explained in the *working definitions* in the research proposal. The researchers should not assume that the readers or experts will naturally follow the intended meaning of terms used in the proposal. For example, if the study uses the term *youth* not in its broad connotation, but referring to late adolescents in psychological terms, this has to be clarified in the section of definitions. Individuals give their own meanings to terms and thus working definitions are essential to communicate the intended functions of terms in the study. For instance, people define terms like *spiritual growth, urban stress, para-church, unreached groups, believing women* in numerous ways. A critical reader will look for the right terms and their proper working definitions.

If researcher's use of the term differs from the commonly framed definitions, that has to be explained. Sometimes, working definitions may be very different than the way certain terms have been conventionally understood. An extensive literature review has to precede the task. Working definitions help the researcher to jumpstart the detailed literature review with deeper clarity in thought and the specific definition of research. Also, if the researcher has consciously avoided certain synonyms of terms, the reasons for the exclusion of such terms and the reasons for the inclusion of the referred terms should be described. Terms that are synonymously used may have different meanings in contexts. For example, are 'mission training' and 'missionary training' the same? Do 'moral development' and 'moral behaviour' convey the same concept?

Likewise, researchers tend to use multiple terms while discussing one idea. In a research on folk religion, the student may use terms interchangeably such as animism, traditional religion, primitive religion, tribal religion and primal religion-terms associated with folk religion. But scholarly writing marks clear distinctions between each of these. Also, terms such as guilt, failure, spirituality, attitudes, feelings, spiritual experience etc. require working definitions based on an existing theoretical framework or the researcher's own new frame of concept.

Let us also consider certain expressions for example, how will a reader understand the phrase *early years of marriage*? In what theoretical framework will one assign that period? Or, for another example, what could be people's concept of *emotional development of children*? These expressions are unclear and hence will be misleading. Good definitions make sense logically and empirically. Clear definitions emerge when researchers illustrate the distinct meanings by reflecting on scholarly literature, theoretical foundations and contextual realities.

Major objectives of the Research: Research objectives are comprehended in two ways: some see them as the clear, concise statements about the specific actions to be taken in the inquiry while others define them as specific aims that will be achieved at the end. Generally, objectives are about the *how* of the research. Proposal writers usually make two or three objectives, indicating the specific tasks to be undertaken. In writing objectives, quantitative researchers use action verbs like test, construct, collect, produce, measure, deconstruct, analyse, document etc., while, qualitative researchers prefer verbs like investigate, evaluate, discuss, compare, analyse, critique, assess, identify and explain. Through tasks specified in the *major objectives*, the researcher achieves the outcomes of the study such as: formulation of a theory, filling the gap between two conceptual frameworks, correct errors in traditional understanding, design a frame of action, develop tools for assessment, develop learning materials, formulate strategies, and, suggest new models for practice and so on. Readers and examiners of thesis particularly evaluate if the researcher had achieved the stated objectives. Ideas in writing objectives of the research:

» To explore (an issue)

» To discuss (an idea)

» To reflect on (a theoretical model)

» To compare (two ideas, theories or phenomenon)

» To examine (a proposal)

» To analyse (some data)

» To systematize (some initial ideas)

» To synthesize (several ideas or propositions)

» To investigate (a range of concepts)

» To propose (a possible explanation)

» To suggest (some solution)

» To test (a hypothesis)

Scope and Limitations of the study: This section in the research proposal helps the researcher and the reader to approximate the scope and limits of the research, which may not be evident otherwise. *Scope* indicates the anticipated impact of the research and the ministerial or social advancement envisioned in the study. *Scope* of the problem precisely indicates the extent to which the study intends to impact the world, for instance, theoretically, socially, practically, geographically, missionally and so on. *Limitation* refers to specific choices of the researcher in limiting the empirical, logical or methodological scope of the inquiry or with regard to concepts, meanings, geographical space or historical periods. Competent researchers are able to see clear boundaries in the process and claims of the inquiry. Nevertheless, mention of limitations are not intended to be apologies for what the researcher is incapable of accomplishing in the process due to personal limitations. These are formal disclaimers that safeguard the research from criticisms by readers, peer-reviewers or the examiners. The section of *scope and limitation* also allows the researcher to make claims on the expected impact of the research, which could be otherwise disregarded. Unrealistic assumptions and goals make a research invalid, while specifying the scope and limitation explains the manageability and potential impact of the research.

Research methodology: This section consists of multiple elements as *methodology* denotes the entire logical process of the study including the type of inquiry, sources of data, methods of data collection, selection of research participants, and analysis. Extensive accounts on each of these elements will need to be given, particularly explaining the *how* and *why* questions. The theoretical framework that is built on the background knowledge, qualitative field data, theological direction and the social research strategies guides the methodology section in the research proposal. How the researcher thinks about the procedure is as important as the details of the procedure. A solid methodology section does not limit itself to field data procedures, rather will present the overall research approach in approaching theology, contextual realities and the literature grounding. It will have incorporated the elements or areas specified below.

- Approach: Qualitative, Quantitative, a combination or any other?
- Genre: Case Study, Grounded Theory, Ethnomethodology, or other?
- Type of the study: Descriptive, Explanatory, Analytical, Critical Comparative, Appreciative Inquiry[8] or other?
- Data sources: Original documents, People, Communities, Events, Official Records, or other?
- Data collection methods: Interviews, Observation, Conversational techniques, or other?
- Data gathering tools: Questionnaires, projective techniques, attitudinal surveys, interview guides, other stimuli?
- Data analysis methods: Coding, content analysis, analytical induction, ratings/graphs, frequency of responses in charts, conversational analysis or other?
- Literature review: what are key divisions expected to underpin the conceptual path?

---

[8] Appreciative Inquiry is a distinct approach allows the researcher to move beyond the conventional problem-centered pattern to identify best of the current practices or build on what went well in the past. It focuses on positive change and the approach is doing more of what is working well in the given situation rather than on problems and new solutions. Refer for more e.g., Jan Reed, *Appreciative Inquiry: Research for Change* (Sage: London, 2007); David L Cooperrider, Diana Whitney, Jacqueline M Stavros, *The Appreciative Inquiry Handbook: For Leaders of Change* (Oakland, CA: Berrett-Koehler Publishers, Inc, 2008).

- Theories: Any particular theory or theory frame used to reinforce the research? How do they operate?

- Biblical-theological matrix: How does the biblical-theological baseline inform, interrelate and direct the processes within the inquiry?

- Social context: Contextual dynamics, possible challenges, number of methods necessary to get a rounded view of the problem, any other

- Procedural pluralities: Researcher critically consider certain methodological questions and clarify the answers to the readers. Questions for example are: Will my historical study a historiography? How many disciplines intersect in my study on the *schizophrenia and demon possession* in the given community? Should my analysis of *identity crises of a given community* take on an *ethnic identity research* or *ethno-historic method*?

Research Question: This is a question that represents the central direction of the inquiry, informed by the preliminary review of literature and contextual analysis. A well-formulated research question focuses and refined the research design. However, approaches like Grounded Theory do not necessarily insist on a pre-research review of literature to base the research question. A research question in the proposal is not intended for specific use in the interviews or focus groups; it is the core query that directs the research. "A research question is a question which the research is designed to address (rather than a question which an interviewer might ask an interviewee) and, taken together, your research question should express the essence of your enquiry."[9] It is structured interrogatively with terminological underpinnings that enable a qualitative search, also indicating the conceptual interrelations through which the inquiry takes place. Framing of a comprehensive research question requires time, and importantly, a wrongly formulated research question will spoil the inquiry and make the researcher move off track from the central purpose.

Although the question is presented in the proposal, prior to the actual field data collection, the researcher revisits the central research question to check if it fits the methodological frame. "Think about the topic in the light of whatever relevant knowledge (historical, theological, common sense, etc.) you may have, and identify as many independent factors (or dimensions) related to that topic as you can. This kind of exercise can help you ask appropriate research questions."[10] Beginner researchers follow simple techniques towards a good research question as follows:

- Write as many vital questions as appear in the inquiry
- Re-read them and short-list them to the most central ones

9   Jennifer Mason, *Qualitative Researching*, (London: Sage, 1996), 15.
10   Richard E Davies, *Handbook for Doctor of Ministry Projects: An Approach to Structured observation of Ministry*, (Lanham: University Press of America, 1984), 116.

- Shuffle again, differentiating the major questions from the subsidiary ones and identifying various logical coherences between these questions
- Formulate the single outstanding question that comprehensively declares the entire task
- Discuss the question with some experts in the field of study and the methodology
- Keep reviewing the question through factors like time, resources, methodology etc.

Tests for the validity of a good research question are, originality, feasibility and expediency. If a struggle persists in formulating the core search in the form of a question, the researcher has to re-examine his/her pattern of approaching the inquiry. A whole different way of thinking becomes necessary in certain cases.

Time Plan: A time plan is an essential element in the research proposal, whereby the researcher communicates how the crucial factor of time will be handled throughout the inquiry. This can be a schedule that is working backwards from the expected time of completion to the present time, probably in specific days, weeks and months. Generally, realistic time estimation and time management are persistent troubles for people. Something may go wrong in the research process or unanticipated problems occur in life, blocking the study. Those who engage full-time in research are able to gather considerable amounts of hours together for focused study while part-time researchers encounter on-going struggles that obstruct the process. When a *time plan* is only broadly imagined and not specifically structured, researchers do not feel the compulsion and motivation to go on with discipline. The perfectionists resist to move from one task to the other while the lethargic always think, there is sufficient time ahead. Unlike the regular degree programs, the researcher in higher theological education does not have the privilege of the academy organizing hours for learning and periodical reviewing etc. The entire research process is left to the vigor and rigour of the researcher. Last minutes experts often face up with distressing experiences with the enormity of data and the complex procedures in interrelating a variety of ends and therefore, a realistic time plan in the proposal document is significant. The whole plan can be drafted in which tasks, durations and possible overlaps can be colour-marked. Above all, we know that the eventual validity of a time plan rests on its diligent application by the researcher.

Defense of the Research Proposal

Preparation of the Research Proposal document marks the beginning of a long journey. Typically in the post-graduate and doctoral level research projects in theology schools, the prospective researchers have to present and defend their proposal before a scholarly panel. This academic exercise in known by different names, the most common of which is, the *Proposal Defense*. A comprehensive, well formulated document is essential for a successful defense. The exhaustive document will have evidences of the realization of relevant issues in the process and thus lays a good foundation for the complex construction of the thesis. Documents of formal consent for research may be submitted to the panel along with the proposal. Studies on specific organizations, churches, schools and so on might demand this. When the inquiry is on participants with mental or physical inadequacies, or those in any of the *at-risk* categories, the researcher has to produce formal consent documents.

Generally in the pre-defense period, the researcher works alongside a mentor, who oversees the preparation of the Proposal document. Absence of expert guidance will reflect on the quality of the work and confidence of the prospective researcher during the defense. Strength of the proposal relies on factors such as the researcher's clarity in thinking, relevance of the topic, skilled guidance from the initial mentor, uniqueness of the topic, comprehensiveness of the proposal document, proficiency of the researcher in presentation and interaction with the academic committee and so on. During the defense, the researcher should:

- Be pleasantly assertive (no arrogance)
- Employ the best methods for presenting the proposal (verbal and visual data, flip charts, PowerPoint presentations, relevant video clips etc. that present the research problem precisely, drawing the theoretical frame on the whiteboard and explaining interconnections among ideas or, just a verbal articulation with the help of the printed document distributed to the panel
- Employ great verbal communication skills such as: Start and wrap up well, articulate solid supportive evidences, ask relevant questions, clarify statements, listen to the points made, recognize the unspoken queries of the panel, communicate with conviction, blend intellectual appeal with ethical and empirical appeals appropriately, make the panel feel free with a highly appropriate point of humour or personal reflection, and, turn the talk to a great time of academic collaboration. Capabilities like these can enhance a judicious conversation at the defense.
- Apply great non-verbal skills such as: pleasantness, relaxed facial and physical posture and communicative eye-contact are highly effective non-verbal competencies. The researcher can overcome nervousness by mentally preparing for the defense and consciously maintaining calmness and confidence even at difficult turns during interaction.

This *proposal defense* exercise offers several benefits for the researcher. It generates significant amounts of scholarly input, helps develop confidence and enthusiasm for the project, and clarifies some of the underlying issues in the design. It becomes the most productive academic experience for those who had worked on the research design scrupulously, valuing it as a matter of life rather than a mere intellectual exercise.

The guidelines above apply in the viva voce (mostly used in its short form *viva*), which is the final oral examination in higher education research, leading to the award of an academic degree. The original meaning for this term in Latin communicates as, 'with the living voice'. Strong and communicative research report arouses little or no agony over the viva procedure. One of the main causes for ambiguity is the researcher's uncertainty about the way in which the examiners must have handled the pre-viva procedures. Purposes of viva are multi-fold:

- To appreciate the researcher for the accomplishment and consistency
- To ensure the entire research is the researcher's own work
- To determine researcher's awareness of how the inquiry is positioned in the existing body of knowledge
- To ensure that there are no gaps or errors in the research procedure and report
- To motivate the researcher for further expansion of the results by publishing or through other strategic actions.

There are other important dimensions in the development of a research design. Following section addresses two of them- types of qualitative research and the selection of the research participants.

Types of Qualitative Research

Three major types are: exploratory, descriptive and explanatory. These signify the nature of the research problem and the level of inquiry undertaken.

Exploratory Research: In exploratory research, as the term suggests, the observed phenomenon is taken through primary exploration. It is exploring a topic, not intending to find conclusive solutions to problems. The researcher targets the initial discovery of ideas and insights of a phenomenon towards the formulation of presuppositions or theories. Issues addressed are relatively new or unique and may not have plenty of supportive literature or evidences available. However, the researcher defines terms and clarifies issues of significance in the phenomenon. Since the task is initial exploration, the study follows a flexible and adaptable methodology by which the basic settings, concerns and data on the topic are provided. It paves the way for further research by informing vital methodological and conceptual directions to take. The exploratory researcher asks questions like, *What are the basic beliefs and faith-based practices in the given community?*

Descriptive research: The major purpose of this research type is to advance knowledge on a social reality by describing its specific functions and characteristics. Presenting facts and giving meaning to the phenomenon is a central task. The study attempts to gather factual details of an existing phenomenon; identify real problems, assumptions, perspectives, practices and justifications; develops contrasts and comparisons; and review other similar situations. The phenomenon is addressed in depth descriptively, towards developing a systematic account of it. Design of the descriptive research is preplanned as the researcher is aware of the existence of the phenomenon to be described. Depending on the topic and contextual feasibilities, the researcher sometimes uses quantitative data partially to facilitate the task of description. In most cases, this *description* characterizes a middle phase in an inquiry, which is between the exploratory and the explanatory types. Question addressed by the researcher may be, *How do people in the given community perceive and define the nature and characteristics of evil?*

Explanatory research: This type of research recognizes the cause and effect relationships by connecting and comparing ideas to offer better explanation to a social reality. It is also known as the causal method. By addressing the *why* question that extends beyond the tasks of exploration and description, explanatory research aims at a more complex search. The inquiry is about areas unknown about a phenomenon. This method is employed to test certain socio-cultural assumptions empirically, by explaining the multi-layered meanings and interconnections of concepts. This type of inquiry assists in identifying reasons behind a phenomenon and accounting for the impact of changes that occur within the context. Explanatory research questions will be for example, *Why do people in the given community shape their daily life around their perception of evil? How does this impact their social, spiritual, physical, emotional, behavioural and mental dimensions of life?*

Figure 14: Types of Qualitative Inquiry

	Exploratory	**Descriptive**	**Explanatory**
Knowledge of the reality	Undefined	Partially defined	Defined well
Origin of inquiry	Basic exploratory question	Research question for description of the issue	Hypothesis statement on cause and effect

Stage of research objective	Beginning of an inquiry	Further development on inquiry	Advanced inquiry
Type of design	Design normally unstructured	Design partially structured	Design normally advanced

These three types are distinctively relevant in handling inquiries. Let us consider the example of a study on people living in the slums. While the exploratory researcher discovers the economic condition of slum-dwellers, the descriptive researcher focuses on systematically unfolding and accounting the nature of life in the slums or what it means to live in a slum in the given context. The explanatory researcher goes still further, addressing factors that keep people in the slums. The researcher critically analyses the claims on *poverty as the major cause of slum-life* or offers explanations as to *why many people prefer living in the slums*. In all three types, data will be gathered from a wide range of sources as given below.

Sources of Data in Qualitative Research

Mason[11] presented a broad spectrum of *data sources* available to the qualitative researcher that includes:

- People (experiences, accounts, interpretations, memories, opinions, understandings, thoughts, ideas, feelings, emotions, perceptions, morals, behaviours, practices, activities, interactions, conversations, relationships, humour, faith, products, secrets, creations)
- Speech
- Language
- Writing
- Texts
- Narratives, stories
- Art, cultural products
- Visual images, diagrams, photographs, maps
- Publications
- Media products
- Documents, archives
- Laws, statues, rules, regulations
- Policies
- Collectivities, groups, clubs

---

[11] Adapted from Jennifer Mason, *Qualitative Researching* (London: Sage, 1996), 37.

- Organizations
- Events
- Socio-geographical locations

Concisely, the sources of data in qualitative study are individuals, groups, phenomena, events, situations, and documents. Locating the most relevant sources is a necessary skill for the qualitative researcher. Another major decision in research is the selection of research participants.

Participant Selection in Research

Sampling is the term commonly used in research to indicate the act of participant selection. It is a vital element in methodological discussions. Sampling is done when the population is very large and it serves to safeguard the process from unnecessary expenditure and effort. *Sample* is the portion selected out of a larger unit that is known as the *population* or *universe* and thus is defined as "the selection of some part of an aggregate or totality"[12]. Decisions regarding sampling are crucial because wrong sampling produces wrong results. It is advisable to follow a relevant criterion in the selection of research participants e.g., a referral source, if available for the particular population and acceptable to the methodology followed.

Quantitative research requires standardization of procedures, random selection of samples and generalization of results. Representative data cannot be obtained from extremely large or too small populations. The researcher aims at a statistically reliable optimum sample to address the problem systematically, ensuring representativeness and reliability of the data. The sample is said to be *representative of the population* if distribution of characteristics of the sample is the same as that of the population. Quantitative undertakings are expected to produce generalizable results if the sample procedures accurately represent the population.

Positivist tradition generally follows quantitative approach, where the sampling method is one of probability. The assumption is, larger the sample, more accurate the findings. "The validity of research findings depends crucially on measurement; but your ability to generalize from valid findings depends crucially on sampling"[13], writes Bernard. Quantitative projects prefer types such as, random sampling, stratified random sampling, and cluster sampling. Probability sampling offers each element in the population the same or a specifiable probability either to be included in or excluded from the study and is employed when the goal is to generalize, make predictions and provide overall explanations. Probability sampling is also known

---

[12]   C R Kothari, *Research Methodology: Methods and Techniques*, (New Delhi: Vishwa Prakashan, 1990), 188.

[13]   H Russell Bernard, *Research Methods in Anthropology: Qualitative and Quantitative Approaches,* 4th Edition, (Lanham: Rowman & Littlefiled Publishers, 2006), ix.

as random or chance sampling and it has well-formulated schemes available. In qualitative research, we speak more in terms of *selection of the research participants*.

Selection of Participants in Qualitative Inquiry

Participant selection in the qualitative approach is done in a different conceptual paradigm. It mostly follows a purposive approach in that the choice is made on who can inform the research question and enhance comprehensive understanding of the phenomenon being studied. Generalization of findings is not the goal in qualitative study, yet, transparency and consistency are required values. Careful thinking has to precede the decision of participant selection criteria lest the process invalidate the purpose. The number of participants and the approaches followed in data gathering need to be realistic and manageable. The qualitative approach offers flexibility for the researcher to choose the number of participants and the type of methods. This, however, should be logically explained in the methodology. Ultimately, decisions regarding the selection of participants depend on the research question, evidences that inform the process and the theoretical frame employed. For instance, the role of the participants in the given community, their diversity in gender, ethnicity, education, marital status or religious background, age-based experience level (for example, child/youth/adult), and their social/religious/political perspectives on the issue investigated can be guiding factors. Participants are chosen on the criterion of their ability to inform the important facets of the study with experience-based evidences. Qualitative studies in general do not predetermine the number of participants, which is generally termed as the *sample size*. The process of inquiry is complete in approaches like grounded theory, when the researcher reaches the point of *data saturation* i.e., when no more new evidences need to be added to the data.

Non-Probability Sampling Design

Non-probability sampling is used in the qualitative domain where the goal of inquiry is not generalization. However, in the case of qualitative surveying, where the researcher estimates a proportion from the sample to a larger population, an unbiased sample could be randomly selected. According to Bernard, "...if your research calls for the collection of data about attributes of individuals (whether those individuals are people or organizations or episodes of a sitcom), then the rule is simple: Collect data from sufficiently large, randomly selected, unbiased sample."[14] Based on flexibility and origination in the process of qualitative inquiry, the researcher chooses participants who will provide relevant data. In methodologies that are intensely qualitative, long-term and in-depth, the exact number of participants will remain uncertain until the point of data saturation is perceived. In this type,

---

[14]   H Russell Bernard, *Research Methods in Anthropology: Qualitative and Quantitative Approaches*, 4th Edition, (Lanham: Rowman & Littlefiled Publishers, 2006), 186.

members in the population do not have equal probability of being a participant as the researcher sets specific criteria for inclusion. Such designs are often criticized for the relatively higher margin of error. Nonetheless, the philosophy and objective of the qualitative study approves the purposive designs in participant selection and its theoretical rationale is different from the probability techniques. Following are types of non-probability design.

Purposive or Judgmental Sampling: Known also as subjective or selective sampling, this sampling method follows two principal aims: "The first is to ensure that all the key constituencies of relevance to the subject matter are covered. The second is to ensure that, within each of the key criteria, enough diversity is included so that the impact of the characteristic concerned can be explored."[15] A range of different approaches to purposive sampling include,

> homogenous samples (chosen to give a detailed picture of a particular phenomenon); heterogeneous samples (deliberate strategy to include cases which vary widely from each other; extreme case/deviant samples (choosing unusual, special cases therefore potentially enlightening; stratified purposive sampling (fairly homogenous groups are chosen in a hybrid approach to display variation on a particular phenomenon); and critical or typical case sampling (cases that specially demonstrate a particular position of are pivotal in the delivery of a process or operation.[16]

Studies on rare populations, intensive case studies and critical case analyses are particularly benefited by this design.

Quota Sampling: The researcher divides the population on certain demographic variables such as gender or educational status; he/she continues to interview them until the quota is complete. Therefore, the first step is determining the key sub-populations in the inquiry and their proportions. Data might be impacted with some amount of subjectivity, but, is appropriate in estimating a general proposition particularly in narrative analysis or investigations on cultural concerns. Like in election polls, this method provides the investigator with a quota of respondents which the sampler can fill from the different strata. The ultimate decision of participant inclusion or exclusion rests with the researcher. Though this method is convenient and relatively inexpensive, the questions of reliability and representativeness are raised especially if/when the data is meant for statistical references.

---

[15]   Jane Richie, Jane Lewis, Carol McNaughtom Nicholls and Rachel Ormston, *Qualitative Research Practice*, 2nd Edition, (London: Sage, 2003), 113.

[16]   Adapted from Richie et al., *Qualitative Research Practice*, 2014, 114. Also refer Michael Quinn Patton, *Qualitative Research and Evaluation Methods* (3rd Edition) (Thousand Oaks, CA: Sage, 2002); and, John W Creswell, *Qualitative Inquiry and Research Design: Choosing among Five Approaches* (London: Sage, 2013).

Convenience Sampling: This is also called the haphazard method referring to the selection process based on convenience i.e., whomever the researcher has access to. The researchers tend to assume that convenient samples are always available and that can be wrong! Participants with specific characteristics may not be readily accessible or willing to be part of the study. For example, the researcher realizes that he barely managed to meet a few young men in his village to talk about the impact of contemporary music on their life. Practical realities in research can be different from what is generally assumed and therefore, sampling techniques need to be handled competently. Convenient sampling is used to gather first stage data on a phenomenon to make it known to the wider public and it affords constraints of time and resources. A specific variety of convenient sampling is the haphazard or accidental sampling, in which the researcher accidently meets potential participants during a formal data gathering procedure. Major criticism of these designs is on the credibility of data generated on convenience because no estimation is possible on the relevance of the data provided by the participants.

Chain Referral Sampling: As the name rightly indicates, the principal technique is networking. Therefore, it is also known as networking sampling. Prominent two methods within this technique are: (i) the snowball sampling, in which the researcher initially decides purposively on a group of participants and seek their assistance in further addition of participants that can inform the research question substantially. Initial participants thus recommend or choose more participants to provide data; and, (ii) the respondent-driven sampling where the *seed* participants are paid or given a coupon for locating more respondents from their own networks for the inquiry.[17] These are regarded as relatively unbiased and technically potential designs that can locate the relevant informants who would not be known to the researcher otherwise. For inquiries on rare topics and hard-to-find samples, this method offers a feasible solution. For example, the researcher who is seeking cases of adolescents rescued from sex-trafficking gangs. While it may be practically impossible for the researcher to find the expected number of cases, the seed participants can support the sampling networking.

Theoretical sampling: This allows the researcher to choose research participants who have significant information related to the phenomenon of inquiry. The design chooses the participants in order to develop, extend, refine or test a theory. Relevant information is drawn from the initial categories of informants and the process of theory progression continues.

---

[17]   Refer Douglas D Heckathorn, 'Respondent-driven Sampling: A New Approach to the Study of Hidden Populations', *Social Problems*, 44: 174-199, 1997.

Theoretical sampling is the process of data collection for generating theory whereby the analyst jointly collects, codes, and analyses his *(sic)* data and decides what data to collect next and where to find them, in order to develop his theory as it emerges. This process of data collection is controlled by the emerging theory, whether substantive or formal.[18]

Participants are carefully selected as the research process is informed and guided by the primary information provided by them. It is from their response that the research elucidates the points for theory development. This method is particularly known in association with the analytical induction procedures in grounded theory. Multiple methods are used in theoretical sampling as the researcher formulates theoretical constructs. Depending on the nature of the theoretical construct, the researcher decides on the particular sampling types and chooses different sample techniques at different steps according to the information sought. For instance, when theoretical construct allows a convenient form, the researcher may use convenience sampling; when it operates in extreme cases, unusual or extreme sampling will be in place; in addressing issues of everyday life, inquirer will follow a paradigm or typical sampling method and a similar case sampling technique may be employed when constructs operate in a range of similar contexts. Grounded Theory approach applies initial sampling, theoretical sampling, constant comparison and theoretical saturation systematically in the inquiry. In the process of analysis, Strauss and Corbin[19] introduced open, axial, selective coding stages to reach grounded theories while Charmaz[20] limited it to the two steps such as initial and focused coding to theory saturation, allowing each to be guided by the sampling procedure.

Sample designs have their own essential strengths and weaknesses and therefore, the researcher needs to attend closely to the procedure. If the sampling design corresponds to the rationale and research question must be put to constant test. The design of study should clearly establish the methodological rationale for the selection of participants –applied initially or through- and how it was guided by the questions of effectiveness and credibility of the data.

---

[18] B G Glaser and A L Strauss, *The Discovery of Grounded Theory: Strategies for Qualitative Research*, (Chicago, IL: Aldine de Gruyter, 1967), 45.

[19] Refer for details, A L Strauss and J Corbin, *Basics of Qualitative Research: Grounded Theory Procedures and Techniques*, 2nd Edition, (Thousand Oaks, CA: Sage, 1998).

[20] Refer, Kathy Charmaz, *Constructing Grounded Theory: A Practical Guide through Qualitative Analysis*, (London: Sage, 2006).

Reflection Box:
Boil it down to FOCUS...

Student C during her summer ministry placement had some most painful encounters with the earthquake victims in place X. A seven year old girl witnessed the tragic death of her best friend, who could not find her way out from the huge concrete pieces that fell off of the building. Student C realized that this second grader is just one among thousands who are alive, yet deprived of life because of lack of any emotional support whatsoever. The community had no information about how to build their lives back to normal and the churches weren't even equipped to consider that they had a role to play. While leaving the medical camp and all the helpless people in their desperation, student C decided to do her research in that community, with a special focus on children's post-trauma disorders and the intervention strategies. Preparing the research design was the challenge. She asked herself: What is the main plot in the research? What should be the theme in the title? Should I address the effects and natural coping strategies children develop or, follow a totally different way with case studies? Should I go with trauma theories, cognitive theories, loss-attachment theories, specific PTSD psychological or sociological theories, emotional processing theory, dual representation theory or which other? What are the relevant subject disciplines to consider? If language, narratives and reactions are crucial, how should I design my data gathering tool in view of that? What could be the difficult part in meeting with children and gathering data from them? How children explain their trauma, how they experience God in all this, do they have questions about God, human suffering and death-addressing all such issues how would I consider my biblical grounding and theological frame in the inquiry? How is PTSD in children heightened by the uninformed interventions by the members within the community or church? What approach will best assist my research purpose? Am I time-conscious about this research? Apart from children, who are important sources of information in the study? What sort of a network will provide significant information for the development of a strategic intervention procedure that can be taken further from the research findings? So, what is the central query?

CHAPTER 6

METHODS OF DATA GATHERING AND ANALYSIS

SECTION CONTENTS:

- Interviews
- Questionnaires
- Observation Methods
- Focus Groups

Methods are specific techniques used in research. The usefulness of the technique is determined largely on the research question and the nature of the data. Choice of method in qualitative data collection is a major decision in the process because each method has implications on the scheme of the project. A researcher who unpreparedly rushes into data gathering is likely to lose quality information. While in-depth interviewing and observational methods are used in qualitative study, the quantitative approach follows statistical analysis.

Qualitative Data Collection Techniques

The qualitative research field is diverse with methodologies such as ethnography, life histories, textual analysis, participant observation, case studies, interviewing, and critical cultural history among many others. Qualitative approach does not assume typically that the ideas gathered are true all the time and in all conditions, rather, it assigns credibility for the derivation of meaning of reality in the given context. It is research that "involves analysing and interpreting texts and interviews in order to discover meaningful patterns descriptive of a particular phenomenon."[1] The

---

[1]   Carl F Auerbach and Louise B Silverstein, *Qualitative Data: An Introduction to Coding and Analysis*, (New York: New York University Press, 2003), 4.

researcher ponders over five *W's*: What? Where? Who? When? Why? And the two *Hs*: How? How much? These questions respectively guide the researcher to the topic, place, participants, the period (past or present) and the reasons/consequences/ conditions, and, the method and the amount of data needed.

An important area of researcher's decision-making is on methods of data collection. Many a time qualitative researchers take this dimension lightly, assuming that 'it's all general knowledge and easy to apply'. It is in the field they realize that they were wrong. One can totally fail the research endeavour by the careless selection of methods. This chapter therefore, discusses four principal methods in qualitative data gathering; interviews, questionnaires, observation and focus groups.

Interviews

Interviews are one of the most commonly recognized methods of qualitative data generation that follow structured, partially structured or open-ended formats. People are considered as the resources of knowledge, evidence and experience. Interviews are selected when open, unstructured conversation becomes crucial to discover the experiences of people. Qualitative interviewing, which uses in-depth, iterative and continuous design of questions, refers to what Burgess calls as the, 'conversations with a purpose'.[2] Designing the flexible qualitative interview format is not a rigid, boxed-in procedure, rather it presumes an overall understanding of a reality.

There are varieties in interviewing. Most prominent type is one-on-one interviews, although certain studies benefit much from group interviews and focused interviews. The researchers use one-on-one interviews (in person or through methods like Skype), telephonic interviews, group interviews and questionnaire interviews (using questionnaires filled-up on-the-spot). Structured interviews are done with structured questions predesigned in a sequence. Qualitative interviewing as a procedural technique requires a careful design from beginning to end.

Mason identifies seven objectives that guide the researcher to the logical choice of qualitative interviewing. She says interviewing is logically chosen when:

- ▶ Your *ontological* position suggests that people's knowledge, views, understandings, interpretations, experiences, and interactions are meaningful properties of the social reality which your research questions are designed to explore.
- ▶ Your *epistemological* position suggests that a legitimate way to generate data on these ontological properties is to interact with people, to talk to them, to listen to them and to gain access to their accounts and articulations.

---

[2]   R G Burgess, *In the Field: An Introduction to Field Research* (London: Allen and Unwin 1984), 102.

► Your view of the ways in which *social explanations* can be constructed lays emphasis on depth, complexity and roundedness in data, rather than the kind of broad surveys of surface patterns which, for example, questionnaires might provide.

► You wish to conceptualize *yourself as active and reflexive* in the process of data generation, rather than as a neutral data collector, and you are going to analyse your role within the process.

► Rather more pragmatically, *the data you want may not be feasibly be available in any other form*, so that asking people for their accounts is the only way to get what you are interested in.

► You may indeed wish to use qualitative interviewing as just *one of several methods* to explore your research questions.

► You may have a particular view of *research ethics and politics* which means that you believe interviewees should be given more freedom in and control of the interview situation that is permitted with 'structured' approaches.[3]

Culture-based interviews set distinct guidelines for the researcher. Rubin and Rubin suggests that the qualitative researcher look at the rules and norms of the culture closely and consider certain guideposts in effective interview procedures.

▷ Ask about the meaning of particular words and phrases because sometimes "words become broader symbols that communicate cultural content."[4]

▷ Consider *topical and cultural arenas*. "A topical arena includes those who are affected by a problem or who interact intensely on a narrow issue... A cultural arena includes those who have similar understandings, expectations, and values; such people usually have had common experiences or a shared history."[5]

▷ "Qualitative interviewing is appropriate when the purpose of the research is to unravel complicated relationships and slowly evolving events... when you need to ring some new light into puzzling questions or when depth understanding is required." [6]

Conduct of the Interview

Interviewing is a skill. It practices two competencies hand-in-hand: concrete understanding of the topic being studied and the capabilities in making a meaningful conversation that is anchored on the research probe. Creating a natural

---

[3]   Extracted from Jennifer Mason, *Qualitative Researching* (London: Sage, 1996), 39-42.

[4]   Herbert J Rubin and Irene S Rubin, *Qualitative Interviewing: The Art of Hearing Data* (London: Sage, 1995), 20.

[5]   Rubin and Rubin, *Qualitative Interviewing*, 1995, 20.

[6]   Rubin and Rubin, *Qualitative Interviewing*, 1995, 51.

atmosphere for conversation is crucial for the participants, who sometimes find this as a nightmare for the fear of knowledge-testing questions or the possibility of researcher's intrusion in personal matters. An informal talk at the start eases further conversation and creates a cordial environment for natural interaction. Expressions of appreciation and respect to the interviewee for the time and availability can add vigor to this introductory talk. Of everything, good rapport with the participants is prerequisite for successful interviewing. Following are certain things to remember about interviewing:

- Obtain prior permission from the interviewees regarding their availability, place and time of interviewing. The researcher does not force interview on participants, rather works with those who consented to share information.

- Exerting unnecessary controls over the participants including that of forcing people to respond quickly or persuading them with *leading questions* that will add favourable evidence for the study are outright violations of research ethics. Participants' agreement to respond to questions does not guarantee that they would do it wholly or efficiently.

- Jokes, unclear comments and complicated questions breed discomfort in the participants. The researcher has to safeguard the interaction from all of these.

- Advantages of flexibility and spontaneity in qualitative data process are not to be used directly or otherwise to lead the interviewee to a pre-determined conclusion on the topic.

- Maintain a truthful and unbiased standpoint throughout the interview and give the participants attending ears and sufficient space to naturally share their experiences or ideas.

- Provide the participants with an environment conducive to genuine conversation free of external interferences and intrusions.

- Be equipped with the devises, tools and materials essential for the task and do not expect of the participant to be accountable for this. Having the tools organized e.g., the printed schedule, pens, blank papers, audio-video recorders, pictures or any other item is solely the responsibility of the interviewer.

- Personal comments or criticisms at the responses and reactions of the interviewees should be avoided.

- Secure the conversation on the design track and guard it from unnecessary self-introductions and discussions on the project.

- Accurately record and transcribe the responses and observations. Distortions of the narratives while transcribing, paraphrasing, and summarizing are against the standard ethical protocol of research.

Several factors play in the design and conduct of interviews. The important considerations on type, mode, length and content are to be laid out precisely in the methodology. For instance, the researcher must be able to recognize situations where face-to-face interviews are not feasible. Sometimes, interviewees may not be always able to use technology assisted modes. Lengthy conversations may not work well in telephonic interviews and also, often fail in maintaining a good rapport. Interviewers might experience difficulties in the field while encountering unanticipated hindrances. Some of these could be detected through careful thinking in advance. Most common examples are: Last minute postponement of the appointment by interviewees, unforeseen circumstances at the interview location, inoperability of electronic devices, failure of the recording devices in the middle of the process, uncertainties in recording data from group interviews and, most unfortunately, the entire data loss before acquiring the comprehensive report.

Approaching Sensitive Issues in Interviews

Methodology classrooms make interesting discussions on dealing with sensitive or personal issues in interviews. This is an aspect the researcher has to keep in mind while choosing the topic for the study. Challenges of the topics of extreme private nature will be clear to the novice researchers only as they start preparing the tools for data collection. One way the experts resolve this is by altering the method from personal interview to confidentially processed questionnaires. However, this shifting will succeed only if participants responsibly fill-in and return the questionnaires. In sensitive topics such as guilt feeing, racial tensions, sibling rivalry, divorce cases and similar others, the inquirer needs to pay attention through the process to protect the participant from feeling violated. Conversations in that line are not easy to begin and end because as Rubin and Rubin says, you are bringing "the interviewee down from the intellectual or emotional high without losing the openness of discussion. After eliciting depth and emotional honesty, you don't want to leave interviewees exposed, but help them calm down and feel protected again."[7]

Effective probes are an added advantage to qualitative interviewing. Probes are tactical follow-up questions to gather deeper information from the interviewees on the topic of inquiry. "Probes encourage the interviewee to expand on the matter at hand, complete an example or narrative, or explain a statement that the interviewer did not understand."[8] Probing should not contaminate the mining process as Kvale

---

[7]   Rubin & Rubin, *Qualitative Interviewing*, 1995, 137.
[8]   Rubin & Rubin, *Qualitative Interviewing*, 1995, 208.

and Brinkman puts it, "The interviewer digs nuggets of knowledge out of a subject's pure experiences, unpolluted by any leading questions."[9] Scholars have listed multiple types of probes used in research. Rubin & Rubin discusses[10] *steering probes* that restrict the questioning to those issues that are of most interest and the *sequence probes* that helps us to reconstruct the order of events. Bernard mentions "the silent probe, the echo probe, the neutral probe, the tell-me-more probe, the long question probe."[11] Experienced researchers use probing to clarify gaps or contradictions and to understand the unspoken standpoint of the respondent. Probing in interviews can use stimuli such as pictures, audio-visuals, narratives, quotes, questions etc. For less experienced researchers, handling the sensitivity of the topic during probes must be a matter of precise caution.

Formulating questions on sensitive issues is a demanding job for the interviewer. Significant areas to consider are: the sequence of questions, specific points of shifts from generic to sensitive probes, number of questions to probe the interviewee to provide additional explanations, methods for winding up the interview, cultural sensitivities in conversation, and the approaches to manage emotional outbursts of the participants during the interview. The researcher may not always know how to present certain important questions to the participants because of the high level of sensitivity attached. Such circumstances could be efficiently handled to a certain extent with the initial rapport building, which prepares the participant to share matters confidently. However, this may not always be the case as individuals process questions in their own ways. The researcher's conversational skills play a big role in understanding this and making further steps. A series of non-threatening questions that allude to sensitive subject matter or raising a delicate point from researcher's own experience are practical resolves. However, these are issues impacted by multiple factors such as the contextual dynamics, the researcher's age and experience, the structure of questions, the way questions are worded and asked and so on. The venue and setting of the interview can provoke more challenges along with the sensitivity of the issue.

Types of Interviews

Structured Interviews: These are fixed interview formats. Closed-ended questions are used with a purpose to develop a statistical frame. Same questions are asked in the same sequence to participants and, assisted by technology, this can process a large number of responses. Structured interviews are feasible option to the researcher for

---

[9]   Steinar Kvale and Svend Brinkmann, *Interviews: Learning the craft of Qualitative Research Interviewing*, (London: Sage, 2009), 48.

[10]   Rubin & Rubin, *Qualitative Interviewing*, 1995, 208-209.

[11]   H Russell Bernard, *Research Methods in Anthropology: Qualitative and Quantitative Approaches*, 4th Edition, (Lanham: Rowman & Littlefiled Publishers, 2006), 218-219.

surveying purposes and also for a quick, not-so-deep analysis of an issue. Bernard clarifies the distinction between structured interviews and interview schedules thus, "in fully structured interviews people are asked to respond to as nearly identical a set of stimuli as possible. One variety of structured interviews involves use of an interview schedule-an explicit set of instructions to interviewers who administer questionnaires orally."[12]

Semi-structured interviews: This method is preferred when researcher wants to ensure that certain information, e.g., specific number of items in the demographic data, is collected similarly from all participants and simultaneously keeping another part of the interview schedule unstructured to maintain adequate flexibility to obtain more details when possible. Interviewer carefully follows two things: the *interview guide* with the instructions and themes, and, *the leads or the topical trajectories during the conversation* to mine in and expand data. Therefore, it has pre-set areas to address but not fully pre-set questions in that providing the researcher freedom to use probes and prompts to deeper analyses.

Open-ended, unstructured Interviews: These are in-depth, open-ended interviews intended to gather the maximum complete data of participants' views and experiences. Ethnographic interviews mostly follow this method". According to Kvale it is "a key venue for exploring the ways in which subjects experience and understand their world. It provides a unique access to the lived world of the subjects, who in their own world describe their activities, experiences and opinions."[13] The qualitative researcher develops rapport with the interviewee and uses relevant stimuli and shifts with perseverance. Open-ended interviews produce massive amounts of data, sometimes making analysis a complex job for the researcher. Simple narrative questions or event-based queries are great stimuli. The researcher can effectively lead the elderly in a community to share their rich insights by using the stimuli of a photograph, a video clip or a simple statement regarding the beginning and growth of a Christian social movement in the given place. Open ended questions that presented appropriately to a participant can provide relevant data for analysis and lead the interview from the periphery to significantly deeper issues. Nonetheless, the researcher who lacks control over the direction of the conversation will end up listening to continuous narratives. Steering the participant from irrelevant digressions and effective management of time are essential capacities of the interviewer. Whenever delicate issues are addressed in the context of ephemeral interactions, the researcher should ensure that non-threatening questions are asked in a way that reduces the possibility

---

[12]   H Russell Bernard, *Research Methods in Anthropology: Qualitative and Quantitative Approaches,* 4th Edition, (Lanham: Rowman & Littlefiled Publishers, 2006), 212.

[13]   Steinar Kvale, 'Doing Interviews', in Graham R Gibbs (ed.), *Qualitative Research Kit,* (Woodland Hills, CA: Sage), 2007, 9.

of hiding, lying or fabricating facts. The researcher has to reflect on the emerging themes and exercise freedom to make necessary alterations in the data collection process to enhance relevance and purpose.

Recording Data in Qualitative Research

- Some researchers use audio-video recorders in interviews. Videos can record verbal and non-verbal information with the reservations of being intimidating to some and requiring more arrangements to setting up. The researcher will have to obtain permission from the participants before setting up any recording devices as it can cause certain inhibitions or offence in some socio-cultural contexts. The researcher might need to show emotional understanding when participants tend to maintain reservations about the use of technological devices, since it may be due to fear of the probable misuse or manipulation of the critical information shared. Importantly, when used, the researcher has to ensure that the devices are in good working condition and the location of interview has facilities to assist (e.g., power supply, sound-control surroundings). Use of recording devices offers high complacency by allowing space for the researcher to listen to the responses on a convenient later time rather than simultaneous transcription of responses. Since chances are there for the failure of digital recordings, it is safe to have an alternative system in place to record the interviews.

- Note-taking is a popular and less expensive method in qualitative data recording. This method helps the researcher to maintain notes of reflections, questions, connections and comparisons even during the interviews. Note-taking done by less-skilled researchers can distract the participant as the researcher tends to pay more attention to transcribing he notes than the person. Manual transcriptions can hinder effective listening and result in missing some important thoughts. In spite of having complete responses transcribed, the researcher may still lose out on the significant non-verbal data that are crucial in qualitative analysis. Prolonged periods of data gathering can make manual transcription hard. Yet, it is a common method followed by interviewers. Writing additional thoughts on the notes can raise confusion in the stage of analysis and therefore, it is advisable to avoid doing this much as possible. The researchers sometimes add ideas that they reconstructed from memory or sentences that are paraphrased on their interview notes. These are to be specially marked or transcribed separately to make sure that the original data is maintained intact.

Managing Data from Interviews

Researcher has to intelligibly *manage* the data that are gathered from various places, persons and times. This intellectual work of managing data involves according to Orna and Stevens "accepting, evaluating, organizing, storage, retrieval, handling, processing, original creation and output information... the work is partly or prevailingly abstract and it contains to some degree an element of creativity."[14] They further articulate how proper managing of data assist the researcher not only to find what is wanted but also to:

- Review our present store of information and spot areas where it's thin and needs adding to
- Identify contradictions (real or apparent) between what we have gathered from different sources
- Verify things that we remember in part but not in detail
- Check if there is support for a 'hunch' or half-formulated hypothesis
- See how our own thinking has developed over a period, what changes it has gone through, what new elements have come into it[15]

Qualitative researchers need to manage and safely keep their original data for any academic scrutiny during or after the period of research. Universities sometime set the minimum period for raw data preservation from three to five years. However, it is desirable for a committed, continuing researcher to keep the rich qualitative data *for life* especially when it is the primary investigation on a cultural or social reality. This not only protects the buoyancy of the researcher but also helps him/her to continue drawing insights from the raw data even after years of the original research. Interview manuscripts made from the recordings and field notes can be well maintained with all necessary information about the interviewee, location and the conduct of the interview. Rubin and Rubin explains it succinctly, "In a log, describe how the transcript was made, whether directly from tape, from notes, or from memory, and indicate when and how the transcripts were verified, and whether the transcript includes pauses and other non-verbal indications of what occurred. If the transcripts are edited versions of the tape recordings, you should also note the kind of material that was left out. Also keep a record of how you organized and analysed the transcripts. Such a record will include the original coding categories, that is, how you sorted out what people said. Maintain the marked-up transcripts

---

[14]   Adapted from Elizabeth Orna with Graham Stevens, *Managing Information for Research* (Buckingham: Open University Press, 1999 reprint), 12.

[15]   Elizabeth Orna with Graham Stevens, *Managing Information for Research* (Buckingham: Open University Press, 1999 reprint), 12.

and include in the transcripts the in-text comments that you jotted down to indicate what was happening in the interview."[16]

Every shift during talk, judgment, reaction, reflection, summary and recommendation is invaluable information for the qualitative researcher. These specifics recorded clearly in the interview logs will help the researcher to recall the precise procedure at any time. Research mentors and examiners can ask for these records to be verified during as part of their professional assignment.

Questionnaires

Questionnaire is a common method for data collection in social research, often used with a quantitative statistical objective. Survey research mostly uses structured questionnaires in "collecting information by asking a set of pre-formulated questions in a pre-determined sequence in a structured questionnaire to a sample of individuals drawn so as to be representative of a defined population."[17] Preferring a blend of qualitative and quantitative methods, questionnaires too are used alongside several qualitative methods. It is used generally in broad surveys of surface patterns. Two major types are: researcher-administered questionnaire (structured interview) and self-administered survey (questionnaire). While researcher-administered questionnaire maintains more completeness, clarity and response rates, self-administered questionnaires often faces concerns of incompleteness, misinterpretation and low response rates.

Types of Questionnaire Administration

- Face-to-face questionnaire administration: Researcher meets with the participant in person and gathers data verbally. This has the advantage of clarifying doubts while administering.
- Printed questionnaire administration: Researcher leaves with the participant the questionnaire on printed format and a pen to provide responses.
- Computerized questionnaire administration: Researcher using the assistance of a computer in sending and receiving the questionnaire.
- Adaptive computerized questionnaire administration: Technology determines where to move the participant from the initial set of questions. This is used on an extensively optimized questionnaire set that gathers data from wide ranging participants.

---

[16] Herbert J Rubin and Irene S Rubin *Qualitative Interviewing: The Art of Hearing the Data* (London: Sage, 1995), 86.

[17] Peter F Hutton, *Survey Research for Managers: How to Use Surveys in Management Decision-making*, 2nd Edition, (Basingstoke: Macmillan, 1990), 8.

There are cases when researchers choose questionnaire method because they lack skills in personal interviewing, conversational capacity and analysis of descriptive data. But there are multiple other capacities required for the formulation of a good questionnaire, which the researcher must be aware of. The research problem needs to be addressed completely through the number of questions presented in the right logical sequence.

Practical Tips for Questionnaire Preparation

- Fixed answer categories make questionnaire administration relatively easy for example response options such as Yes/No, Right/Wrong and so on. For the multiple answer categories, the researcher's challenge is the preparation of the exhaustive list of response options. This means all key imaginable answers and a category to let the participant add *any other*. Well-designed check-boxes or circling numbers are commonly used. In fixed answer-format, the participant chooses answers from the exhaustive and mutually exclusive options provided.

- Keep reorganizing the questions until the logical sequence is clear. Place preparatory questions at the beginning and make sure every single question is important for data analysis. The researcher should not be going by *questions of personal interest*. It might be wise to keep the sensitive questions until preceding questions have prepared the participant to respond to them. A logical flow from fact to behaviour, from behaviour to attitude, and from there to evaluative type questions is very capable of gathering comprehensive information.

- First few questions capture the attention and determine the interest of participants in filling-in the questionnaire. Therefore, much thoughtfulness required. Long sentences, difficult vocabularies, expressions with double meanings and multiple issues in one question are examples of ineffective questions.

- Researcher should know the particular categories of queries intended to explore each aspect of the research question or hypothesis. Placing some of the very important questions in the first half will serve the researcher gather crucially important data even if the respondent had returned it partially done.

- Questionnaire must look tidy and the answer categories should be shown in the same page rather than split up into two pages. There must be enough space to give the responses. When things appear messy, participants might choose to do away with rather than wrestle with it.

- Questionnaire needs to reflect good skills in communication and presentation. To maintain interest in the participant, the researcher can use different ways of asking questions and a variety of interesting terms and themes running through the questions.

- In the making of each question, keep the participants in mind. Their lifestyle, educational level, cultural dynamics, faith assumptions, social values- all have roles to play in the formulation of a good questionnaire.

- A pilot survey is helpful to make sure the reader comprehends the questions with their intended meanings. Self-administered questionnaires leave no room for real time clarification.

- Make the questionnaire as short as possible. Lengthy questionnaires normally receive few feedbacks. Respondents get exhausted by glancing through the several pages. It is a false estimation that by increasing the number of questions we enhance comprehensiveness. The researcher should revise questions and categories until the minimum number of questions are prepared for maximum amount of data in a manageable form for the participant.

- Response rate is mostly unpredictable, but researcher can attempt to foresee the common reasons that cause low-response rates to the questionnaire. Response rate depends on the participants' commitment, their values and life style, the length and clarity of the tool, nature of the issue investigated and many other.

- Decision on the analysis method is a guiding factor in the formulation of the questionnaire. The researcher handles each question with the analysis procedure in mind. Open-ended question will not provide data for statistical survey unless everyone's responses include numbers. Assigning numbers to questions and pre-numbering the answer categories aids the researcher at the time of tabulation and analysis.

- Regarding survey questionnaires aiming at generalizations, the researchers central tasks include the assigning of specific variables to attributes in the questions. For instance, the researcher may develop variables relevant to a fact (ethnicity), a behaviour (alcoholism), or develop questions to aggregate responses into an index or scale e.g., measuring an attitude (attitude towards virtual worship communities), or personality traits (low self-esteem). Responses from the open-ended questions in a questionnaire are coded into a standard scale after the data collection. Compared to the interview method, questionnaires require more concrete preliminary works in making the tool ready for use and a standard analysis.

- Title of the questionnaire and researcher's note of introduction have huge impacts on the response rates. Instead of a long cover letter, researchers now use a short, great paragraph that persuades and guides the participants to do their part in the study. Relevant guidelines for the completion of the questionnaire and the data and method to return the responses need to be given in direct and understandable language. Statements of ensuring confidentiality for responses if any, should be made in the introductory note. Any relevant instruction regarding the modes to fill-in the format, the date and method to return the response are to be included.

- Design of envelop of the printed questionnaire and inclusion of return postage are matters to consider in mailing questionnaires. Follow-up mails normally help to secure higher response rates.

- Translation of the questionnaire into local languages is a necessary assignment in certain studies.

- Expert help and reference to standard tools can provide helpful roadmaps for the researcher in the making of a rational questionnaire.

Effective questionnaires are formed from clearly specified goals, appropriate background concepts that define these goals and meaningful splits of queries from each concept. The researchers who know how the research findings will be used, will have clarity about the major goals, the concepts and the specific questions relevant towards that direction. In other words, on every question the researcher asks, 'how will the response to this question guide the study to its intended goal?'

Guidelines for Questions in a Questionnaire

- Develop a flow of questions from less delicate to most delicate. Creativity is intrinsically significant in questionnaire design.

- Sentence completion exercises can be very useful in attitudinal analysis

- Statement-feedback type questions are powerful means to gather perspectives and evaluations

- Always remember to include the *any other* option after the exhaustive list of answers

- While constructing the question sentences, keep in mind that participants are of different age, capability, educational qualifications and social skills.

- Present questions with formal punctuations and correct grammar and spelling. Avoid double-barrelled questions and jargons and technical terms.

- Eliminating ambiguity is central to the task. All response options must be mutually exclusive to safeguard the participant from getting confused about similarly meaning terms or expressions. Davies presents two basic questions that help to eliminate ambiguity thus, "First, will the respondent understand the words you use? Second, will the words convey the meaning you intended?"[18] Meanings and aims can be extremely subtle at times. Consider the possible implications for the two questions such as, 'Do you think church should allow public speeches against divorce?' and 'Do you think the church should forbid public speeches against divorce?'

- Operationalization of special terms used is a major task. "If you want to change accepted operationalizations, you should accept the burden of proof for your decision."[19] Working definition denotes a definition that is modified to suit the research task undertaken. Distinguishing 'working definition' and 'operationalization' Neuman says, "After you have a working definition, you are ready for *operationalization*, the process of developing an operational definition for the construct or variable."[20] This procedure is vital for question making, as it enables researcher to define specific operations of concepts and techniques of measurements. Operationalization, therefore, connects theory and experience in research. These variables and operationalizations take form from the literature review and the review of available reports of research.

- Fixing the rating scale is another task in the questionnaire formulation. For example, attitudinal data may use response options such as:

- Always/Most of the time/Sometimes/Never

- Excellent/Good/Fair/Poor

- Strongly agree/Agree/ Disagree/ Strongly Disagree

- Rating or measuring variables is a meticulous job. "Five suggestions for coming up with a measure

  1. Remember the conceptual definition. The underlying principle for any measure is to match it to the specific conceptual definition of the construct that will be used in the study.

  2. Keep an open mind. Do not get locked into a single measure or type of measure. Be creative and constantly look for better measures

  3. Borrow from others. Do not be afraid to borrow from other researchers, as long as credit is given. Good ideas for measures can be found in other studies or modified from other measures.

---

[18]   Richard E Davies, *Handbook for Doctor of Ministry Projects: An Approach to Structured Observation of Ministry*, (University Press of America, 1984), 129.

[19]   Davies, *Handbook for Doctor of Ministry Projects,* 1984, 104.

[20]   W Lawrence Neuman, *Social Research: Qualitative and Quantitative Approaches,* 2nd Edition, (Boston: Allyn & Bacon, 1994), 124.

4. Anticipate difficulties. Logical and practical problems often arise when trying to measure variables of interest. Sometimes a problem can be anticipated and avoided with careful forethought and planning.

5. Do not forget your units of analysis. Your measure should fit with the units of analysis of the study and permit you to generalize to the universe of interest."[21]

- Open ended questions have their own advantages says Davies, "The first decision is whether a question will be "open-ended" or not. An open-ended" question has the advantage of allowing the respondent to introduce the points of view that may not have occurred to you. Because of this, such questions are particularly useful in pilot studies. But is it difficult to compare "open-ended" responses from different people."[22]

- Questionnaire development is initially a cyclic process involving multiple tasks such as formulation, assigning ratings, revising, testing, determining on analysis, estimating the response rates. Expert consultation can always add some useful insights to ensure effectiveness in a questionnaire as Davies argues, "Apart from your own good sense of writing style and logic, and the friendly criticism of your neighbours, one of the best ways to learn to write good questionnaire is to study questionnaires written by others. Beyond that, there is a large literature on questionnaire design."[23]

- Piloting the tool helps the researcher discover linguistic errors, need for revision in the question sequence, relevance for more response options, and any negative ramifications. The task of piloting a questionnaire is simple. Dawson explains the piloting process thus.

> Ask people who have not been involved in its construction to read it through and see if there are any ambiguities which have not noticed. Once this has been done, alter the questions accordingly, then send out a number of questionnaires to the type of people who will be taking part in the main survey. Make sure they know it is a pilot test and ask them to forward any comments they may have about the length, structure and wording of the questionnaire. Go through each response very carefully, noting comments and looking at the answers to the questions as this will help you to discover whether there are still ambiguities present. Alter the questionnaire again. If you have had to undertake major alterations, you may need to pilot the questionnaire again.[24]

---

[21] Neuman, *Social Research,* 1994, 125.
[22] Richard E Davies, *Handbook for Doctor of Ministry Projects: An Approach to Structured Observation of Ministry,* (University Press of America, 1984), 129.
[23] Davies, *Handbook for Doctor of Ministry Projects,* 1984, 129.
[24] Catherine Dawson, *Practical Research Methods* (New Delhi: UBSPD, 2002), 95.

- Pilots have other advantages in the process of research as Sampson says, "While pilots can be used to refine research instruments such as questionnaires and interview schedules, they have greater use still in ethnographic approaches to data collection in foreshadowing research problems and questions, in highlighting gaps and wastage in data collection, and in considering broader and highly significant issues such as research validity, ethics, representation, and research health and safety."[25]

- Participant's rights may be indicated, if any, e.g., the right to know the results of the study, the right to be anonymous, the researcher's compliance with the specifications of Data Protection Act and so on.

- Analysis of data is done by taking the average of response rates.

- Sometimes same set of questions is given to distinct categories of participants. For instance, on the critical study of foreign mission funding procedures in the church, responses of the ministers may significantly vary from the members in the pew. The researcher has to anticipate the possible implications of this on the analysis of the data?

- Qualitative social researcher while preparing a questionnaire undertakes the task of measuring or weighing concepts or constructs that explain the function of the social reality. This has inherent complexities as it sounds.

Questionnaire method is being used beside other methods in qualitative undertakings increasingly. The researchers continue to explore the efficient integration of this method in the qualitative domain while simultaneously developing competencies required for the task.

Observation Methods

As a dynamic method in qualitative data gathering, *observation* "sits somewhere along the continuum between generated and naturally occurring data in that it involves an interaction in which the researcher is present, and sometimes an active participant."[26] According to Marshall and Rossman, "Observation is a fundamental and highly important method in all qualitative inquiry."[27] Researcher as the observer spends extensive time in the research context, takes consistent field notes on what is seen and add reflections on them in the light of the stated research questions. General advantages of this method are:

---

[25]   H Sampson, 'Navigating the Waves: The Usefulness of a Pilot in Qualitative Research', 383-402 in *Qualitative Research*, 4 (3), 383.

[26]   Jane Lewis and Carol McNaughton Nicholls, 'Design Issues' 47-69 Chapter 3 in J Richie, J Lewis, C M Nicholls & R Ormston, *Qualitative Research Practice*, 2nd edition, (London: Sage, 2014), 54.

[27]   Catherine Marshall and Gretchen B Rossman, *Designing Qualitative Research* (5th edn), (Thousand Oaks, CA: Sage, 2011), 140.

- researcher does not have to wait or rely on participant's willingness to provide data;
- a reality can be observed as it naturally is; and
- researcher's data is first hand rather than what is collected from others.

Observation method has the intrinsic problem of obtrusiveness and observer bias. The researcher as a stranger entering into a community will have restraints in observing life in its natural style. Participants will tend to behave better if they realize being observed. The researcher's active presence is an essential feature of this method but to varying degrees. Mills & Kotecha listed the four variations as occurring along the spectrum of the method outlined by Gold (1958) in which the researcher could be a: Complete participant, Participant as observer, Observer as participant, and, Complete observer.[28] Researcher has to make objective judgments on the significance of what is being observed and in what situation it is observed and the reliability of the interpretation of the observation. All types of observations cannot be methodologically validated but authentic qualitative research designs are used to systematically observe and explain a phenomenon. Observation as a research method may bring about significant data underlying a social reality that are not attainable through methods like interviews and questionnaires.

Types of Observation

Observation techniques vary on factors like, the information available to the researcher about the context, the purpose and design of the study, and the feasibility of the type of observation anticipated. Observes follow methods such as:

- Structured (Items to observe/record are defined) and unstructured (everything is observed)
- Direct (observes behaviour as it happens) and non-direct (observes the results of behaviour)
- Participant (joins, participates and observe) and non-participant (Observes without participating)
- Disguised (observation is unknown to the observed) and undisguised (participant is aware)

Rather than communicating with the participants in interviews and other methods, the researcher uses his/her own power of observation to capture the reality as it is in a natural setting. Observing a phenomenon normally assumes extended time spent in the context of inquiry. To understand and experience the cultural sub-systems, we must allow time. Therefore, the researcher's choice of observation

---

[28]   Lisa Mills & Mehul Kotecha, 'Observation' 243-264, Chapter 9 in J Richie, J Lewis, C M Nicholls & R Ormston, *Qualitative Research Practice* (2ⁿᵈ Edition) (London: Sage, 2014), 246.

methods, naturally assumes a commitment for prolonged stay in the context. The method has little chance for recall error because data is gathered first hand and, not reported.

As mentioned earlier, in *structured* procedures, the observer uses a format that has specific details of what and how to observe, how to record the data, and what procedure to follow in the analysis and so on. For example, regarding the *social dilemmas of ministers from the lower class communities serving among the predominantly higher classes*, observer who has primary knowledge of the situation begins with a clearly structured format to observe aspects such as social interactions among the ministers, between ministers and church members, attitudes in the administrative and ministry spheres of church life, conversations and behavioural patterns of persons, relevant events or activities, and interpretations and implementations of policies. Alongside the formulation of the research problem and observational procedures, the observer decides on the analysis plans as well.

If observer is not entirely sure about what data to be gathered from observation, the process will start in an *unstructured* method. As observation of the situation progresses in the natural course of events, the researcher will identify certain areas for focused observation that helps the formulation of a solid structure. Alternatively, the researcher who begins with basic knowledge of the situation will follow a fairly structured blueprint for observation. For example, exploring the ethical implications of the *street feeding projects of various social service groups in a given city*, the researcher may start with an unstructured observation method. From the initial impressions, observation proceeds to more specific dynamics such as hygienic issues, quality of services, abuses, financial manipulations and so on. Thus, an exploratory observation technique can open up before the observer a wide ranging data for further inquiry. The term *observation* itself implies activities that range from "hanging around in the setting, getting to know people, and learning the routines to using strict sampling to record actions and interactions and using a checklist to tick off pre-established actions."[29]

In *participant observation*, the researcher is an accepted participant in the life of the context being observed. Observation can be done with or without the knowledge of the observed, following structured or non-structured procedures. A skilled participant observer develops competencies for not to be intimidated or influenced by sensitive forces present in the context. Sociological, anthropological studies employ the participant observation method widely. To draw an example, the researcher becomes part of a Christian aid work group serving in a highly antagonistic religious setting to explore the *challenges faced by Christian aid workers*

---

[29]   Marshall and Rossman, *Designing Qualitative Research*, 2011, 139.

there. As a participant, the researcher immerses him/herself in the research context, systematically observing activities, relations, interactions, talks and events. Social anthropologists employ the term ethnography or field research, where participant observation takes place as an on-going method. Ethnographer participates in people's lives for an extended period, "watching what happens, listening to what is said, asking questions; in fact collecting whatever data are available to throw light on the issues."[30] Researcher observes how people in their normal settings view things, understand their meanings, interpret the dynamics and respond to them. Participant observation design takes into account features like: the number of persons, events or situations to be observed, the size of the social world that is represented by the observed, the categories to be observed, the method of knowing and engaging, and, interpreting the process of observation. A well implemented participant observation produces authentic data.

In *disguised observation*, identity of the researcher as the observer is not known by the participants. Not only that, the participants do not realize that they are being observed. Since observer takes a disguised role, the study cannot use direct interviews and other methods for data gathering. The method raises questions regarding its ethical justification, particularly about the use of hidden devices by researchers. The inherent criticisms on the participant observation methods are around the biases, possible subjectivity and researcher's influence on the behaviour of those being observed. The social, political or religious biases of the researcher may impact the way a situation or a person or system is observed. Conscious attempt to put aside one's own prejudices, cultural bias and presuppositions is central to observation techniques. The researcher participates in the life of the observed and simultaneously record their actions and reactions while exerting no control or influence on the normal patterns of their behaviour directly or indirectly. There are several skills that the participant observer can develop, says Bernard with his extended outline consisting of: 'learning the language, building explicit awareness of little details in life, building memory, maintaining naiveté, building writing skills, hanging out, gaining rapport, maintaining objectivity'.[31] Since participating with the observed in certain activities may narrow down the range of research experience, there should be constant realization of the limits and angles of the observation.

Focus Groups

Focus groups are "small structured groups with selected participants, normally led by a moderator. They are set up in order to explore specific topics, and individuals'

---

[30] Martyn Hammersley and Paul Atkinson, *Ethnography: Principles in Practice*, (3rd Edition) (London: Routledge, 2007), 3.

[31] Extracted from H Russell Bernard, *Research Methods in Anthropology*, 359-370.

views and experiences, through group interaction."[32] Researcher instigates a focused, moderated time of discussion on an issue with a group of an average size of 6-8 members who have relevant information to share about the given topic. Primary steps in the process are:

- identify the central purpose of the focus group,
- formulate 4-5 lead questions or areas for discussion,
- develop a rational frame for the time, and
- invite potential participants.

Scheduling, sharing general guidelines, fixing the venue, arranging for refreshments, setting the recording methods are other practical tasks. The researchers prefer this method as they can gather solid data from relevant informants in a single session. *Primary rules* for the group consist of specific instructions to be followed during the meeting. For instance,

- share ideas clearly and briefly
- listen to others before proceeding
- Don't dominate the discussion; help the group freely share perspectives & experiences
- Speak only what is relevant to the topic and avoid interrupting
- Accept critical statements from others and follow moderator's directions kindly

The group is usually homogeneous. We may think of focus groups of Christian youth in the political arena, individuals who publish biblical responses to a contemporary cult, missionaries who facilitate the culture-exclusive insider Christian faith movements etc. Morgan introduces focus groups as a method occupying a middle ground between participant observation and in-depth interviewing.[33] Group dynamics and the process of arriving at points of consensus vary from group to group, often depending on how the conversational styles work together and how much of openness was exercised in the talk.

Conversational openness and flexibility and the focus in the direction of discussion is a unique strength factor. It is a self-contained method, but can also be used effectively in conjunction with other methods. Number of questions or areas covered in a focus group may be limited as the researcher seeks rich, deeper interaction within the group. In the non-threatening situation of being in a group, participants feel at ease to share their problems and respond to comments and criticisms etc. Basic characteristics of these groups are that they are focused and

---

32 Lia Litosseliti, *Using Focus Groups in Research* (London: Continuum, 2005), 1.
33 David L Morgan & Richard A Krueger, *The Focus Group Kit* (London: Sage, 1997).

interactive. The purpose of focus group is to provide the participants a well-planned environment to share their opinions and not to bring the group into consensus or common conclusions. It often produces rich data from the confident sharing of views, experiences and stories. An outstanding advantage of focus group method is the potential for internal quality-control where participants provide checks and balances on one another. This natural trend within the group serves to curtail false or extreme views. Group dynamics are an added strength in this technique, stimulating people to respond, react, criticize or agree. Fear of public manipulation might cause negative results in cases of particularly sensitive issues.

Efficiency in designing and directing the conversation determines the outcome of focus groups. The more structured the talk, the less questions asked for depth of information. The researcher as the facilitator and moderator should consider factors like time, finance, nature of the topic and effective ways for discussion. Focus groups normally take about two hours. The number of themes or issues to be addressed within this time needs to be estimated. Use of audio/video recordings helps the researcher to carefully attend the natural occurrences and reactions in the conversations rather than getting engaging in concurrent transcribing of data. Manual transcription in group discussions do not always work well due to the difficulty in listening and recording multiple comments concurrently and in following up with the non-verbal data and insights that are significant in qualitative inquiry. For instance, focus group with *highly influential young male evangelists in the corporate technology world* will provide much more than verbal data. Video recordings will help the researcher to carefully process how they use language to express ideas and how interactions develop among the participants. Maintaining supplementary personal notes enhances efficiency. The researcher may organize meetings with several groups or the same group on several times to discuss the issue of inquiry. The researchers sometimes find this method particularly helpful in the study of attitudes and opinions. However, it does not fit well in certain situations for example, when participants are not cooperative for mature, objective interaction, potential participants resist to join or are unavailable, or, the researcher fails to execute the conversational design competently. Moreover, focus group method will not be suitable for inquiries that sees quantitative data. The qualitative researcher in most of these methods processes narratives of the participants. The following brief section on narrative analysis will substantiate this discussion.

Narratives

Scholars use narrative technique as a research genre and/or as a research method.

> Narrative generally refers to a particular kind of text organized around consequential events in the teller's life. It then includes characters and a plot that evolves over time.

The teller takes the listener into a past-time world, and recapitulates what happened then to make a point, often a moral one. No formal model of story actually exists. However, personal narratives depend on certain structures to hold them together.[34]

Variety of terms such as narrative analysis, narrative method, narrative inquiry etc. are in use in methodological discussions. Actual meaning of the term is determined by the process and purpose in an inquiry and in the current discussion it refers to a method. Literary analysts and folklorists favoured this method as they stepped away from the structured social scientific methods to deeper investigation into the consistent and meaningful development of *story lines* by people. Narratives include particular elicitation techniques such as natural conversations, differently from the traditional survey method that lacked enough space to draw the intended meanings in participant's words. This method aims to surface the untold, hard life experiences of persons and giving voice to those whose stories are never heard or accounted for. It aims to configure from the variety of descriptions of participants a fine story line.

The narrative approach appears in distinct techniques across the humanities disciplines, using variety of analysis methods. Creswell refers to Polkinghorne's description of narrative analysis in which the researcher collecting descriptions of events or phenomenon from people and configure them into a story using a plot line.[35] Narrative analysis uses varied sources like conversations, biographical study (a person narrates the story of another), autobiography (one's own story narrated), life history (narration of a person's entire life story rather than limiting it into select episodes), oral history (narrating the reflections of events and their causes and effects by one person or more), journals, focus groups, family histories and so on. These are useful when the researcher needs to formulate themes from narratives and when these narratives are key to understanding the people and their realities.

Sometimes the entire research design uses the narrative method where the researchers follow certain steps in which they: [36]

- Determine if the research problem or question best fits narrative research. Narrative research is best for capturing the detailed stories or life experiences of a single life or the lives of a small number of individuals.

---

[34]   Margareta Hyden and Carolina Overlien, '"Doing" Narrative Analysis' 250-268 in Deborah k Padgett (ed), *The Qualitative Research Experience,* Australia: Thomson Brooks/Cole, 2004), 253.

[35]   John W Creswell & Cheryl N Poth, *Qualitative Inquiry and Research Design: Choosing Among five Approaches* (London: Sage, 2017), 67-69. Creswell's mention of Polkinghorne in Chapter 4, 68. http://www.sagepub.com/upm-data/13421_Chapter4.pdf

[36]   Adapted from D. J. Clandinin & F. M. Connelly, *Narrative inquiry: Experience and Story in Qualitative Research* (San Francisco: Jossey-Bass, 2000), 17-20.

- Select one or more individuals who have stories or life experiences to tell, and spend considerable time with them gathering their stories through multiples types of information.

- Collect information about these stories through participants' personal experiences, work and home, their culture and historical settings.

- Analyse the participants' stories, and then re-story them into a framework that makes sense. Re-storying is the process of reorganizing the stories into some general type of framework.

- Collaborate with participants by actively involving them in the research

Disciplines of psychology and feminist studies are using narrative methods widely. Since it helps individuals to explain their identity, problems and experiences in their own terms and interpretations, this is particularly useful in deriving perspectives from the marginalized people and draw meaning from accounts of their experiences and memories. People normally like to give a narrative form to their experiences and such stories are significant contributions to social formation and transformation. Nonetheless, the qualitative researcher may find narratives as extensive data with multi-layered meanings. While the active cooperation of the participant is crucial, the researcher has to be conscious of possible subjectivity in handling the data. The researcher keep asking: Whose voice is heard? Is it what needs to be heard? What are the latent meanings the story conveys? Will there someone to present a different story? What is most highlighted in the narration? What are emphases neglected knowingly or otherwise?

Reflection Box:
There is always more to consider...

Young researcher Z presented the research proposal on 'People's Methods of Resolving Marital Problems in Christian Families'. He enthusiastically articulated the importance of understanding how holistically families would approach the question and how he wanted to correlate the inquiry to the role of premarital expectations and preparations impacting their methods of problem resolution within marriage. The pastoral ministry purpose of the inquiry was obvious - all sounded incredible! Is there anything more for him to consider before proceeding?

CONSIDER:

- What would it imply for the unmarried young man interviewing couples in a rather closed, shame/blame-grounded cultural setting?
- How much of openness would he assume about resolving marital issues in the light of premarital expectations and preparations? Is the correlation reasonable in the context of study?
- How is he planning the interviews? What are the implications for the couple taking the interview together? Is it culturally acceptable to ask for separate interviews?
- Do these families represent one particular denomination or place? What are methodological concerns otherwise?
- What type of questions would be non-intrusive, less-intimidating or non-threatening to the couple? Can the researcher articulate a few key questions for personal interviews?
- Does Researcher Z speak the same language of the participants? Is vernacular being used during data collection, using tools translated and tested for clarity?
- Are there existing theories or concepts in the literature that correlated the impact of premarital experiences on the problem-solving dimension in marriage? How well does he locate his research on this?
- Will the researcher be able to gather reliable data as he anticipates? What specific skills are essential to get there?

- Whose voice is he mainly planning to heed? Whose voice is going to be neglected?
- Is he thinking of generalizing the result? What are the implications?

CHAPTER 7

COMPETENCIES IN QUALITATIVE STUDY

SECTION CONTENTS:

- Reading Skills
- Writing Skills
- Thinking Skills
- Data Process and Analysis Skills
- Self-management Skills
- Theological Skills

Research requires skills. Yet, the encouraging note is that no one starts researching after having acquired all the skills. The keen researcher develops each of them during the process. Creswell outlined 30 essential skills[1] for the qualitative researcher offering "how to" information for beginners in social, behavioural and humanities fields. This chapter discusses six areas of skill development that the theology researcher should be consistently working on. The figure below provides a bird's-eye-view of several points of which certain ideas are further elaborated in sections following.

---

[1] John W Creswell, *30 Essential Skills for the Qualitative Researcher,* (Sage: London, 2015).

Figure 15: Research Skills Overview

Reading: Previewing, discussing, comparing, contrasting, evaluating, construting, interrogating, inferring, anotating, refleceing, critiquing, analysing, synthesizing, judging

Writing: Language, expressions, narrative techniques, genres, relevance, interconnections, effective links, coherent logic, clarity, conviction, justice, honesty

Thinking: Grasping, outlining, creating, criticising, reflecting, classifying, assuming, inferring, hypothezing, finding patterns of relationship, comparing, testing, making judgments

Data process: Planning, organizing, gaining access, legal functioning, selection of methods and participants, decision-making on direction, note-taking and management, epistemological assumptions, theological underpinning, right questions, solid interconnections, ongoing analysis and data saturation, reinforcement of research question through the process

Self-management: Time management, trust in God, immersion in data, organized journaling and reflection, effective breaks, socio-cultural, religious and political sensitivity, health and exercise, attending family & ministry

Theology: Grounded theological wisdom, seeking wisdom from peers/experts. engaging personal epistemological assumptions, critical cross-disciplinary interfacing, theological inter-departmental reflections, aligning the study with God's eternal plan for the world, exploring strategic missional interventions to guide the way forward.

Reading Skills

Critical reading capacity is integral to the researcher's task. Many have wrongly assumed that qualitative research has nothing to do with critical reading or rigorous analysis. Although not of the same nature as in the quantitative, research in this domain needs to build the study on these pillars, aligning with the epistemological foundations. *Critical readers*[2] never read passively. Their reading progresses with engagement in the text, analysis and synthesis. Real engagement happens when the reader makes personal notes, asks critical questions, classify key thoughts, compare/contrast concepts, and check each idea against personal standpoints and values. In focused reading, large categories of information are split into smaller units, specific components are identified, and sub-themes and their intertwining recognized in order to make sense of the information. Therefore, reading and thinking happens together.

Reading in this style develops by keen practice. First, the qualitative researcher recognizes the existence of a problem to be investigated, then, starts off the task with critical reading and reviewing of the literature. Topic for the research can be proposed to the academic committee only alongside this component of reading. There is no stage for the qualitative researcher is accomplished with reading. In fact reading gets its horizons further expanded when the researcher keeps discovering deeper wisdom turn-by-turn. The two major comprehension strategies are: Grounding in background knowledge and asking critical questions. Types of reading comprehension vary from person to person. However, the capacity in reading comprehension will develop significantly in the process of a good research and the research report will vividly reflect this.

- **Literal** comprehension of a text helps the researcher understand the 5Ws and the 2Hs (who, what, when, where, why, how and how much)
- **Interpretive** comprehension refers to the *why, what if* (conditions set), and *how* of the information
- **Practical** comprehension of the text expects the impact of the text to make the researcher act upon
- **Affective** comprehension denotes the knowing of the content in emotional and social dimensions of life
- **Lexical** comprehension has to do with the definitions of vocabularies in the reading

---

[2] Refer Deanne Spears, *Developing Critical Reading*, 9th Edition, (New York: McGraw Hill Companies Inc., 2012). Also, Nolan J Weil, *Thinking Beyond the Content: Critical Reading for Academic Success* (Michigan: University of Michigan Press, 2008).

- **Reflective** comprehension of a text makes the researcher critically reflect upon the impact of the text on the crucial aspects of life and service

Figure 16: Dimensions in Reading

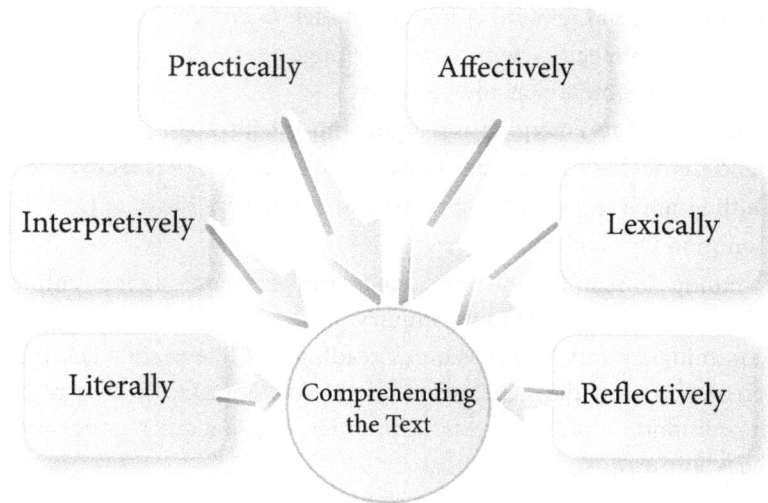

Those who are unable to recognize key thoughts or the points of critical questions to ask normally have difficulty in constructing meaning of what they read. One of the reasons for this is the unskillfulness in gathering the background knowledge. With concrete knowledge of the background data, it is relatively easy for researchers to identify the conceptual and practical interconnections between ideas. The researchers, who never had received coaching in strategic, critical reading, are more likely to approach and interpret various genres of reading on the same preconceptions. The researchers should be able to see the distinctions in literature in their particular forms as history, criticism, popular theology, systematic theology, biography, autobiography, missionary narratives, and the like. Research undertakings in higher education presuppose critical reading competencies. Some simple steps are shown below:

- Preview the text prior to reading. This background knowledge contributes much to further reading
- Place the content in its context. Reading makes sense only when the context in and to which it is written.

- Visualize the content. Creating mental images improves comprehension.[3] Visualizing the language and verbalizing the imagery are two sides of skillful reading.
- Interrogate the text at every important point. This helps the researcher to comprehend and remember important themes and concepts
- Annotate connectors with other writings in similar directions and see elements of comparison and contrast
- Infer viewpoints emerging and arguments established
- Reflect how these impact one's own personal values, perspectives or beliefs
- Outline, analyse, compare, contrast and summarize ideas
- Common types of reading are:
- Scanning: In scanning, the researcher reads fast, looking for specific pieces of information relevant to the inquiry.
- Skimming: Skimming too is quick reading, but like in milk skimming, the researcher takes the richest part off the top. Specifically, it is reading the most important parts or sections in order to gain a quick understanding of the whole text.
- Intensive reading: This is known as the *zoom lens* reading. Going deep into short passages or articles also fall in this category. Rhetorical, grammatical, discourse analytical, and literal dynamics are closely looked at by the researcher.
- Extensive reading: This is done when researchers have a large amount of useful material for the quick grasp of the general content. The researcher does not look for specific details or important terms, rather gathers the gist of each text in a generic form.

Writing Skills

A great deal of qualitative research is writing. The term *note-taking* has won special approval in the qualitative domain. Moreover, the review of literature, data analysis and interpretation, reporting of the findings require strategic writing skills. Writing is a nightmare for the unskillful, unorganized readers and thinkers. The researchers who are educated in the vernaculars often face much difficulty in transferring ideas to another language, especially using academic terms and styles. However, generally we understand writing as a competency that can be developed by consistent writing and re-writing.

The SEEE approach is a wide known sequence that helps to develop a solid style in writing by carefully substantiating each statement. SEEE stands for Statement,

---

[3]   Nanci Bell, *Visualizing and Verbalizing for Language Comprehension and Thinking* (CA: Gander Publishing, 2007), 303-314.

Explanation, Evidence and Evaluation. The writer is always to keep the reader in mind as each sentence is framed. Reading and interpreting a written page involves a complex hermeneutical process that varies according to the level of mental development, knowledge, and attitudes of whoever reads it. The researcher therefore has to employ foundational principles of efficiency in written communication in order to make the inquiry relevant.

Critical academic writing is different from general descriptive writing. Descriptive writers do not analyse the text or engage in critical reflection. What they do is present the material or context as it stands. Critical writing on the other hand, is capable of assessing, comparing, integrating, interrogating and synthesizing, along with many other tasks. The researchers follow the strategic academic style that is coherently arranged, problem-response method, addressing critical issues and assessing them from multiple perspectives. The hallmark of good research writing is the ability to examine the different aspects of the research question and to present the data and findings as clearly inferred from the logical evidences. It presents complex information with clarity, analytical strength and a high level of precision and carefully safeguards writing from unnecessary expressions of personal feelings and the not-so-crucial snippets of attitudinal details.

Academic writing has certain characteristics. A most common question in writing is on the use of person pronouns in grammar. The researchers follow institution's guidelines or their own preferences in this.

> Traditional approach to academic writing uses the third person singular rather than the first person. However, many interpretative approaches to research, typically has an effect upon other research participants during the collection of data. Hence interpretative researchers often feel that it is permissible, and even desirable, to write at least partially in the first person. Such reflexive accounts are often seen as being a very desirable element in accounts of interpretative research.[4]

Also, we note that suggestive language may be preferred over the prescriptive and assertive expressions. Good writing avoids sweeping comments and present claims of truth in terms of data, in preference to more definite claims, one might say, 'it appears from the data that' 'the evidence would appear to indicate...' 'One might argue from these words that...' While using technical theological vocabulary, the researcher makes sure that ideas are presented in an understandable manner. Writing is ultimately, the development of one's voice. Wellington et al refers to the development of one's academic voice in writing as:

- healthy scepticism ... but not cynicism;

---

4 Paul Oliver, *Writing your Thesis*, (Sage: London, 2008), 13.

- confidence ... but not 'cockiness' or arrogance;
- judgment which is critical ... but not dismissive;
- opinions ... without being opinionated;
- careful evaluation of published work ... not serial shooting at random targets;
- being 'fair': assessing fairly the strengths and weaknesses of other people's ideas and writing ... without prejudice; and
- making judgments on the basis of considerable thought and all the available evidence ... as opposed to assertions without reason.[5]

There are many ways to enhance quality of writing. The qualitative researcher whose work is mostly about the meanings and interpretations needs to carefully craft each word and expression so that the writing will communicate the intended meaning qualitatively. Sometimes explicit parts of the study may have been impacted by researcher-bias in certain ways with regard to assumptions of faith and practice. Consistent articulation of such values or assumptions with self-critical accounts adds great quality to academic writing. Ability to develop concise summary and a convincing theory from numerous forms of evidences is particularly desirable in academic writing. Presenting various sections in the research report proportionately is another desirable skill in writing. Sections that are too disproportionate can heighten ambiguity. Using gender-inclusive language is another mark of academic writing.

Qualitative research writing does not read like a flavourless compilation of information. It has evidences of critical interaction, meaning constructions, comparisons of theories, exploration of the relations between observations and realities and many more. Writing the implications of the study requires still other capacities like strategic theory-practice integration and the insight to imagine the way forward based on God's mission in the world. What makes the qualitative research unique is the essential message it carries for the world's difficult quests. In this the researcher needs to see as Ott suggests, the integration of the Greek categories of Theoria, Praxis and Poiesis denotes respectively, the Reflection (Knowledge), Action (Responsibility) and Production (Ability)[6]. The universal standards of intellectual reasoning by Paul and Elder present the elements that determine the quality of reasoning as follows:

---

[5]   J Wellington, A Bathmaker, C Hunt, G McCulloch and P Sikes. *Succeeding with your Doctorate* (London: Sage, 2005), 84.

[6]   Bernhard Ott, *Understanding and Developing Theological Education* (Cumbria: ICETE Series, 2016), 203. Cf. Stackhouse, *Apologia*, 84-135.

Clarity: Could you elaborate? Could you illustrate what you mean? Could you give me an example?

Accuracy: How could we check on that? How could we find out if that is true? How could we verify or test that?

Precision: Could you be more specific? Could you give me more details? Could you be more exact?

Relevance: How does that relate to the problem? How does that bear on the question? How does that help us with the issue?

Depth: What factors make this difficult? What are some of the complexities of this question? What are some of the difficulties we need to deal with?

Breadth: Do we need to look at this from another perspective? Do we need to consider another point of view? Do we need to look at this in other ways?

Logic: Does all of this make sense together? Does your first paragraph fit in with your last one? Does what you say follow from the evidence?

Significance: Is this the most important problem to consider? Is this the central idea to focus on? Which of these facts are most important?

Fairness: Is my thinking justifiable in context? Am I taking into account the thinking of others? Is my purpose fair given the situation? Am I using my concepts in keeping with educated usage, or am I distorting them to get what I want?[7]

Significant research reports are produced when these elements are critically applied to the purpose of research, the research question, assumptions, inferences and implications.

Thinking Skills

The spine of the entire process of research can be defined as *thinking*. Independent and original thinking is the hallmark of a competent researcher. Formulating one's own views and expressing one's own voice are cognitive abilities essential for transformative learning. The researcher consistently handles arguments, inferences, comparisons, deductions and propositions. Coherent inferences of the data take form in the researcher's mind while handling the rich qualitative data. The researcher reflects on the theological/philosophical assumptions, evaluates them against the social realities and draws conclusions from reliable evidences from the data.

---

[7] Richard Paul and Linda Elder, *The Miniature Guide to Critical Thinking Concepts and Tools,* 7th Edition, (Foundation for Critical Thinking Publishing, 2014), 12. https://www.criticalthinking.org/files/Concepts_Tools.pdf accessed on June 2, 2017.

Thinking patterns of the researcher play a big role in developing a coherent research strategy that includes the formulation of the research question, methodology and philosophical (theological and practical) underpinnings and so on. Splitting ideas into small specific elements, identifying patterns of relationship and drawing justifiable inferences are ongoing thinking tasks. Grasping, identifying, outlining, creating, criticizing, reflecting, classifying, assuming, inferring, hypothesizing, finding patterns of relationship, comparing, testing, evaluating, and making judgments are various activities in thinking.

Interpretative or hermeneutical skill is of paramount significance in qualitative researching. Hans-Georg Gadamer, one of Heidegger's students, recognized the interpretive dimension of scholarship as something open to encountering and learning genuinely new things. The following are the five moments he recognized in the hermeneutical task:

Preunderstanding: understandings that come from the past with which one starts interpretation

The experience of being brought up short: Experiencing something that calls into question certain aspect of the preunderstanding.

Dialogical interplay: the back and forth interplay between the horizon of the interpreter and the horizon of the person, or the object being interpreted.

Fusion of horizons: emergent new insights when the horizons of the interpreter and the interpreted meet together when both make their contributions

Application: New insights give rise to new ways of thinking and acting in the world[8] [emphasis added].

Enhancing critical quality of research practically starts with *thinking*. "Scholarly research assumes that…existing understandings will need to be subjected to critical scrutiny. This does not mean that existing knowledge is to be automatically regarded as erroneous."[9] Critical thinking as some might assume, is not about criticism. It is not always referring to the adverse or censorious judgments people make on others. In academic thinking and writing, it simply means the reviewing the merits and demerits of specific theories, lines of argument or activities. Critical thinking presupposes open interaction with other dimensions, disciplines, concepts and actions. The following comparison chart shows the two ways of making good judgments.[10]

---

[8]   Adapted from Hans-Georg Gadamer, *Truth and Method* (New York: Continuum, 1975), 310-325.

[9]   Hunter P Mabry, *A Manual for Researchers and Writers* (Bangalore: The BTESSC, 1999), 3.

[10]   Adapted from The Association of Theological Education by Extension (TAFTEE)'s Research Guide (2000), Archives at New India Bible Seminary Library, Kerala.

Figure 17: Ordinary Thinking vs Critical Thinking

Ordinary Thinking	Critical Thinking
Guessing	Estimating
Preferring	Evaluating
Grouping	Classifying
Believing	Assuming
Inferring	Inferring Logically
Associating Concepts	Grasping Principles
Noting Relationships	Noting Relationships among other relationships
Supposing	Hypothesizing
Offering Opinions without reasons	Offering opinions with Reasons
Making Judgments without Criteria	Making Judgments with Criteria

There are multiple ways to enhance critical thinking capacity. According to Mabry, a critical approach to study presupposes that

- We have a questioning mind which critically interrogates the existing level of understanding.
- We avoid being overwhelmed by what other scholars have said on a subject and at the same time are prepared to deal seriously with their arguments.
- We seriously consider materials which challenge any hypothesis, bias or personal interest with which we began our research we well as materials which confirm these.
- We have the intellectual and moral courage to seriously consider the full range of material relevant to the research problem.
- We conceive new and persuasive solutions or envision new theories to deal with the problem with which we struggle. [11]

There are enormous data a student analyses in the whole process of research in the form of literature. Major claims are determined on particular stages and these are substantiated well with primary evidences drawn by the researcher from primary and secondary sources. However, there are stages in the research process, where the study has to see beyond such lists of evidences and reach the stage of

---

[11]   Mabry, *A Manual for Researchers and Writers*, 1999, 3.

165

making judgments of the data. This is a skill that researchers develop not necessarily by reading but very much through interacting with scholarly writings.

Development of the skill of reflexivity is crucial in research. It is the thinking pattern that helps the researcher to objectively explain the production of knowledge and the theological, biblical, ministerial, social, worldviews of the researcher or other scholars.

> Concept development is an important dimension in thinking. Pattison, discussing the losses and threats in Practical Theology while following the empirical data, mentions the centrality of conceptual development.

> Conceptual work seems much more difficult for average research students to do well than empirical work where the road is well mapped, the methods are well honed and useful results are more or less guaranteed. Part of the reason for this is that critical insight the product of conceptual research, takes a long time to emerge and does not appear to order. If it is misconceived or poorly presented, it is worthless.[12]

Researchers are said to be able to make a sensible judgment when the inquiry: *is based upon supportive evidences* (standards, procedures, findings and anything that can guide one's judgment); is *contextually relevant* (takes into account cultural realities and contextual evidences); and, is *self-critical* (assuming a critical standpoint at one's own arguments and foreseeing the possible counter-arguments). How to create good arguments is a question that most researchers grapple with at various stages of their research process. An argument should offer

- a *claim*
- *evidence* or *grounds* that support it
- something we call a *warrant*, a general principle that explains why you think your evidence is relevant to your claim
- *qualifications* that make your claim and evidence more precise[13]

Readers of the research report are interested to know precisely, why there is a claim and how well these claims help them to understand the argument better. It also enables them to think with the researcher in developing and testing new ideas. All through the reasoning process, the researcher should be upholding what is known as *the intellectual morals*, termed by Paul and Elder as, the intellectual traits or virtues as "Intellectual humility, Intellectual courage, Intellectual empathy, Intellectual

---

12   Stephen Pattison, *The Challenge of Practical Theology*, (London: Jessica Kingsley Publishers, 2007), 274.
13   Wayne C Booth, Gregory G Colomb and Joseph M Williams. *The Craft of Research* (Chicago: the University of Chicago Press, 1995), 89.

autonomy, Intellectual integrity, Intellectual perseverance, Confidence in reason, and, Fair-mindedness."[14]

The researcher as a multi-tasker needs multiple competencies. The following diagram summarizes the tasks and skills in the transformative research practice.

Data Process and Analysis Skills

Qualitative data skills are not limited to the writing of methodology and the collection and analysis of the data. This methodology is more than what many would assume it to be. Therefore, training in the methodology, purposes, wide-ranging methods, epistemological assumptions and outcomes is essential. When learning is facilitated to a group of ongoing or immediate prospective researchers, there is usually great impact through active reflections and interactions. Skills in planning, organizing, decision-making, altering to better strategies, field note-taking and managing, effective use of language and communication, consistent embodying of logical coherence in thinking, coding and interpreting, ongoing processing of beliefs, values and assumptions, prominent debates on the topic and interdisciplinary issues, and, the efficient reinforcing of the research question to run through the entire process are particularly central to the task. The capacity to build in each of these is substantial, for instance, as Taylor and Bogdan says, "Those who want to use qualitative methods because they seem easier than statistics are in for a rude awakening."[15] Moreover, for the theology researcher, this form of inquiry corresponds to the quintessence of incarnational mission, which assumes more skills in reflection and hermeneutics.

Data processing skills are varied in qualitative inquiry. Data gathering is designed on interpersonal skills. The researcher has to develop skills in gaining access to data sources, maintain prolonged contact and build efficient rapport with the participants. The researcher's analysis is done concurrently with the generation of data. The quality of the inquiry lies heavily on the analytical ability and skills training of the researcher. Processing of the rich, descriptive data to specific concepts and constructs seeks multiple skills of coding, sense-making and analysis. Balancing sensitivity and objectivity in the procedure is a skillful work. Development of conceptual interconnections and meaningful inferences depends largely on the analytical skill of the researcher.

The term *analysis* refers to the computation of certain measures to organize the data systematically so that interpretive ideas can emerge and simultaneously

---

[14]   Richard Paul and Linda Elder, *The Miniature Guide to Critical Thinking Concepts and Tools* (7th Edition), (Foundation for Critical Thinking Publishing, 2014), 15. https://www.criticalthinking.org/files/Concepts_Tools.pdf accessed on June 2, 2017.

[15]   Steven J Taylor and Robert Bogdan, *Introduction to Qualitative Research Methods,* 2nd Edition, (New York: Wiley, 1984), 53.

researcher can look for patterns of relationship within the data. It is simultaneously an exciting and challenging task with rich data from qualitative interviewing and other techniques like observation, narration etc. Qualitative data analysis usually takes into account, not just what is available on paper, but what the non-verbal responses recorded, the actual and complete detail of the conduct of the research. According to the preference of the researcher, the data are transferred into a manageable format. The researcher may use a number of transcripts from personal interviews, focus groups, semi-structured questionnaires and observation techniques along with personal memos and notes. Simultaneously with data gathering, the researcher is vigilant to identify and note down certain themes emerging from the data. Overall theorizing in the research is about "thinking through the data"[16] as Silverman says. The researcher induces theoretically based observations and linkages to grand models. Regarding the positioning of such grand theoretical models in cultural studies Alassutari writes,

> One preferably starts directly from empirical examples, develops the questions by discussing them, and gradually leads the reader into interpretations of the material and to more general implications of the results. If one feels like discussing and constructing them, the best position for grand theoretical modes is in the final pages.[17]

Many withdraw from qualitative approaches fearing the large amount of data to be analysed and the long process of coding towards developing the theory. The nature of qualitative data demands certain kinds of analytical expertise from the researcher. Summarizing previous chapters, we see the characteristics of the qualitative data as:

- Inductive
- Focused on context
- Open inquiry
- Naturalistic
- Descriptive and interpretive
- Often cyclic
- Multiple perspectives
- Attention to individual experience

How Different is the Qualitative Data Analysis?

In certain genres of qualitative data, the researcher starts analysing simultaneously with the gathering of data where as in the quantitative, the process of analysis starts when the data gathering is complete. However, coding in methods like Grounded

---

[16]   David Silverman, *Doing Qualitative Research: A Practical handbook*, (London: Sage, 2000), 252.

[17]   Pertti Alasuutari, *Researching Culture: Qualitative Method and Cultural Studies*, (London: Sage, 1995), 183.

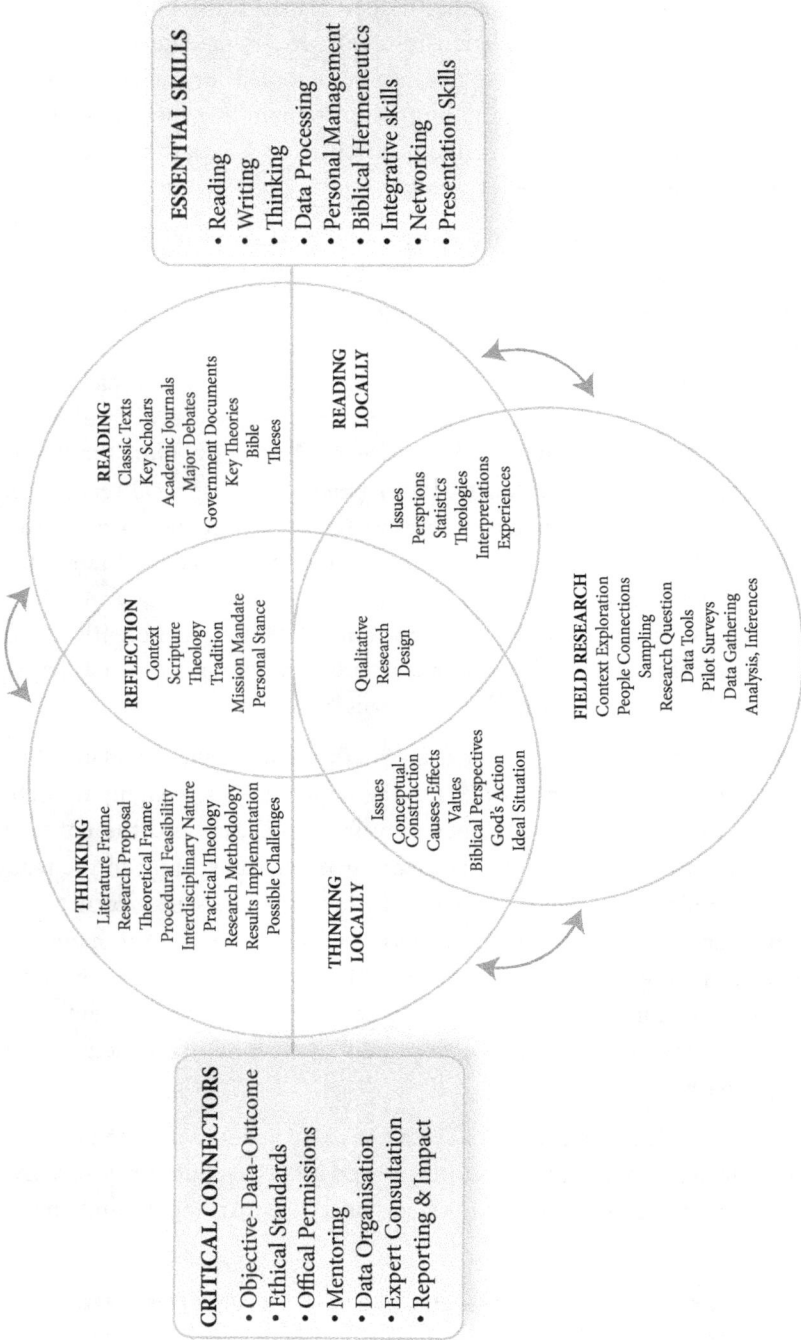

Figure 18: Tasks and Skills in Transformative Research Practice

Process of Transformative Qualitative Research

ESSENTIAL SKILLS
- Reading
- Writing
- Thinking
- Data Processing
- Personal Management
- Biblical Hermeneutics
- Integrative skills
- Networking
- Presentation Skills

READING
Classic Texts
Key Scholars
Academic Journals
Major Debates
Government Documents
Key Theories
Bible
Theses

READING LOCALLY

Issues
Persptions
Statistics
Theologies
Interpretations
Experiences

REFLECTION
Context
Scripture
Theology
Tradition
Mission Mandate
Personal Stance

Qualitative Research Design

THINKING
Literature Frame
Research Proposal
Theoretical Frame
Procedural Feasibility
Interdisciplinary Nature
Practical Theology
Research Methodology
Results Implementation
Possible Challenges

THINKING LOCALLY

Issues
Conceptual-Construction
Causes-Effects
Values
Biblical Perspectives
God's Action
Ideal Situation

FIELD RESEARCH
Context Exploration
People Connections
Sampling
Research Question
Data Tools
Pilot Surveys
Data Gathering
Analysis, Inferences

CRITICAL CONNECTORS
- Objective-Data-Outcome
- Ethical Standards
- Offical Permissions
- Mentoring
- Data Organisation
- Expert Consultation
- Reporting & Impact

169

Theory in the qualitative mode must begin with the complete data in hand. Careful thinking through the data, making judgments on themes emerging, interpreting data by locating patterns of relationships and processing data towards the argument are major tasks. Software assistance can be obtained for qualitative analysis but it can sometimes encounter certain limitations in handling the varied and rich data.[18] In cases of highly complex data, the researchers seek expert help to attach numeric codes and locate occurrences of terms.

Qualitative and quantitative analyses differ as their approaches and objectives are essentially different. While quantitative follows a highly developed, standardized set of analysis techniques, qualitative is less standardized and can adapt from a multiple analyses approaches. Quantitative analysis, as its name indicates, follows a predictable analytical procedure with mathematical, statistical precision while qualitative analysis allows its analysis method to evolve as the data collection progresses, mostly adapting to inductive methodology. Quantitative researchers use numbers and variable constructs that represent empirical realities in order to test abstract hypotheses when qualitative researchers focus on the formulation of concepts, theories or models with the help of empirical facts. Quantitative analysis highlights variables, statistics, hypotheses, patterns deriving from numbers and causal relationships between variables and attributes. Differently, in qualitative analysis, we find words, themes or concepts developing from the descriptive raw data, mostly context based and less abstract.[19]

Dawson articulated three analysis methods in qualitative data, the thematic, content and discourse analyses[20]. The thematic analysis is highly inductive in that it allows the emergence of themes only from the data and the entire process of the development of themes or the theory is made transparent to the reader. When emergent poles in ideas are recognized, the researchers may turn to the tasks of comparison or contrast. Content analysis is seen more as a mechanical procedure in which the researcher analyses the material carefully, assigns codes in the form of words or numerals to ideas, develops categories of themes and presents the responses with frequency numbers. Such data presentations look like a blend of quantitative and qualitative.

Discourse analysis considers discourse as an action which can be analysed and themes derived. "Much of this is intuitive and reflective, but it may also involve some form of counting, such as counting instances of turn-taking and their influence

---

[18]   Catherine Dawson, *Practical Research Methods* (New Delhi, UBSPD, 2002), 122.

[19]   W. Lawrence Neuman, *Social Research: Qualitative and Quantitative Approaches*, 2nd Edition, (Boston: Allyn & Bacon, 1994), 405.

[20]   Dawson, *Practical Research Methods*, 2002, 119.

on the conversation and the way in which people speak to others."[21] Analysing a discourse means analysing what people say or write. This method gained wide attention in the 1970s with the linguistic focus in social sciences that brought to the centre of thought, the discourses of people. Discourse analysts do not limit language simply as a means to express ideas rather they see it as a consequence of experiences of the reality, which extends further from the basic functions of conversation. The four key features of discourse analysis according to Antaki[22] are:

- The talk or text to be naturally found
- Words are to be understood in their co-text and their more distant context
- Analyst to be sensitive to the words' non-literal meaning or force
- Analyst to reveal the social actions and consequences achieved by the words' use- as enjoyed by those responsible for the words, and suffered by their addressees, or the world at large

Qualitative data can be analysed both in reflective method and in quantifying method. This choice is made often according to the personal preference, educational background of the researcher and the nature of the topic. The following is Dawson's Qualitative Analysis Continuum.

Figure 19: Qualitative Analysis Continuum (Dawson)[23]

Highly Qualitative		Almost Quantitative
e.g., thematic and comparative analysis	e.g., discourse and conversational analysis	e.g., content analysis
Reflexive Intuitive Takes place throughout data collection	Uses a combination of reflexivity and counting	Code and count Mechanical Can be left until end of data collection

Qualitative data is varied and follow different analysis methods. Questionnaire survey method may follow statistical analysis. Data gathered from interviews, focus groups and observations can be processed through Grounded Theory analysis. Conversational data may use ethnomethodological techniques, since, the analysis

---

[21] Dawson, *Practical Research Methods*, 2002, 119.

[22] Taken from Charles Antaki, 'Discourse Analysis and Conversational Analysis' in Alassutari, P., Bickman L, and Brunnen J (eds), *The Sage Handbook of Social Research Methods* (London: Sage, 2008), 435 cited also in web source https://dspace.lboro.ac.uk/dspace-jspui/bitstream/2134/5435/1/antaki%201.pdf on May 31, 2017.

[23] Dawson, *Practical Research Methods*, 2002, 115.

takes into account the social meanings within the talks, by carefully integrating the non-verbal aspects of the interaction. Both discourse analysis and conversational analysis are used in ethnomethodology and they centre on the meaning-making function of language. How people truly make sense of their life experience through conversation in the real time is the focus in this method. Conversational analysts handle ordinary language of people to realize how individuals make sense of interpersonal actions and how these actions are organized socially.[24] It considers the specific terms, their repetitions and their placing in the ongoing interaction.

In critical textual analysis of narratives, researchers like psychologists, linguistic ethnographers, ethnomethodologists and sociological researchers who study oppressive social structures analyse texts from multiple angles. They look for the linguistic structure of the participant's narration, that is, the words, sentences and the topical cohesiveness, and the narratives as cognitive structures made by the participants that have significant themes, plots and underpinnings of concepts. They address issues that are buried in the narratives in excavating why this story here and now.

Focus group data analysis starts with the completed transcription of the recordings from the discussion. It follows some interpretive code mapping method in which the research list the key topics in the discussion, then identify sub-divisions to each topic, search for patterns of interconnections and draw inferences in order to develop themes, issues and concerns. Observations of people's interactions, their lines of reasoning, expressions and reactions during the talk attribute insights to the data.

Observational data is typically analysed on the recorded content, its criteria and theoretical construct in the research. Being hands-on exploration of the context, the observation method is considered more objective; yet the way the data is recorded and analysed could be criticized for observer-bias. Inter-observer and intra observer objectivity are decisive factors in the analysis of observational data.

The Coding Task

Various tools of data collection provide the researcher with extensive data that cannot be presented anywhere in the research report as it is. These data consist of different kinds of information such as perspectives, beliefs, opinions, feelings, evaluations etc. By analysing the data, the researcher derives fresh information, insights, themes and specific findings. Inquirers may formulate theories or create models for improved practice as the result of data analysis. The process of analysis, therefore, speaks of the

---

[24]   Robin Wooffitt, *Conversation Analysis and Discourse Analysis: A Comparative and Critical Introduction* (London: Sage, 2005), 186.

organization of the data in a particular manner that enables the researcher to develop interpretative ideas that lead to findings. In analysis, the qualitative researcher carefully groups the verbal and non-verbal responses of the informants. The large body of information is grouped into a limited number of categories without losing or adding anything from the actual content of what has been obtained.[25]

'Coding' further assists the process. Responses may be given particular codes that can be tabulated. Unclear and incomplete responses increase coding errors. Researchers therefore ensure that the intended amount of information was gathered and the data tools are complete. Since the research report cannot contain responses descriptively, researcher aims at forming theme clusters out of the data code the ideas correctly in a coding sheet. Frequency of the responses is coded in this coding chart. A careful evaluation of the coding chart with the frequency distribution of various opinions and observations helps the researcher to formulate the theme clusters. Manual sorting out of the data may be done with word description but mechanical tabulation requires numerical symbols.

After categorizing the data and coding every theme of the responses in those categories, the researcher can choose a viable method to present the derived information in statistical tables. Tabulation is a significant part of the analysis process. Tabulated data conserves space in the thesis. Quantitative and qualitative researchers adapt tabular methods that are appropriate for their data. The compact form of presenting the data enables the reader make comparisons or contrasts. Tabulation of relatively small inquiries can be done manually while large research attempts require the help of mechanic devices. Simple tabulation presents one set of thoughts at a time. Cross tabulation provides the reader with the presentation of manifold information in one chart. An experienced social researcher can accurately present more than three inter-related characteristics of information (any large number of variables) in one table. Having a clear idea of the kind of data to be gathered, the researcher will be able to develop an appropriate tabulation plan even before the collection of data.

Tabulation done by electronic devices facilitates speed, cross classifications and safeguards the coder from tabulation errors. This is widely used by quantitative inquirers. Hand tabulation has the advantage of doing the tabulation aright from the field from where the investigator secures the data. Organizing and presenting the material in the most appropriate and effective manner is the responsibility of the coder. Experts in research speak of the vast possibility of using various methods of presenting the data. Diagrams and graphs are notable among them.

Sequences diagrams of interaction and sequence flow charts of events are easy to read and understand but they require a certain level of knowledge from the part

---

[25] Jessy Jaison, *Enjoy Your Research* (Trivandrum: New India Publications, 2000), 82.

of the reader. It is of profound importance that the researcher integrates the most appropriate method to present the data. Coding and tabulation enable the researcher to present the data in understandable and compact form. The statistical analysis in quantitative inquiries undertakes the greater task of estimating the reliability of generalizations of the larger unit (population) from the secured data.

The process of data analysis therefore starts with recording the data from the questionnaire or an interview guide. This is transcribed from the questionnaire to a coding sheet where the responses of each question are systematically coded with symbols or numerals. Then on the basis of common characteristics, the major themes are identified and theme clusters formulated. When the mass of raw data is reduced to a small number of classes, the coder should ensure that every theme is recorded in a category. Charts, diagrams and graphs should be intelligibly presented for the potential reader. Further interpretation for the concisely shown data should be given. It is from the analysed and interpreted data, the researcher obtains themes for further discussion.

From a large amount of data transcripts, the researcher moves to coding, which is not a mechanical act but rather, a step in a careful process that helps him/her develop a concept, theory or a model. As already established, qualitative data analysis does not set a single, rigid pattern as *the* method of analysis. The researchers generally assign numerals or other symbols to themes in answers and put responses into a limited number of categories. Data are then organized into conceptual categories and themes are formulated wherever patterns of relationship between such categories are detected. This process, however, is guided by the major research question. For example, a study on conflicts within the organization may provide the researcher with data from conversational methods. Initial codes are assigned to the various problems identified in the data. Then the researcher sees the possibility of classifying them into a limited number of categories such as family issues, lack of clarity in verbal communication, complexities in written communication, dissatisfaction about payments, misunderstandings due to language differences, cultural conflicts among workers, burn-out of individuals and many more. These categories can be further organized into themes such as exterior factors, communication gaps, personality clashes, and so on. Interconnections between these themes can be explored in view of overall psychological, sociological, organizational, communication-related aspects and finally develop the theory that explains the research question in the given context of the organization.

Analysing interview data is possible only with a completed transcript on which the coding starts. These codes derive from "standard external categories or drawn from the interview themselves (often repeated words or concepts across the corpus)."[26] Analysis is always done with the central point of search in mind as Shaw puts it,

> ...identifying internal terms, topics, or categories repeated by the informants provides the initial coding that leads to further analysis and interviewing. Once coded, the categories of material may be entered into a chart or other device appropriate for displaying the categories that reflect these data. This information can be enhanced with further increasingly focused questioning in order to determine its meaning.[27]

The researcher's move from the raw text to the key research concerns in the Grounded Theory is depicted thus by Auerbach and Silverstein,

> From the raw text, to the relevant text (text that is relevant to the specific research interest), then to the repeating ideas (ideas repeated by participants in same or similar way), from there to themes (groups of repeating ideas that had something in common and call them theme), then to theoretical constructs (organize the themes into larger, more abstract ideas as researcher gets closer to research concerns), then to theoretical narrative (theoretical constructs are organized into theoretical narratives that summarize what researcher had learnt about the research concerns), and, finally, research concerns are established.[28]

These are various ways of looking at the analysis task.

Presentation of Analysed Data

A largely qualitative research normally have a lengthy section of data analysis and by this, the reader might miss connections between key themes or concepts in between. Qualitative data analysis takes careful time of organization, breakdown of concepts, reflection, meaning-making, correlation, interpretation, synthesis and so on. This often monotonous process, therefore, requires in the first place, a clear guideline of the design of the section. How headings, sub-headings, explanations between data tables or diagrams and other helpful signposts relate to each other can offer significant support the reader. There should be clear evidences that each theme presented from the analysis process is drawn correctly from the data. New information or interpretation at this stage will negate the entire procedure.

Transcription of data is an important task in research in the cases of tape/video recorded personal interviews or focus groups. Additions and omissions are equally damaging. Emotions, reactions, varieties of expressions, emphases and certain

---

[26] R Daniel Shaw, 'Qualitative Social Science Methods in Research Design' 141-151 in Edgar J Elliston, *Introduction to Missiological Research Design* (Pasadena, CA: William Carey Library, 2011), 148.

[27] Shaw, in Edgar J Elliston, *Introduction to Missiological Research Design,* 2011, 149.

[28] Adapted from Carl F Auerbach and Louise B Silverstein, *Qualitative Data: An Introduction to Coding and Analysis,* (New York: New York University Press, 2003), 35.

terminologies are significant data in qualitative research. Even while transcribing data in the researcher-administered interviews, these are to be recorded clearly for effective analysis task. Accuracy in data gathering is essential for authentic data analysis.

Ethical principles in qualitative research are to be followed while presenting the data. For instance, privacy safeguards needs to be kept if anonymity or confidentiality was assured during data collection. This is also true with locations of research or names of organizations or institutions took part in the study. When data analysis uses references to official records of organizations or institutions, it has to be done in perfect alignment with their official policies.

While the quantitative researcher uses well-presented graphs, pie charts and tables to show the statistical content, the qualitative researcher describes and explains data in the form of concepts, taxonomies and themes. However, these can be presented in charts and diagrams as the nature of the data permits. The quantitative approach typically reduces verbal, non-verbal data into numerical forms and notations and the analysis appears in numbers, statistics, pie diagrams, graphs and so on, whereas, the qualitative data is descriptive and interpretive, using lots of narratives in understanding the representative aspects in a phenomenon. Presentation of analysed data appears in cluster analysis format, flow charts, frequency distribution tables, and various types of diagrams and figures. Compared to the quantitative, qualitative data analysis is seen as a process with few fixed rules.

The analysis section in the report may use numerous extracts that help the researcher to explain the themes. Theoretically speaking, the multi-dimensional matrices in the rich data makes the process complex because it uses multiple methods in data gathering and hence provides multiple perspectives from the various categories of the participants. In order to assist the reader to understand the story line that helped in the formulation of theories or arguments, the researcher should be using effective markers during the process of analysis. This will help avoid contradictions in the account. Analysed data need to be presented most effectively.

While presenting the analysed data, actual quotes and inferences must be directly connected to the whole. The researcher must remind him/herself that the study is addressing a real issue of real people in real time. The report should be safe guarded from moving away from the main crux of the research problem to other matters of secondary significance. Presenting quotes while extracting ideas from interview data and avoiding unsubstantiated comments are marks of effective analysis as Oliver puts it, "An interesting addition to the process of analysing qualitative data is to include in the thesis a reflexive or reflective account."[29]

---

[29]   Paul Oliver, *Writing Your Thesis* (London: Sage, 2008), 21.

As the researcher develops a specific line of argument, a search on what is omitted and discarded from the data would be necessary. Apart from the obvious arguments extracted from the transcribed/recorded data, there may be potential, embedded, implicit or alternative arguments indicated. Qualitative researchers need not fear presenting alternative views because it is embedded in its philosophy. Whether qualitative or quantitative methodology, the omission practices in data analysis are to be subject to thorough ethical scrutiny. In attaining the coherent knowledge of an issue, it is unjustifiable to omit the embedded or alternative arguments. The researcher in presenting the data will do a better job in suggesting the preliminary analysis result (admitting the possibility of alternative arguments) rather than making debatable sweeping statements.

While quantitative researchers in their data analysis aim the exclusion of subjectivity, interpretation and context, qualitative researchers count on a certain amount of essential subjectivity, interpretation and context as a necessary feature in the analysis. The quantitative researchers' general preference is to communicate evidences visually, while qualitative researchers do it mostly verbally. Decision is made on basic questions: What is the kind of data that I am going to present? Will this be presented better in charts/diagrams/graphs or in descriptive style verbally or, both? Which will be more beneficial for my readers? Essentially, qualitative research makes sense only if it becomes part of the life and vision of the researcher even when it is to be done with certain constraints of time. It is not about finishing a certain amount of the data process hastily and moving on with other things in life. Therefore, skillful analysis is central to the process.

Self-Management Skills

Skills for successful qualitative research are primarily in the area of self-management. Due to the massive amount of planning needed in the entire practice, time management must become a major consideration. Nonetheless, speed does not signify good qualitative research. The researcher has to give time for deep thinking and reflection all through the process, preferably with a journal that records personal queries, implications, biases, interpretations etc. Awareness of personal prejudices, values and standpoints and how these are allowed in the process of the inquiry is to be addressed. In the constant cycle of planning, decision-making, implementing, reviewing and continuing with more rigour, the researcher has to balance dependence and independence at various angles of relationships.

Qualitative research that usually requires a relatively prolonged time on the field requires researcher's attention to the legal and ethical measures to be considered in the process. Some studies are socially and politically more sensitive than others. An ethnographer or a researcher who studies religious issues must have the wisdom in action to guard the research participants from being unnecessarily dragged into public annoyance.

Clarity of thought is the product of a calm mind. Silence, rest and relaxation are important personal habits for the researcher. Unless sufficient time is given for deep reflection and careful inferences, the study will easily get misguided from its intended aim. Meaningful break times help the researcher to stand back to evaluate how the assumptions, hopes and claims are being laid out in the real setting of research. This kind of a *soaking in the framework of the study* requires considerable measures of self-awareness and depth. Mere gathering of data and its mechanical organization will not make a good qualitative study.

The area of self-care is also of vital importance with all the striving and sweat involved in the qualitative study. Self-care and sufficient space for reflections and revisions in the practice are crucial factors for effectiveness.

As indicated already, interactive skills determine the efficiency of the inquiry all through the process. The researcher, who communicates and shares ideas with others in the early stages of design are relatively quicker in recognizing the focuses and challenges, ensuring greater clarity for the design. Having a supportive people network is one of the best ways to view effective self-management. Networking with peers, friends and experts has immense potential in the qualitative process. The researcher develops deep awareness of numerous issues through the relevant collaborations formed in the larger schema of inquiry. Qualitative research cannot be done in isolation; it is all about reality, life and people.

A question that runs through the process of a research is, 'How do I present the information?' It begins with the literature review, takes on the presentations of the theoretical frame, field data and closes with the final report and, the viva, in cases of the doctoral programs. The presentation part of the process is usually taken lightly by researchers, who spend all their time 'doing the data'. However, in a later stage, they realize the importance of how well the personal management skills of the researcher reflect in the presentation and defense of the work. Looking at the viva event, for instance, much of the direction of discussion is based on how the researcher manages thinking, ordering, articulation and arrangement of the information.

The researcher's disorganization in any dimension of life will adversely impact the research being undertaken. Of all the skills that the researcher aspires, self-management is the one at the centre that holds everything else together. At the very centre of all these, the theologian identifies the need to rely on God's wisdom and purpose while he/she is addressing the human problems and making interpretations and judgments for forward trajectory.

Theological Skills

The outstanding skill for the theology researcher is undoubtedly the skill to think theologically and to do theology. Theology academia has to review its way of perceiving theology as purely 'thinking' and perceiving practical subjects separate and in many contexts, less significant. The primary mode of theology has been "think-ing"[30] as Farley remarked. Miller-McLemore wrote, "The modern academy, shaped by Western views of rationality, often assumes (or at least is dominated by teaching methods that assume), that one thinks one's way into acting".[31] We know that the inquirer cannot take a pack of abstract theology to help those who wrestle with real questions in life or blindly reiterate scattered truth points to handle the complex situations. Inquirer continues seeking: What is God doing in the world today? How should we see this research problem in the light of God's purposes and working in human life? What should we be doing? What hinders us from doing it? What is the resolve? Theology researcher's ultimate competency is in discovering and voicing the divine perspective as revealed in the scripture about human problems and the search for direction. Affirming the central role of biblical framework understanding the world's problems, Peck and Strohmer wrote, "Christians cannot faithfully meet the radical questions and crises that beset life today without an adequate understanding of how the world and human culture works. The only satisfactory framework of thought for this is the one which underlies the Gospel; that is, a biblical one."[32] These authors made succinct observations that meaningfully define our reflections on theological matrix in qualitative study. For them, "learning about one's God is to discover what governs one's conscience in secular life…A biblical teaching method is centered on asking and raising ultimate questions."[33] However, theological reflections in qualitative inquiries also depend largely on the theological position one takes. For instance, those who approach the Bible as the fundamental and final authority for faith and living will follow a different reflective and interpretative methodology from those who incorporate Biblical references as one of the supportive referential evidences.

Humans can use cultural understandings to make sense of their problems; yet finding the way out is through exploring the divine perspective and purpose. Framing this essential path is the task of the theologian. To get there, one must learn to see,

---

[30]   Edward Farley, "Four Pedagogical Mistakes: A Mea Culpa", *Teaching Theology and Religion* 8, No. 4, 2005, 202.

[31]   Bonnie J Miller-Mclemore, "Practical Theology and Pedagogy" 170-194 in *For Life Abundant: Practical Theology, Theological Education and Christian Ministry*, Edited by Dorothy C Bass and Craig Dykstra (Cambridge: William B Eerdmans, 2008), 176.

[32]   John Peck and Charles Strohmer, *Uncommon Sense: God's Wisdom for our Complex and Changing World* (Tennessee: The Wise Press, 2000), Abstract, ix.

[33]   John Peck and Charles Strohmer, *Uncommon Sense: God's Wisdom for our Complex and Changing World* (Tennessee: The Wise Press, 2000), 234-235.

listen, understand, interact, reflect, interrogate, with other things. The baseline of God's purpose for humanity irrespective of the culture and creed is the direction for theologian. Presenting this direction in a research, however, is to be done with humility, wisdom and conviction that the divine purposes are not violated by human knowledge structures. George Zachariah emphasizes on academic commitment, social engagement and ministerial commitment in a theologian's horizon of development.[34] The theological vision as rooted in the scripture needs to fortify the repercussions of the inquiry. This skill has to develop during the training time in a theology school through courses, course works and every activity or discussion on campus that one gets involved with. From formal learning the qualitative researcher steps into informal and non-formal settings, to make this integration possible. When the interworking of the practical theologian's vigorous formation –as explained earlier in Chapter 1 of this book- is absent, the research endeavour reduces itself to nothing more than a naive collection of information.

The absolute skill of the researcher is in enhancing the functional connectedness of the academy, church and the world in the context of the inquiry. Mentioning Asia Theological Association's core value of biblical grounding and contextual rooting says Harkness,

> We must together take immediate and urgent steps to seek, elaborate and possess a biblically informed theological basis for our calling and engagement in theological education and allow every aspect of our service to become rooted and nurtured in this soil.[35]

Critical queries across disciplines are viewed through the lens of God's eternal plan for humanity and tested against the entire schema of the scripture. Theology is only an abstract reality if it is not grounded in and aimed for dynamic relationship with God and people. Therefore, theological education in its fundamental sense, is about actualizing the situation where the society, church and family are able to articulate, affirm, interrogate and evaluate their life's reality towards getting fully reconciled to the purposes of God. In this, the qualitative researcher is not proof-texting to establish some theories, but rather concretely engaging in mining the missional panorama of the kingdom of God in Biblical Studies, Church History, Religion, Theology, Christian Ethics, Pastoral Theology and across the body of knowledge.

---

[34] George Zachariah, 'Discernment, Vocation, and Commitment: A Call to Repentance and Transformation' 71-85 in Theological Education: Ploughing the Field for New Life to Sprout (Bangalore: BTE-SSC & CLS, 2014), 80-83.

[35] Allan Harkness, 'Introduction', 7-22, in *Tending the Seedbeds: Educational Perspectives on Theological Education in Asia*, by Allan Harkness (ed.), (Quezon City: Philippines: Asia Theological Association, 2010), 12.

This non-negotiable aspect of research has been neglected for too long by the ultimate splitting up and dividing of the departments and courses. Theological integration is a vital skill of the inquirer. The inquirer in theology keeps on excavating life's reality through history, philosophy, politics, sociology, psychology, ecclesiology, ethics, hermeneutics among many others, ultimately engaging in the mission of uncovering the eternal plan of God for the world.

Let us consider the terms that describe the task of a theological researcher. Familiar expressions are *thinking theologically, doing theology* or *theologizing*, which indicate generally, the making of theology the frame and foundation of the learning exercise. In other words, it is thinking in God's perspectives and connecting the inquiry fully to comply with how God views things in human life. This refers to the principles of practice rather than mere amassing of theoretical knowledge. Theological researcher recognizes theology as the overarching design for human life and service and as the foundation of knowledge of the divine. This we call the theological reflection.

Ballard and Pritchard outline four models of practical theology that correspond to the four methods of theological reflection: applied theology, critical correlation, praxis and habitus.[36] Borrowing Farley's terminology of *habitus*, they set the core question in theological reflection which we might correlate with the current discussion. "How can a student, lay person or reflective practitioner bring her whole Christian being to bear on the action or experience she has chosen to review?"[37] The skill to think and reflect theologically is also termed as the ability to theologize, which denotes the act of having God-centeredness in thought, word and action.

For a theology researcher, the learning process is partnering with God in the way He sees, acts and wills for the world. Qualitative researchers in theology increasingly realizes of being partners with God in the *Missio Dei*, the mission of God. The qualitative researcher develops the skill to observe anything that reflects on who God is and what God is doing in the world. This is faith seeking understanding and it has dimensions beyond human reasoning. Based on the scripture, the researcher builds capacities to: apprehend (take hold of the truth with deep awareness, experience and not like formulated philosophical reasoning), analyse (reflect, ponder, critically evaluate), articulate (express in words for anyone in their context and capacity to comprehend) and, apply (practice in life each day with clear perception of being firmly scriptural, experiential, missiological and lived out truth of God).

---

[36]   Paul Ballard and John Pritchard, *Practical Theology in Action: Christian Thinking in the Service of Church and Society* (London: SPCK, 1996), 57-68, 119-134.

[37]   Ballard and Pritchard, *Practical Theology in Action: Christian Thinking in the Service of Church and Society*, 1996, 133.

A theology researcher must develop skills to do theological interpretation, distinguishing between cultural and supra-cultural, local and universal, and, temporal and normative foundations in the scripture. Gerben Heitink attempts to explain the function and position of practical theology within theology as a whole and said that its method can be summed up in three word pairs: "Historical-interpretive, hermeneutical-critical and practical-constructive."[38] These we realize as the primary theological competencies of the qualitative researcher. He called practical theology 'an empirically oriented theological theory' explaining the empirical-critical or critical-empirical nature of inquiry,

> A practical theology, which chooses its point of departure in the experience of human beings and in the current state of church and society, is indeed characterized by a methodology that takes empirical data with utter seriousness, takes these as its starting point and keeps them in mind as it develops its theory. This manner of "doing" theology differs from exegetical, historical or philosophical approaches, which are distinctive for other subjects, even though practical theology does use exegetical, systematic and historical methods.[39]

Doing qualitative inquiry that requires multiple interactions and observations, the theology researcher must develop skills from guarding the hermeneutic from becoming captive to anything that is not rooted and tested out in the scripture such as, denominational pet doctrines, cultural concepts, church traditions and practices, charisma of certain leaders, or the proof-texting method in approaching the scripture. The researcher undertakes the inquiry realizing that fundamentally, all true theology holds the mission focus at the centre. Charles Van Engen affirms the skill of doing biblical theology of mission saying,

> One of the most profound differences in the way biblical theology of mission does its research as compared with social science-based research in missiology is that biblical theology of mission is more intentionally and strongly prescriptive as well as descriptive. It is synthetic (bringing about synthesis) and integrational (bringing about new conjunctions and interrelations of ideas).[40]

He also explains how this mission theology is done by being, knowing and doing.

> When mission theology is abstracted from mission practice-and when missiological research is abstracted from mission encounter- it seems strange and far removed from the concrete places and specific people that are at the heart of God's mission.

---

[38]   Gerben Heitink, *Practical Theology: History, Theory, Action Domains* (Michigan: William B Eerdmans, 1999), 5.

[39]   Gerben Heitink, *Practical Theology: History, Theory, Action Domains* (Michigan: William B Eerdmans, 1999), 7.

[40]   Charles Van Engen, 'Biblical Theology of Mission's Research Method'113-118 in Edgar J Elliston, *Introduction to Missiological Research Design*, (Pasadena: William Carey Library, 2011), 118.

Such "objective" removal itself may lead the research astray from understanding the wisdom of the way God wants to work in mission. Mission theology is at its best when it is intimately involved in the being, knowing, doing, and serving of the church's mission in a particular context.[41]

Researchers safeguard themselves from being unthinkingly drifted away by constructed theologies because they can be solely cultural, personal and hence, fallible.

Theological researcher learns to wrestle with the interplay of four different cultures in doing theology in human situations: culture of the Biblical world, culture of the contemporary world that endlessly strives to systematize the truth, the researcher's own culture and the research participants' culture. Thinking theologically is as big as perceiving the meaning of the kingdom of God and what we call the Missio Dei. There is virtually nothing outside its scope for the researcher who is addressing real human problems. When the theological underpinning is weak in theological research, it produces only empty descriptions, decayed morals and incomplete view of God and his mission.

---

[41]   Charles Van Engen, 'Biblical Theology of Mission's Research Method', 2011, 118.

Reflection Box:
Creatively Handling Vigil of the
Unexpected

Student X went inside the rural village through her contact with one of the members in the tribe, hearing the story of a group from inside started believing in Jesus. Her descriptive ethnography using narrative techniques and observations hoping to understand how they successfully adapted the new faith in their deep rooted cultural reality. Surprisingly, she soon realized that none of them would talk about Jesus anymore because they had denounced their faith in Jesus. The unexpected! Student X, then re-designed her research plan and shifted to the explanatory ethno identity dimension, where she would do an in-depth case study of the community to find the causal factors of their shift. Her results pointed to the blind imposing of conventional mission approaches by the churches outside who intervened unthinkingly into a highly sensitive cultural context.

CONSIDER:

What strategies student X must have used? How had she developed a cohesive design for research methodology including that of the categories of research participants and the methods of interaction with them?

CHAPTER 8

THE PERSONNEL AND THE PROJECT

SECTION CONTENTS:

- The Qualitative Researcher
- Shape of a Significant Research Project
- The Mentoring Practice

The Qualitative Researcher

The dream could be the big day, the day of graduation! Normally it is a lone and longer path than what we initially had assumed it to be. The researcher should consistently explore on the essential expectations and the qualities and competencies of the task. The researcher's cutting edge question, above all else, is the question of motivation. What motivates me in this research? It can be an intellectual/academic quest, ambition on a higher degree and benefits, passion about improving one's ministry involvement, or professional requirement from higher authorities.[1] Is it the degree itself or the honours, recognition and possible elevation in service that are attached? Or, am I driven toward improved practice in ministry? The real motivating factor plays an important role throughout the process. That is why when someone starts off with a research prospect just by the pressure from leadership of a theology school or merely driven by monetary passions in the field of service finds frustration and conflict. In spite of the initial source of motivation, if a researcher makes learning a matter of personal choice and commitment, the best results can still be achieved. However, if the choice of research evolves from exterior forces, it can make the process extremely energy-straining or boring since personal commitment is less or even totally missing. Ideally in theological education, the researcher is driven by theological conviction, ministerial commitment and personal calling.

---

[1] Jessy Jaison, *Enjoy Your Research* (Trivandrum: New India Publications, 2000), 10.

The qualitative researcher demonstrates unique characteristics. Intellectual freedom has to be exercised by the researcher and this happens with a mentor who facilitates learning in that direction. In Palmer's words,

> to study with a teacher who not only gives answers but asks questions and welcomes our insights, who provides information and theories that do not close but open new ones, who encourages students to help each other learn-to study with such a teacher is to know the power of a learning exercise.[2]

The researcher is not technophobic even though technological facilities are used in the study and the report. The basic tenets of flexibility, naturalism and immersion place the researcher in a very distinct position from researchers in other approaches. The researcher is a thinking, reflective practitioner, who "not only thinks and acts in ways which are situated and contextual, but also strategic."[3] The four typical stances of a qualitative researcher according to Rossman and Rallis[4] are to:

- View social worlds as holistic and complex,
- Engage in systematic reflection on the conduct of the research,
- Remain sensitive to their own biographies/social identities and how these shape the study (i.e., they are reflexive), and
- Rely on complex reasoning that moves dialectically between deduction and induction.

Data collection in qualitative research is immensely deep and rich so that the unanticipated responses and twists can go on surprising the researcher. Therefore, the researcher should carefully guard the data process from getting too quickly done. The qualitative researcher, particularly in the data process, has to have developed certain traits. The researcher ensures that a lot of preparatory work is done before getting to the field to gather data, where he/she often the unanticipated feedback is awaiting. Recognizing the institution's policies, government restrictions, and codes of ethics that are relevant in the context of study is crucial particularly, when the research participants belong to any of the *at-risk* groups. On the procedural dimension, pilot study and the subsequent revision of the data gathering tool are vital steps.

Every qualitative research in theological education is built on a ministerial-social responsibility, which the researcher has to keep in mind all through the stages of the study. Constant reflection on the theoretical and practical implications of the study

---

[2] Parker Palmer, *To Know as We are Known: Education as Spiritual Journey*, (San Francisco: HarperCollins, 1993), 70.

[3] Jennifer Mason, *Qualitative Researching* (Thousand Oaks, CA: 1996), 165.

[4] G B Rossman & S F Rallis, *Learning in the Field: An Introduction to Qualitative Research*, 2nd Edition, (Thousand Oaks, CA: Sage, 2003), 10.

characterizes the qualitative researcher. In spite of all that is happening around, the researcher is processing and analysing the data that emerges from conversations, observations and reflections. Real time experience among people in their own life settings can make unlimited surprises to the researcher, for which he/she should be always open. At times beyond the prevailing fears, respondents will participate with excitement and passion while in the middle of interaction, some may leave the site without saying a word. There can be tears, sobbing, laughter or angry outbursts. Things may not go entirely organized as per the schedules and the researcher learns how to handle such uncertainties and disorganizations. The researcher remains calm, friendly and appreciative in the midst of possible discomposure and uneasiness but keeps reflecting over what went wrong, what is working well, and, how to move on.

The researcher needs to be time-conscious, organized, and determined about the collection of data and all the challenges involved. An enormous amount of homework needs to be done prior to the field visit especially with data collection tools, data recording devices (if any), data back-up settings and so on. In contexts that require special assistance with transcription, multiple forms of recording the talks and observations, conveyance and language translation, the researcher has to arrange all of these in advance rather than desperately searching for help on the spot. Creating a calm, peaceful climate for the participants is crucial in qualitative data gathering and, key to this is the researcher's own preparedness and calmness.

The qualitative researcher should be conscious about the essential balance to be maintained in relating to the research participants. As the participants show closeness and trust to the researcher as a dependable friend rather than a distanced professional, the researcher should recognize the importance of relationships as well as the professional commitments in research. A critical balance is to be maintained between the two. During data gathering, the researcher maintains an unwavering consistency in recording, analysing, reflecting and synthesizing. The researcher is keen to the end of inquiry that the systematic examination of relevant similarities in order to develop sensitizing concepts is called analytic induction.[5] Glaser and Strauss termed this analytical skill as constant comparative method.[6]

Personal qualities of the researcher often have serious implications in the qualitative study. Task-organizing and time-managing are outstanding among the virtues. Qualitative research process can go unendingly long and hence, only an efficient work pattern can resolve this. Naturally demotivated, tardy and withdrawn students need to realize the detrimental effects of these traits on their research pursuit.

---

[5]   Charles C Ragin, *Constructing Social Research: The Unity and Diversity of Method* (Thousand Oaks, CA: Pine Forge Press, 1994), 93.

[6]   B G Glaser & A L Strauss, *The Discovery of Grounded Theory: Strategies for Qualitative Research,* (New York: Aldine Publishing Company, 1967).

Another overall virtue is a responsible and balanced approach to life beyond the task of research. Life is much more than research. The highly ambitious and the very lazy can spoil their life and relationships. The researcher who fails in redeeming time in a balanced way for all of life's responsibilities is likely to struggle on the way. In fact, when a researcher neglects important responsibilities in life, it naturally results in more stress rather than gaining more support to learning. The timing pattern as well as the work style that best balance life's responsibilities and the demands of research has to be rigorously worked out by the researcher.

As fluid and complex as the process is with all the scheduling, travels, interviews, and multifaceted analyses, the researcher's personal qualities are a key determinant in achieving a successful completion. To make simultaneous thinking, reading, data gathering, writing and reflecting happen, life has to be managed with resolute consistency. Great networking advances great learning. Discussing issues/concepts with others, receiving critical feedback and improving skills to gather wide-ranging information through people networks are exceptionally suitable because qualitative study does not happen in isolation. Academic humility and intellectual astuteness should go hand-in-hand, towards accomplishing the task.

Those who return to theology research after a break as senior students in ministry or building their family, normally takes more time to recapture their learning skills. Lack of confidence in catching up the current academic methods and developments, intensified demands from family/work, economic/health constraints and poor concentration will require special attention from the beginning. Novices in the field need to obtain substantial knowledge and skills in the multi-layered processes of qualitative research.

Core to the research task are the theoretical and hermeneutical skills. How the researcher thinks theologically, how the biblical accounts are discussed and how the socio-analytical part is reflected on the theological core are central components in theological studies. The researcher is expected to develop hermeneutical capacities to address the biblical-theological content in the conceptual task and socio-empirical skills in handling the life related inquiry.

Lack of knowledge about the nature of researcher-participant dynamic might direct the researcher to the wrong conclusions. Every researcher should have primary understanding about the workings of these dynamics in this domain[7]:

- The qualitative paradigm focuses on the voices of the participants. Therefore, the experts are the participants, rather than the researchers.

---

[7] Carl F Auerbach and Louise B Silverstein, *Qualitative Data: An Introduction to Coding and Analysis*, (New York: New York University Press, 2003), 126.

- The research is hypothesis-generating, rather than hypothesis testing. This acknowledges that:
  - ▷ There are variations in experience, rather than a universal form
  - ▷ The researcher may not know enough about the phenomenon under study to generate a valid hypothesis
- There is an assumption of collaboration and partnership between the researcher and the participants. This makes it more likely that the outcome of the research may be relevant to improving the lives of the participants, and not simply furthering the career of the researcher.
- The qualitative paradigm includes a reflexive stance that provides the opportunity for the researcher to examine her or his biases. Accepting the responsibility for examining oneself increases the probability that the research process will not be exploitative or oppressive for the participants.[8]

Shape of a Significant Research Project

Qualitative research originates from an inquisitive mind that responds to the need for transformation and development in a real situation. What defines research as significant? Defining an exemplary qualitative study in its theoretical construction, Janice Beyer offers the following[9]:

1. The study appears to spring from genuine curiosity

2. It both acknowledges and questions existing theory

3. It seeks new insights from immersion in the phenomena in question

4. It uses research methods flexibly and imaginatively, as a tool serving the questions pursued

5. It is an unstinting effort, doing whatever it takes to arrive at a credible answer to the research question.

The ten distinctive qualities of qualitative research identified by Roller and Lavrakas are worth considering in the assessment of the *total quality framework* of the inquiry[10]:

1. Plausibility of interpretations rather than truth claims on the findings

2. Importance of context; outcomes hinge greatly on the context of inquiry

---

[8] Adapted from Auerbach and Silverstein, *Qualitative Data*, 2003, 126.

[9] Janice M Beyer, 'Researchers are not Cats: They can Survive and Succeed by being Curious'65-72 In P J Frost and R E Stablein (Eds), *Doing Exemplary Research* (Newbury Park, C A: Sage), 1992, 65.

[10] Adapted from Margaret R Roller and Paul J Lavrakas, *Applied Qualitative Research Design: A Total Quality Framework Approach* (New York: Guilford Press, 2015), 15-49, 332-340.

3. Importance of meaning: Derivation of meaning from the data from multiple sources, variables (e.g., language, context, participant-researcher relationship, the researcher bias, participant bias) and methods

4. Researcher-as-instrument in data gathering: Places the researcher at the centre of the data process

5. Researcher-Participant relationship: The way researcher and participants share the research space

6. Skill set required for the researcher: Beyond the usual qualities of organization and analysis, qualitative researcher needs skills to build rapport, to undertake the messy analysis where the context, social interactions and several other complex variables play roles in the understanding of reality

7. Flexibility of the research design: Researcher is called to be as unobtrusive and flexible as possible

8. Types of issues or questions effectively addressed in qualitative research: Scope to study sensitive and personal issues

9. Messy analysis and inductive approach: Not a single cause-effect reality, but multi-layered data with inconsistencies, illogical inputs and complex interconnections

10. Unique capabilities of online and mobile qualitative research: Online or mobile participant in the inquiry as a rather recent development is thought to be enjoying more flexibility, power and convenience

Necessary Conditions for a Significant Research Endeavour

- A solid research proposal
- Efficient presentation of the proposal in which the researcher owns the study and shows a personal commitment for its accomplishment.
- Consistency in the process exemplified by astute maintenance of deadlines as a personal discipline.
- A scholarly and genuine mentoring support that provides critical evaluations and strengthening of the overall theoretical frame happen.
- Access to relevant literature resources.
- Time to read, reflect, write, travel and meet with people.
- Financial and moral support from family and work place.
- Linguistic support in the making of data tools, gathering of data and writing the thesis when dome in researcher's second language.

- Ability to visually and verbally present the work before the academic committee or the *viva voce* panel.

Simple yet Crucial Tips

Qualitative research requires extensive planning and decision-making. Beginning from the selection of topic, till the decision about publishing the results, the researcher's life revolves around decision-making. This makes the task relatively less complex for students who are naturally organized in thinking, decision-making and initiation.

Deep thinking for right focus: Researchers sometimes decide too quickly on their topic, out of initial excitement, without estimating what it would take for them through the process. The one central determinant of a significant qualitative project is the amount of initial deep thinking given to the design. From there crucial debates on the issue are thought through, the actual research procedures are weighed, and the focus of the study emerges. Hurried decisions invite confusion in qualitative study and it can produce totally disadvantageous results.

Talking it over: For those who realize qualitative research as the form of *theological education between the academy and the world*, this practice is crucial. Presenting our unrefined thoughts with academic experts, peers in ministry and the people who live in the context of inquiry in itself is an eye-opener to the researcher. Often fear obstructs the researcher, evoking hesitancy within him/her regarding the workability, theoretical strength, and receptivity of the proposal. Those who fearlessly discuss their ideas with others get their design modified and perfected relatively quickly.

Analysing relevant literature: Prospective researchers sometimes tend to spend long hours in their own limited world of knowledge, ignoring the rich content available in the literature. The research topic must be proposed after the comprehensive analysis and reflection on the literature. Moreover, there is no better way for the researcher to gain confidence on the research design.

Formulating the major research question: Hassled researchers tend to undermine the importance of time to be spent initially for the formulation of the central research question. Ideas and the question frame take time and effort to get into shape. Without the right research question, the entire process may lose direction and fall off track from its unified purpose.

Knowing what it takes to get there: Instead of assuming the requirements, the researcher should know exactly the requirements for a successful completion of the project, for example, the academic, university-related, methodological, theological, sociological and practical requirements. The researchers who begin with *interesting* topics may later find several areas in the inquiry beyond their capacity to reach.

Estimating the financial commitment involved: Financial demands involved in academic research need to be considered at the beginning of the process. Apart from fees at the school or the university, the qualitative researcher incurs many other expenses, ranging from library visits to photocopying materials, extensive travels and data recording from multiple venues and sources, printing of the report and so on. When the researcher is not employed or proceeds without a substantial scholarship for the study, financial liability can obstruct the process at any time.

Considering health or work related roadblocks: Concerns of health and ministry are yet another matter for consideration. The researcher should attend to issues that are known and find ways to handle them during the course of study although life for the next day might bring more uncertainties. One's own family responsibilities, and health and work related issues of other members in the family also need to be thought through. Many schools have supportive policies and procedural assistances for their research students in cases of disability, terminal illness and other demanding situations in life.

Recognizing factors that demotivate: Individuals have their own unique reasons to lose interest in a study in spite of a fervent start. Qualitative research with its intrinsic disorderliness particularly in the long-term data process is sustained by the consistency of the researcher. Disinterest and boredom can overshadow from time to time for reasons such as, topic being realized difficult, procedures unclear and lengthy, change in job, loss of income, lack of support from immediate family, emotional trauma, poor supervision, and negative comments from peers/scholars. It is particularly helpful to view the natural tendencies in oneself that provoke discouragement and set sustainable safeguards.

Considering the mentoring support: Institutions follow their own procedures in mentoring support. Whether mentors are chosen, associated, or assigned, their task is to deliver formative and transformative guidance. There are newer integrated methods in mentoring mentioned elsewhere in the chapter but the researcher has to foresee the advantages and probable perils in each. For instance, joint mentoring by two scholars in two contexts can either provide a rich learning experience or drown the researcher in absolute confusion due to the perspectival differences between the two. In principle, credibility of a mentor is determined primarily on degrees and academic achievements while for a qualitative study, field exposure and ministerial involvement of the mentor could be an added credential.

Time, commitment, and, careful and creative thought are key to the design of a significant research project. Experience testifies that students who closely attend to each of these aspects obtain clarity and confidence relatively sooner.

The Mentoring Practice

Research forms a vital dimension in transformative learning and hence, purposeful action with dedicated mentoring support. There are schools that routinely practice research mentoring without realizing its meaning, purpose or scope for enhancement. We may contend that phenomenal development could have been realized in the church's mission, with our research practices in higher education comprehensively analysed and improved. This paper starts with the meaning of the term *mentoring* and proceeds to discuss a few pertinent areas of the practice in theology schools.

Terms such as supervisor, guide and mentor are used to denote the faculty or expert who assists a student in the process of research. These roles virtually fulfil the same expectations, yet the term *mentor* connoting *a trusted guide* and *an experienced coach* is used in the current discussion for its ministerial preference. Guide is the one that travelled the path of research before, gained coherent knowledge about the threats and prospects in the journey and is willing to provide authentic support to another traveller.

> The metaphor of the guide best pictures the multi-faceted role of the teacher in Proverbs 1-9. As a guide, the teacher uses his knowledge and experience to provide direction for the learner. The ultimate goal, however, is that the learner will develop independent competence in living responsibly in Yahweh's world. The teacher's progression from expert authority to facilitator parallels the intellectual and moral development of the learner. When the learner is a novice, the teacher must exert a higher degree of direction, but as the learner grows in wisdom, the teacher is able to become more of an enabler to assist the learner as he makes his own decisions. Thus the teacher's role is to be a guide, to motivate the learners on to maturity. The teacher is at times an expert, at times a facilitator, but always the guide, pointing the learners toward their own independent competence.[11]

Characteristic images of a mentor may be found in the gospel accounts on several occasions. One instance of addressing a real time issue is on the road to Emmaus where Jesus guides the disciples to reflect deeply and discover tolerantly and choose determinedly for life and mission. This we comprehend not merely as an accomplishment of a given duty rather, a spiritual act of wisdom implanted in a missional core. In word and action, the mentoring relation realized theological insight, practical wisdom, prophetic affirmation and courage for decision-making.

The term *coach* represents an expert who trains another person with rigour, patience and determination to make significant growth in knowledge and skills in a certain

---

[11] Daniel J Estes, *Hear, my Son: Teaching and Learning in Proverbs 1-9*, (Downers Grove, IL: Inter Varsity Press, 1997), 134.

practice. A good mentor will use all he/she has in terms of knowledge, skills and guidance while simultaneously making sure that the mentee is not a recreation of the image of the mentor. A common flaw of our educational system is that of viewing the mentor as the one who fixes the deficiencies of the researcher, which increases a feeling of inadequacy, leading to an unhealthy form of dependency. In fact, what the mentor should be nurturing are efficacy and confidence. Ziegenhals says there are faculty who see students, "…that they often identify as problems-the unprepared, the ungifted for ministry, the "Teflon student" who will not change. Faculty are coming to recognize that the importance of liking our students for who they are and accepting them as they are, rather than wishing them to be what they are not."[12]

The term *mentor* is said to have derived from Homer's Odyssey in Greek mythology where Odysseus entrusted the education and care of his son Telemachus to a friend named Mentor, while the father departed to the war of the siege of Troy. It denotes the relationship of a coach, guide, supporter, confidant and a role model. The inherent task is that of developing the mentee in personal formation, social engagement, and skills development towards realizing his/her ministerial and professional goals. Mentoring is a power-free relationship between two people who desire mutual development in the field of their learning and service where the mentor serves with greater experience, wisdom and skills to help the mentee reach the heights of God-given potential in life. It is also contended as, "… a protected relationship in which learning and experimentation can transpire; potential skills can be developed and in which results can be measured in terms of competencies maintained."[13]

We recognize the role of mentor as central to the process of qualitative research. As methodologies multiply, the standards for rigour change too. In this, mentoring as a supportive pedagogy emerges as an essential element of theological education as Chiroma and Cloete[14] argue, with reference to the spiritual growth, character development and ministry formation of the students. While there are theology schools that virtually ignore *mentoring* in their teaching-learning practice, those that offer *mentoring* often tend to set their exclusive focus on academics. This has certainly done much damage to the learning process and moreover, the very purpose of the theological endeavour.

---

[12]   Gretchen E Ziegenhals, 'Faculty Life and Seminary Culture' 49-66 in *Practical Wisdom on Theological Teaching and Learning*, Malcolm L Warford (ed.) (New York: Peter Lang, 2004), 60.

[13]   Ian L Cesa and Scott C Frazer, 'A method for encouraging the development of good mentor-protégé relationships', 125-128 in *Teaching of Psychology*, Vol. 16, 125.

[14]   N H Chiroma, and A Cloete, 2015, 'Mentoring as a supportive pedagogy in theological training', HTS Teologiese Studies/ Theological Studies 71(3), Art. #2695, 8 pages. http:// dx.doi.org/10.4102/hts. v71i3.2695 accessed on 06 May, 2017.

Therefore, the proposal here is for all levels of academic mentoring to facilitate holistic formation to the students. Intentionality is the primary value to be added to reach that end. Mentoring needs to be a core vision at the school, where faculty receives progressive coaching to put into practice the formational mandate in theological training. Also, faculty being the expert authority in the field and scholarly leader is undoubtedly significant in this. Seeking to transcend the age-old debate on *teaching versus research,* Boyer expanded the teacher's scholarship into four essential tasks; scholarship of discovery, scholarship of integration, scholarship of application and scholarship of teaching.[15] The meanings of Boyer's themes in teaching set a challenge for theology schools to review their concept of a *scholarly mentor.* For Boyer,

- *The scholarship of discovery*, which refers to the specialized research contributions in a particular discipline.

- *The scholarship of integration* is outstanding undertakings that fills gap and connects disciplines or larger settings of meanings.

- *The scholarship of application* is about relating knowledge to real situations, what Boyer calls the civic life.

- *The scholarship of teaching* views teaching as the highest form of understanding.

Assessing our mentoring practices thoroughly, there could be admissions that our understandings tend to be shallow and that the scheme of mediocrity often surpasses the vision. In a mentoring relationship, research students seek to build confidence with a professional friend, to share new ideas, find inspiration for the study, receive feedback and explore new directions in thinking. What they experience instead is the increase of 'over-projecting yet under-delivering' mentors in the field of study, particularly in contexts where primary discussions on mentoring standards are yet to begin.

Faculty formation in theology school needs to have this research mentoring practice as a central component. The figure below presents a design for the on-going formation of faculty in theology schools, where *research and learning* is one of the four primary tasks. In order to develop effective mentoring skills, faculty members are to actively contribute in all four service dimensions in the diagram.

From this overall design, each of the features can be explained separately in figures, highlighting the purposes, functions and the interconnections that make an integrated whole.

---

[15] Ernest L Boyer, *Scholarship Reconsidered: Priorities of the Professoriate* (San Francisco: Jossey Bass, 1997), 23.

The theological milieu and method in qualitative research is another important dimension, where practical theology as an academic discipline has much to contribute. As the following points suggest, the values that guide practical theological research can serve as significant signposts to the mentor. From the discussion on Practical Theology in Chapter 1, the following figure draws major indicators for the qualitative research undertaking.

Figure 21: Practical Theology's Reinforcement in Transformative Research Practice

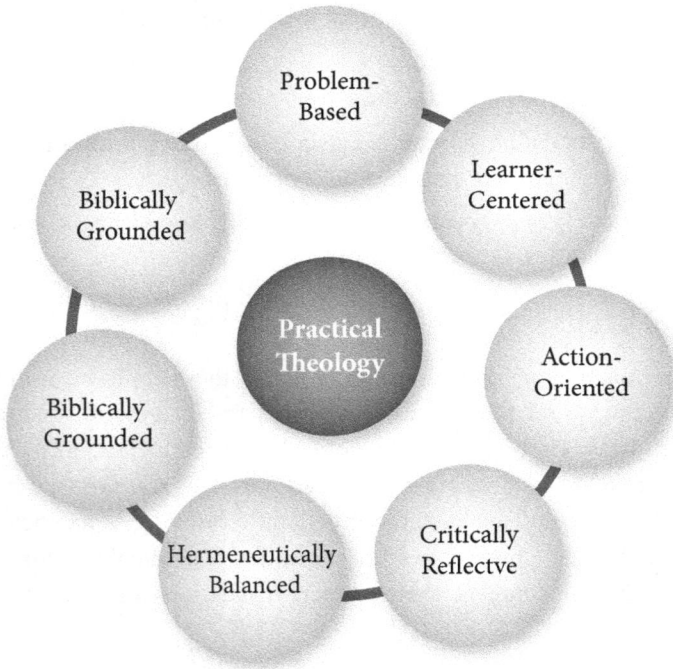

Contribution of the research mentor in the process, however, is not necessarily by means of meticulous prescriptions, but rather by purposeful listening and facilitation. The mentor might need to integrate certain predominant themes to reach the vision of transformative research practice as the following section imagines.

Research in theological education as envisioned here therefore, does not refer to a set of abstract data. Using relevant qualitative methods it attempts to excavate the not-so-obvious realities of human experience and reflect on them theologically in seeking practical interventions. This comprehensive analysis of the social reality requires the methodology that surpasses a simplistic treatment of demography or frequency of responses. In theological studies, this also points to a responsive

Figure 20: Framework for Transformative Faculty Formation in Theology Schools

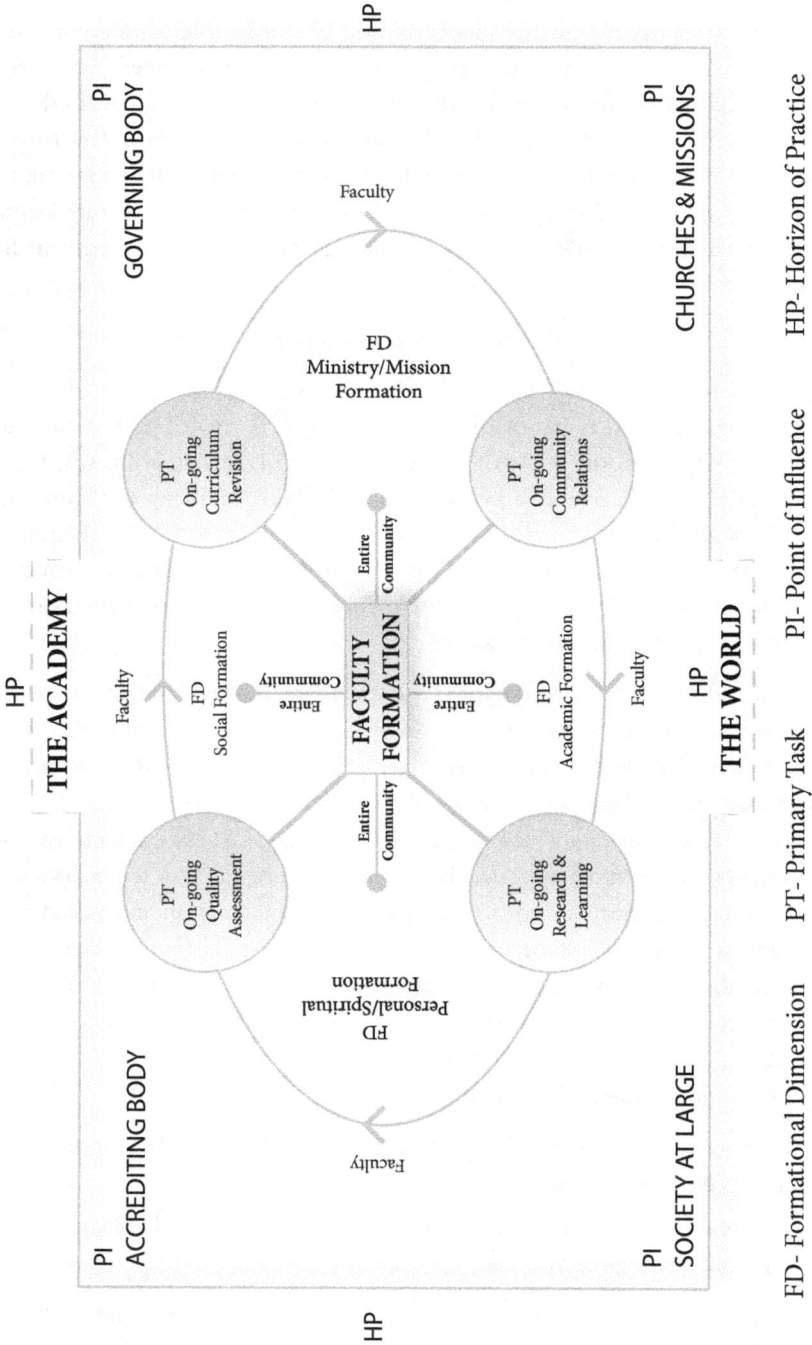

GOVERNING BODY

CHURCHES & MISSIONS

THE ACADEMY

THE WORLD

ACCREDITING BODY

SOCIETY AT LARGE

Faculty

FD
Ministry/Mission
Formation

PT
On-going
Curriculum
Revision

PT
On-going
Community
Relations

FD
Social Formation

Entire Community

FACULTY
FORMATION

Entire Community

Entire Community

FD
Academic Formation

Faculty

Faculty

PT
On-going
Quality
Assessment

PT
On-going
Research &
Learning

FD
Personal/Spiritual
Formation

Faculty

HP

HP

HP

HP

PI

PI

PI

PI

FD- Formational Dimension   PT- Primary Task   PI- Point of Influence   HP- Horizon of Practice

197

outcome to facilitate the multi-faceted mission of the church. Ministry impact is at the heart of a good mentoring practice in theological education. The mentor's own commitment to ministry and the incorporation of ministerial essence in research makes the difference. The answer to 'what great mentoring in higher education should do' depends ultimately on our definition of the purpose of theological education. We have seen how important it is for the mentoring practice to expand from its routine patterns of assessments to higher themes such as personal formation, ethics and impact on mission. Considering the *head-heart-hand balance* in transformative learning, we will now consider some of the qualities that the theology mentor should possess.

Personal Qualities of the Mentor in Theological Research

A mentor owns a treasure of knowledge in the field of study. Mentoring is void without knowledge. Yet, it is not only the amount of knowledge, but the quality of the person who lives out a life of wisdom is what ultimately counts in terms of effective mentoring experience. Basically, humility, i.e., realizing that one person does not have all the answers, docility i.e., the ability to appreciate the insights and resourcefulness of others, and, hospitality i.e., willingness to allow authentic space for learning and reflection are qualities that reinforce the task of a mentor. David Lose imagined teacher as a rafting guide,

> who takes students through both the placid waters and the rapids, neither doing the work for them nor abandoning them to the white water, but using his her experience on the river to guide, prompt, challenge and coach them to draw from themselves more than they had previously imagined they could do as they navigate their way downstream. One can only play such a role, of course, if one is willing to get wet, not only talking with others about the raft trip but jumping into the boat to be a participant in the journey. For teachers, this means abandoning an understanding of teaching as the transmission of knowledge and embracing, instead, the notion that teaching about active participation, struggle and confession, with all the ambiguities and vulnerabilities of such a pedagogy intact. This may take some time to get used to; leaving the comfortable confines of objective truth is surely risky. But then the pursuit of truth has never been for the faith of heart.[16]

In theology, mentoring will have little impact if it is not about reflecting the divine nature. We therefore, expect that the research mentor:

- Has real joy in walking closer with someone younger and seeing the person thriving in learning and life.

---

[16] David J Lose, 'How do we Make Space for Students to Seek Truth? Teaching with Conviction' 19-31 Chapter 2 in Mary E Hess and Stephen D Brookfield (eds), *Teaching Reflectively in Theological Contexts: Promises and Contradictions* (Florida: Krieger Publishing, 2008), 30.

- Makes genuine responses to meeting schedules and offer solid comments on the queries or information put forth by the researcher.
- Is willing to do erudite groundwork in exploring the context of the research question.
- Offers adequate space for the researcher to handle the fluid process of qualitative data.
- Displays preparedness in extending professional support and openness in appraising the researcher's perspective.
- Discovers how creativity is stimulated as problems are discussed and ideas shared.
- Is attentive and understanding and have the researcher's best interests at heart.
- Exhibits confidence in the researcher and an unswerving faith in God.
- Expands the researcher's learning experience to the larger body of researchers/professionals by which accountability standards are heightened.
- Inspires the researcher to transcend the tiresome data process duly into a sound integration of knowledge and wisdom for lasting impact in mission.
- Sets the model of the person who can be trusted fully in terms of personal and professional morality.

Basic Skills in Mentoring Qualitative Research

Mentoring is central to advancing rigour in the entire qualitative process and therefore, it should not be seen as a task in the periphery. Shelby speaks of mentoring relationship as "… an integral aspect of promoting rigour in qualitative endeavors" and that the mentor models "a stance with the student that the student needs to maintain with the data."[17] A mentor facilitates the self-efficacy of the researcher by showing brighter light, guiding the path and building confidence, as the qualitative inquiry progresses. Daloz observes that "mentors give us the magic that allows us to enter the darkness; a talisman to protect us from evil, spells a gem of wise advice, a map, and sometimes simply courage."[18] Overall, listening to the field experiences of the researcher and making appropriate interventions to promote deep explorations of the data are vital skills of the qualitative researcher. Even in doing this, how the mentor perceives the developmental process will determine the direction of the research. The following points present some of the indispensable skills for mentoring in qualitative theological research. An effective qualitative research mentor will:

---

[17] R D Shelby, 'Using the Mentoring Relationship to Facilitate Rigor in Qualitative Research', 315-327 Smith College *Studies in Social Work*, 702 (2), 315, 319.DOI:1080/00377310009517595.

[18] L A Daloz, *Mentor: Guiding the Journey of Adult Learners* (San Francisco, C A, Jossey-Bass, 1999), 18.

- Know the qualitative researcher as a "bricoleur, as a maker of quilts, or as in film making, a person who assembles images into montages"[19] rather than the one who does experiments, predictions and statistics.
- Direct the researcher to the roots of authentic wisdom which is the fear of and dependence on God.
- Assist the researcher with the standards of rigour expected in the process.
- Recognize and employ the logical reinforcements of methodology in practical theology.
- Guide the researcher who strives to achieve balance between objectivity and sensitivity, while researcher immerses in the qualitative data and the self is actively engaged in all of the process.
- Cultivate understanding of the experiences of the researcher in the given cultural context of the study.
- Set the pattern of moving further from mere emotional empathies and cheering habits to a more professional pattern of inquiry.
- Guide the researcher to careful construction of interpretations of the data rather than a quick and disconnected writing up of findings.
- Caution the researcher of the hazard of *overuse of the self* in qualitative data processing.
- Keep constant watch over the process that while going beyond the master narrative to discover new and different meanings, the researcher maintains credibility and balance.
- Foster creative, analytical interaction during meetings rather than fixed patterns of talk.
- Help researcher's self-assessment of the work with difficult questions on the reliability of data process, efficiency of the hermeneutical grids and the articulation of the findings.
- Assist to enhance researcher's network with peers or other experts in availing critical evaluations prior to the final examination, where an expert from elsewhere weighs the work based on his/her standards and expectations.
- Finally, build capacities of the researcher in the several integration tasks in qualitative researching as depicted below.

---

[19]   N K Denzin and Y S Lincoln, 'Introduction: The Discipline and Practice of Qualitative Research' in N K Denzin and Y S Lincoln (eds) *The Landscape of Qualitative Research*, 3rd Edition,1-43 (Thousand Oaks: CA, 2008), 5.

Figure 22: Dimensions of Mentoring in Qualitative Theological Research

Personal Formation of Researcher

Ethical Soundness of Research

Strategic Dissemination of Results

Personal Formation	Ethical Soundness	Strategic Impact
Pointing to God, divine wisdom	Personal-interpersonal ethics, addressing biases	Writing and publication
Shaping analytical thinking	Handling mentoring relations	Awareness programs on campus
Developing skills in learning	Research design and sampling	Interventions in & through church
Enlightening to social action	Data gathering and credibility	Social actions & networking
Building confidence	Data process, interpretation & report	Strategic Focus Groups
Motivating to serve church	Contribution to research context	Long-term service in the context
Enhancing vision for mission	Commitment to the church	Taking further on action research

Figure 23: Multiple Integration Tasks in Qualitative Research

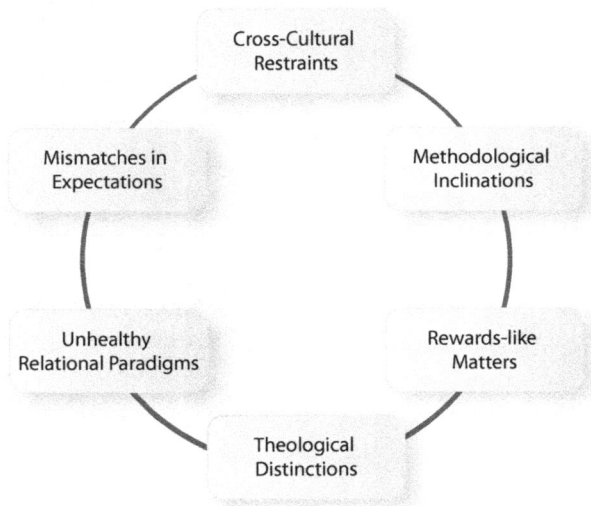

Critical Interfaces in the Mentoring Relationship

Both the mentor and the researcher should be interested in the subject chosen and need to have a concrete sense of the requirements from the theology school or the university. There are administrative and writing style/referencing snippets that the mentor must provide expert guidance for. A mentor has to be a strong guide in the process of research proposal development especially in the formulation of theoretical frame, data procedures and development of arguments. A central contribution of the mentor is in enabling the researcher to set and act upon realistic and meaningful goals. Two key events to which the mentor provides focused coaching are the research proposal defense and the viva voce in doctoral studies. This relationship can be highly motivational and transformative. However, this also can go extremely troublesome due to lack of empathy, behavioural issues and personality conflicts. See below some of those critical areas.

- Cross-cultural mentor-mentee interactions can set unique dilemmas. Mentor would find certain areas in the research process unclear or unacceptable while for the mentee those may be the most relevant contextual realities. Mentors in such projects need to enhance their cross-cultural knowledge and competencies. Culturally oriented behavioural and communicative patterns too can hinder effective mentoring practices.

Figure 24: Potential Crisis Zones in the Research Mentoring Practice

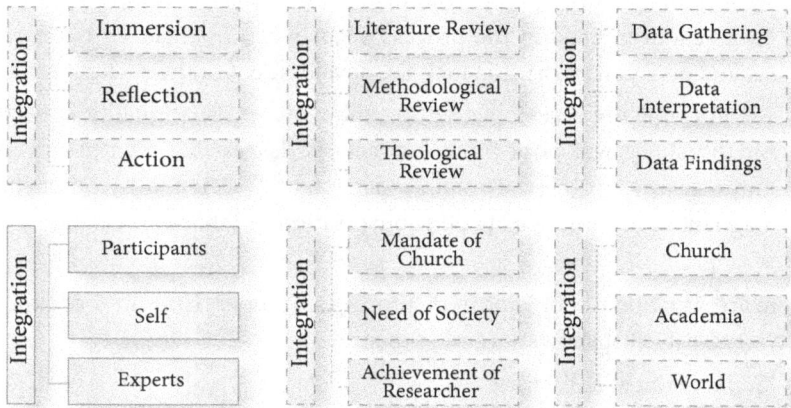

- Qualitative research projects are not well endorsed and administered in many theology schools primarily due to methodological suspicions prevailing among the faculty members. For instance, mentors who are trained in quantitative genre might tend to resist explicitly or internally, what the qualitative researcher proposes for the study. The danger of being pulled to what is familiar to the mentor can obstruct the research prospect in such situations where the methodology requires a different form of inquiry and analysis.

- Research in theology has inherent challenges pertaining to possible doctrinal/ ideological incongruities in mentoring interactions. These could at time provoke serious set-backs in the development of the task. Conservative-liberal dichotomies in scholarship, driving the researcher even to quit in the middle of the journey too is not uncommon. Faculty who cordially enlist to the academic and administrative procedures can simultaneously cultivate sharp distinctions in their ideological preferences. When mentoring relationship fails to handle these differences wisely towards facilitating deeper learning, it becomes a persisting predicament.

- Differences in denominational affiliation are also at times reasons for certain quandaries spoken or unspoken. These distinctions can actually be an advantage for mutual growth but when approached immaturely, they foster a sense of irrelevance and detachment in mentoring interactions.

- Unhealthy relational paradigms allowed in the professional activity makes it difficult to guard the personal and moral boundaries for both the mentor and the researcher, and, to stay focused on the judicious completion of the task.

- Conflicts of interest in the process occur when financial or other reward-related personal priorities block the development of the research.
- Mentor and the researcher setting different levels of quality expectations on the study will pose intense concerns. Issues like mentor's disinterest and mentee's tardiness are equally detrimental. Mentoring relationship gets stagnant in the absence of open conversations often, not realizing what goes wrong.

There are situational problems in mentoring and supervising an academic work. McCarty's extensive list shows several of them.

- 'Supervision at a distance
- Cross generational supervision
- Supervising older people
- Supervising younger people
- Supervising cross gender
- Supervising friends
- Supervising emotionally unhealthy people
- Supervising underqualified
- Supervising over qualified
- Supervising in an inadequate system
- Supervising in a task-oriented system
- Supervising in a person oriented system
- Supervising cross vocationally'[20]

Mentoring Expectations and Misconceptions

Mentoring is a relational dynamic and it sets expectations. The mentor's expectation of the qualitative researcher is that he/she should be committed to the study and able to take relevant initiatives in each phase of the process. A self-motivated, hardworking researcher motivates the mentor to be intentional about the task. Mentors are usually appreciative of students who consistently carry on their tasks in spite of delays on the part of the mentor in commenting on the work. Mentors are encouraged by students who know their research design and the frame of thought clearly. Students are expected to submit their periodical written reports well-done and edited, also allowing sufficient time for the mentor to study and comment on them. The researchers are to grow from mere writing tasks to making critical discourses with their mentor as the research progresses. They are to respect and be

---

[20] Extracted from Doran C McCarty, *Supervision: Developing and Directing People in Ministry* (Florida: McCarty Services, 2001), 130-145.

open to critical comments and take responsibility for the strengths and weaknesses in the inquiry. Mentors in qualitative research seek to find the researcher flourishing in theological reflections, practical solutions and ministerial strategies as learning progresses.

> Don't we look at many events of our lives as big or small interruptions, interrupting many of plans, projects and life schemes? Don't we feel an inner protest when a student interrupts our reading... And doesn't this unending row of interruptions build in our hearts feelings of anger, frustration and even revenge so much so that at times we see the real possibility that growing old can become synonymous with growing bitter? But what if our interruptions are in fact our opportunities, if they are challenges to an inner response by which growth takes place and through which we come to the fullness of being?21

The researcher also has expectations of the mentor. One of the loudest cries of students is the lack of meaningful availability and accessibility of mentors. The researchers expect that the mentor is an expert in terms of knowledge and practice in the subject area investigated. Another aspect is that the mentor should thoroughly know the academic expectations of the research endeavour and guide the student accordingly. In cultures where appreciative expressions are limited, we hear students say how much they want to hear from their mentor a word of appreciation amidst the rows of criticisms. On the other hand, researchers feel utter helplessness with a mentor who is not keen in guiding and chooses to make all positive comments to keep things going. They are losers at the final stage when realizing that the mentor failed to point out the crucial gaps in the theory frame. The most defeating struggles occur when it is felt that the mentor does not seek the success of the work, consistently delays in feedbacks, lacks clarity in most comments, is unavailable for tutorials, and carelessly nominates examiner/s from fields outside the subject area.

Students maintain certain misconceptions regarding mentoring as shown below:

- I can expect my mentor to do the work for me may be with some of the writing and data collection tasks.
- I'm a typical last-minute person. It will be fine to do it together at the end rather than strictly keeping to all the deadlines set.
- Mentor has to keep encouraging me and schedule appointments so that I can get it done.
- Mentoring is all about someone tells me what to do and I just follow it.
- When mentor's comments are incorporated, the work naturally turns out perfect. (keep improving your work in every possible way because mentor

---

21   Henry J M Nouwen, *Reaching Out: The Three Movements of the Spiritual Life*, 1975, (Bantam Doubleday: New York, 1966 reprint),30.

is not the examiner. Moreover, the readers are out there, who will read your work from multiple perspectives and queries).

- If I am consistently smart in defending and proving my views right to the mentor, that's how it works.
- I must please my mentor somehow to make sure I get through the process successfully.
- Part of the job of the mentor is to edit my writing.

Apart from the above larger issues, the mentor-researcher relation can encounter many set-backs. It can get really tough for many reasons. A good mentoring support is denied when the mentor:

1. Is overly committed on other responsibilities and engages in extensive travels.

2. Does not respond to queries or submissions of sections on time, leaving the student in anxiety and uncertainty.

3. Maintains an ever negative and cold attitude to the research prospect by which the researcher loses motivation.

4. Changes job and the venue and sometimes moves out of the country.

5. Falls ill and the work cannot be technically handed over to another person for technicalities and thus causing stagnation.

6. Keeps shifting opinions on methodological preferences and processes. The researcher moves back and forth with no clear direction.

7. Fails to capture the overall frame of the study or point out the detrimental flaws in the theoretical underpinning but reads sections separately and make judgments.

8. Is not methodologically equipped or gifted to guide the work (in spite of his degrees).

9. Never wills to trust the ability of the student to complete the work successfully.

10. Fails to be empathetic and attentive at least minimally to the personal struggles of the researcher.

11. While appreciating the qualities and skills of the mentor in theological research, we also recognize that mentoring does not just take place in a one-on-one, closed setting. The following section lists some of the paradigms.

Mentoring Paradigms

Mentoring paradigms are in constant re-shaping in the twenty-first century. Added flexibility, openness, multiple perspectives, and, questions over norms and absolutes and many other features contribute to this. In spite of the inherent concerns, there are several opportunities the field of theology could discover to strengthen the mentoring pattern. A few helpful layouts are:

- The *formal mentoring* pattern in theological education is where a senior faculty is assigned for a one-to-one mentoring responsibility.

- The *multiple mentoring* paradigm in the twenty-first century epitomizes multiple mentoring relationships that make the researcher draw support from diverse team of resource people.

- *Peer mentoring* is another practice where the researcher has the advantage of walking the journey together with a peer who might be more empathetic, more attentive than anyone else.

- *Interdepartmental mentoring* is another transformative way of mentoring that takes the researcher to break through the boundaries of other departments and gain confidence and clarity in the research process.

- *Collective mentoring* is usually designed by an institutional or departmental leadership who develops a pattern for mentoring based on a collective effort to their students.

The impact of mentoring is a crucial theme in the context of research. We close with the proposition that the theology school that pledges to transformative higher education needs a discerning eye on the practice of research and also, on the content and direction of mentoring. Often, mentoring occurs as a subsidiary task that does not have much to do with deep learning and reflection, vision direction, person formation or, the lasting impact of the study. The transformative learning design of qualitative research in theology proposes solid mentoring support and for this, faculty formation is suggested as a foremost consideration for theology schools. The role of faculty growing deep from expert authority to transformative learning facilitator is what is envisioned. When the mentoring practice grows deep enough to impact life, moving beyond the generic academic procedures, we achieve the purpose of theological education. Moreover, with regard to the mission in the church and society, this can serve as the accountability check-point for the theology school. Any bidding to deepen our teaching-learning practice would apparently exert more practical demands on the school. Yet, to determine the missional tenacity of the school, it is worth pursuing.

We reiterate that good mentoring practice will rightfully place our intellectual lives in academic collegiality and in the fear of God, which is the essence of all genuine understanding, ethics and mission. Together, the mentor and the researcher realize that they deal with the matters of God and walk alongside the other in search of His infinite wisdom. Therefore, every moment in the mentoring task is to be approached with the deep sense of transmission of God's grace. This is particularly important because our theological conclusions regarding the intricate realities of human dilemmas cannot be made in anyway violating the divine standards. We therefore see mentoring not simply in terms of academic or analytical competency (which are of course, indispensable features), but beyond that as faithful participation in God's eternal project of wisdom and action in reconciling the world. Doing this, we keep asking 'What is happening?' 'Why is this happening?' 'What ought to be happening?' and therefore, 'How should we respond?'

Reflection Box:
Theologian's *learning* does not stand aloof from the spiritual/faith convictions...

While writing this book, I had the privilege of spending some invaluable hours with the cognitive cultural anthropologist Dr. Daniel Shaw at Fuller Theological Seminary in California who lived among the Samo group in the East Strickland Plain of Papua New Guinea and became one among them in an elaborate three-day formal ceremony called *initiation*[1]. Shaw's research was engrained in the exploration of the scripture and the daily life lived in "the relationship with God through Jesus Christ in the power of the Holy Spirit". He wrote, "My own research among the Samo has taught me the value of qualitative research and its application to the development of the Church and local theology. Understanding the intent of Samo initiation with its focus on interpersonal relationships and the need to counteract spiritual power, has brought new insights to my appreciation of Paul's letters to Ephesians and Thessalonians."[2] Matters of faith and spiritual commitments are central to the research endeavour and the researcher is the one who confidently affirms God and his Word as the foundation of all wisdom and direction.

Student C in a multi-faith Asian context selected the most adventurous topic in the Master's program that year. The inquiry and methodology on a fast-growing cult in the given context had won for him special recognitions already. During discussions in the class, his comments on research methodology were acclaimed *exceptional*. To get inside of a closed religious cult group that claimed to have the messiah incarnated among them, C selected a disguised participant method. Pretending to be a devotee and entering that closed compound was not as easy as it first appeared. While moving step by step, doing all what the actual devotees did, he realized he was hurling himself into a serious encounter with demonic forces. Due to intense confusion, stress, physical stress and fatigue experienced inside that place, he said he had to leave the place without completing the task. Poor C!

CONSIDER: Student C had always understood theology research merely as an academic exercise that anyone can accomplish with a brilliant methodology; he never anticipated that theology, research, spirituality, morality and community inseparably blend in the life and learning of the theologian!

CONCLUSION

REINVIGORATING RESEARCH TOWARDS TRANSFORMATIVE RESULTS

SECTION CONTENTS:

- Schools to Critically Revisit their own Research Component
- Unlimited Potential of a Curriculum that Embed Qualitative Research
- Perceptions that Cripple Practice

The indispensable challenge before theology schools therefore, is to revisit their research and learning processes more intensively, defining the *what, when, where, who, why* and the *how* questions around it. Theory and practice are no dichotomies for the theology researcher; neither are knowledge and mission. If theological knowledge cannot address the real life concerns of the church and the society or, sensibly communicate to the realities, it needs to be critically evaluated. If a missiology research does not impact the actual grounds of mission, it is only a hollow drudgery. Every bit of knowledge we claim to have processed or produced in and through the theological enterprise has meaning only to the extent of it being used, reflected upon and refined to make sense in our world today, and above all, to direct the world towards knowing and loving God.

This book on Qualitative Research, aimed to: (1) inform students of the need and method of qualitative researching and instil interest in them to undertake transformative research projects that correspond to the relevant issues in ministry (2) invite the faculty and academic-administrative leadership to pay closer attention to several features of research/learning practices towards greater appreciations on the academic-ministerial formation of the student.

Theology Schools to Critically Consider Their Research Component

What goes well and *what does not* in the school's own philosophy and practice of academic formation would need a thorough reviewing in the first place. The overriding debates in theological education in the past few decades have been on topics like: Contextualization, Integration, Critical Reflection, Pastoral-Leadership Formation, Theology-Culture Hermeneutics, Assessment, Outcome, Impact, Sustainability, Life-long Education, Online Education, and Distance Education, among many others. Any school that critically reconsiders these areas spontaneously starts addressing the formational patterns and philosophy of its training. Otherwise, detrimental learning practices continue and the schools fail their students in achieving the intended level of formation and transformation. As far as the research curriculum is concerned, there are areas that require the schools' immediate attention as the following points illustrate.

- *Research* as a crucial area of formation for the student is not a widely commended perspective in theological settings. Even schools that maintain relatively high regard for research, tend to emphasize its abstract academic dimensions, while, knowingly or otherwise, ignore the transformative methodological potential of qualitative researching.

- Faculty members generally maintain a cold response at least internally, when it comes to mentoring and assessing research and thesis. It often feels burdensome for many of them as these assignments come on the top of heavy workloads, and, without reasonable compensation. Certain projects thus reflect the mentor's indifference as students go away contented with convenience rather than relevance.

- Crowded academic batches allow little attention to individual learners. With the absence of a genuine mentoring system, students eventually fade into mediocrity in their desire to *learn for a change*.

- Courses and departments are often so gravely separated that they compete rather than integrate, interact or intersect to strengthen one another. Departments and courses are in an unremitting attempt to retain uniqueness in their contents and achievements. In doing so, they consciously stay detached. This unhelpful competition to win over the other hinders any prospect for learning/research integration that is cognitively and practically transformative.

- Over emphases on classrooms, exams, library-based assignments and the neglect of student's self-learning and reflection have indorsed an obstinate resistance on the field-based qualitative research undertakings.

- Mentor-mentee formational dimensions need more explorations; faculty's image and role as the facilitator, co-learner, enabler and hospitable helper is to be enhanced.
- Conveniently overlooking the dearth of the qualitative learning domain, several learning contexts grow ill-equipped in terms of nurturing responsiveness, sensitivity and creativity.
- Holistic formation of students is ignored when learning is restricted to academic procedures within the classrooms and libraries. The fragmented, abstract, and modular culture adopted in theology schools needs to be replaced with transformative research practices that integrate learning in and towards essential action.

Rethinking of the learning philosophy and practices, therefore, appears to be the very first step forward. Adapting the qualitative research approach through the entire theology curriculum is deeply transformative, yet could set a huge demand on the schools in terms of curricular revision and faculty formation. Yet, as presented in the previous chapters, it can ensure that the student is not only gaining knowledge but is simultaneously acting upon it. The risky divide prevalent between the theology school and the world has done enormous damage to the minds, missions and the masses. Reparatory procedures in learning and research have thus become indispensable in order to sustain relevance. The methodology of qualitative research in practical theological approach has crucial roles to play in this by facilitating the *curricular redesign that integrates the conventional banking of knowledge and the critical pedagogy of reflection and engagement*. This is identical to the effective blending of:

- Theory and ministry praxis
- Focus on technicalities of learning process and a training methodology that is based on the outcome-impact assessment
- Formal education patterns and the non-formal, informal learning experiences
- Classroom exposure and field experience
- Information and the on-going, active engagement in reality

Salvaging theological education from getting reduced into an unrealistic theoretical exercise is to start with the teaching-learning philosophy and objectives. Both the learner and the teacher need to develop a research mindset in all that happens in the school. This is not about facilitating a critical approach to everything, rather a keen mind that asks the essential questions for constructive change and growth. An essential criterion for this, however, is a steady academic leadership that equips the faculty to redesign the curriculum to reflect the vision, mission, objectives, core values, input, output, outcome and impact. Mutual enabling of formal and non-formal theological trainings might become a strategic move in the renewal of theological education. Expectations from the *world*—where the church and the society situate—call theology schools for mutuality, dialogue, debates and, often, real tough engagement. We are ever more aware that this sort of an active response to the church and the world is not a natural trait in the traditional educational setting.

The rather safe resolve for many schools is to stand aloof of all such transformative, responsive engagement, doing one's own things in one's own way, hence ending up building factories that produce knowledge for one's own sake. In other words, we build up centres were bundles of knowledge are accumulated to be kept in the stacks, made accessible for intellectual elites who manage to make their way there. Hence, even dissertations that were awarded doctoral degrees for *the contribution of original knowledge* might remain unused forever. Nonetheless, we know the irresistible vocation of a theology school is engagement rather than escaping from the ground reality. It is the permeation of wisdom in daily dimensions of life and not the establishment of an intellectual world of its own right.

This book sets the issue on the desk in order to enable us to start pondering on reshaping our learning patterns to grow into a methodology where realistic dialogues and interconnections take place between theology schools and the real life of the society and the church. Typical, large-scale consultations may have certain limitations in facilitating this; while individual schools or a group of schools can achieve this transformation by working at least around the following four areas:

Figure 25: Key Dimensions of Learning/ Research Sustainability in Theology Schools

Curriculum Reformation with qualitative research underpinning, focusing on intersections of learning, reflection and practice dimensions	**Faculty Formation** incorporating the research vision through lessons, courses and programs, and, in mentoring and assessment
Churches-Missions Integration in making churches/missions crucial accountability partners (including significant role in project assessment)with theology schools in field research procedures	**Research Orientation** to students in critical integration of theory, context, action and grounded theological wisdom

Perceptions that Cripple the Learning Practice

Theological education is flourishing in depth and width everywhere and the media keeps projecting this substantially. Faculty with long years of experience engaging in persistent writing and research, outstanding infrastructures, great libraries with advanced learning facilities that offer knowledge from anywhere at your fingertip, beautiful campuses, newer academic programs year after year, affiliations with universities, and, the list of achievements continues. Nonetheless, in spite of all these, there are areas that go unattended as we get immersed in doing the same thing over and over. Like any institution, theology schools too can stagnate, where they stop impacting lives but claim to contribute many things. Practising theological education without assessing the outcome and impact challenges the very purpose of our existence.

Learning is approached in a way that it ends at one point and there has been a consistent want for effective means to assess how the learning impacted the person and his/her mission prospects. Sadly, the mindset that 'learning stops as the course ends' is still strong in many learning contexts. Disintegration of the learning practices sets another big challenge for the learner. Courses, research activities and assessments are often poorly integrated to make a whole experience. Selection of modules done according to the availability of the faculty and sequence of the subjects done to suit the convenience of the faculty are evidence for this. By this, students receive a fragmented learning, where learning feels more like a burden and boredom rather than a life-giving experience.

Assessment of learning sets multiple challenges. The amount of knowledge accumulated is assessed in tests and exams; the rest is unclear and so, we go by assumptions. Critical learning that is expected to happen in research has to touch people out there—their questions, problems and experiences—beyond library knowledge. Only through comprehensive assessment methods, can we get formed and reformed in this transformed research/learning pattern. Formation presupposes information but only when that information impacts the whole person in thinking, reflection, interpretation and action. Self-learning, deep learning, life-long learning, multi-dimensional learning, problem solving learning—all are hidden in the curriculum of research. The unique challenges of the context of the student demands innovation and responsiveness in learning practice.

The formal theological system pulls out the student from his/her life context for a minimum of 2–3 years, and challengingly, requires learning in a second language. Lack of deep reflection and ground-touch with reality during this period can create a huge vacuum in the student's perception of ministry and life. For practical wisdom to advance, the student has to engage in the real context, and experts in the field are to account for the direction of learning that takes place there. Real time practical engagement and deep reflection on life's questions from multiple angles is facilitated in theological education only by intention. For theology schools in their intellectual-practical mission, this pedagogical adaptation seems indispensable. Individuals are different in their learning approaches. Students in theological education differ much in their life experiences and in their understanding of God and the Scripture as they hail from variety of cultures, languages, formal education levels, theological perspectives and secular worldviews. Normally, the faculty members in theology schools who lack field ministry expertise struggle in designing holistic learning practices that blend knowledge and practical wisdom. Contextual, structural, socio-political, vocational, personal, spiritual issues in real life can be very different from what a student is taught at a school. Therefore, for meaningful learning interactions, deep engagement is vital.

At the end of an academic program, we often see a discontented faculty who thinks the student has not reached the expected level in learning and an unhappy student who complaints that his/her expectations in learning were not being met. Even more dreadful is the situation where students frantically talk about their fear of being ill-equipped for the new ministry assignments ahead. For them, field ministry requires a different kind of training. I have known students, who upon completion of a theology program in a formal setting, get enrolled for a short-term non-formal pastoral or leadership training. Students increasingly find themselves unfit to face the real world despite their academic qualifications. Flexibility, adaptability and the ability to see, hear, and talk in ways people understand are important capacities of the graduate. Known answers may not always work well in the context of service. It is not just the context of our society that changes, but the church too is changing in terms of needs, expectations and challenges. Demands put forth by various constituencies in theological education are also shifting. Contextual problems associated to ministry formation in Asian cultures (e.g., pluralism, terrorism, fast changing socio-political scenario, proliferation of denominations, cults and life styles, impact of the digital culture on discipleship and witnessing) set a whole new level of threat to the contents and patterns in training. Information gets too easily outdated and the student returns to the ground of ministry with a disconnected body, soul and spirit.

For students to develop skills and capacities, carefully designed research practices are essential. It aids to develop several factors including:

- analytical ability to understand the situation
- responsiveness in addressing issues and undertaking challenges
- set goals and execute them
- responsible self-learning and on-going reflection

- ability to integrate theological knowledge with real life, and,
- the capacity to engage meaningfully in the real ground of human realities

Unlimited Potential of a Curriculum that Embeds Qualitative Research

Properly implemented qualitative research methodology has unlimited potential in the reformation of theological education. The challenge we have addressed in this book is simply this: Can we converge the streams of academy and the world through carefully crafted research practices? If so, what would this mean to the school, the faculty and the student?

STUDENT FOCUS

Qualitative research experience helps students engage in real life and respond to real issues:

- It trains students to pose the right and transformative questions
- It has essential requirements for practical networking and reflective interactions
- It enhances leader-development capacities and skills
- It instils courage to face problems, confidence to venture into uncertainties rather than making one feel less prepared, less equipped, less confident and, fearful about facing the world
- It can refine the student's perception of calling in ministry, by its very prerequisite the student takes responsibility for learning
- It provokes critical thinking naturally, without getting overburdened with the massive amount of information to be processed in the syllabus; always mentored and guided by experienced faculty.
- It leads the student to venture fearlessly into situations where his/her theological convictions are put into the test

FACULTY AND ACADEMIC ADMINISTRATION OF THEOLOGY SCHOOL

Qualitative research transforms the faculty. Great mentors exuberantly *learn with their students*. Qualitative research motivates mentors for more authentic social engagements:

- It facilitates newer transformative practices in teaching and learning
- It encourages collaborative learning procedures between departments, practicums reflected across academic disciplines, and, potential integrations within subject areas and thinking styles

- It calls for a full-fledged revisit to the curriculum and teaching practices at the school to see how efficiently learning is connected to student's context in each lesson, course and program

CHURCH, SOCIETY AND THE ACCREDITING AGENCY

- It calls for the maintenance of dynamic accountability measures of theology schools with churches and missions
- Mission intervention of theology school is practically advanced and the gap between the school and church is minimized
- Church and the larger society start experiencing and exploring meaningful interactions with the theology school
- Qualitative research calls for more rigorous quality control by newer criteria of assessment and examination prepared within the school or set by the accrediting agencies
- It enhances social and legal awareness by establishing ethical standards and policies for the Human Subject Research (HSR)

Theology schools, churches and missions need to break down the walls of separation and, build bridges. The participatory and grounded nature of qualitative research nurtures this concept of mutuality credibly. The pervasive attitudinal problem with teaching is the way in which teaching and mentoring is seen as the teacher passing the knowledge on to the student. In fact, transformative teaching is enabling and facilitating the student to explore the best ways to reach the right information. The biggest fault is made when we assume that the students understand the cultural background of the teacher, the scripture and the society, and that they will process the knowledge accordingly. In fact, the faculty's context, educational path, thinking methods, challenges, questions and all are usually drastically different from the students'. Only when the student is made to engage and think through his/her own contextual reality, to they start processing information in a holistic manner. When this insight is lacking, students wonder why they study what they study.

Therefore, propositions to guide further thinking are:

1. Current research practices in theological education need a critical revisit as to assess its theory-practice coherence and hence transformative results

2. For theological education to be missionally relevant, the on-going practice of qualitative researching would require a distinctive level of visionary mentoring, alongside accountability standards maintained with missions/churches.

3. We might otherwise consider doing theological education in a radically different hue and milieu to be relevant in the diversified world of ours.

Gaining right propositions is important. Qualitative researching is about getting down to earth, knowing people in the context of their searches, troubles, strivings, needs and challenges. It is in this task the students understand articulate and examine their theology. When each student reaches out to the world with their own areas of concern in ministry, research practice will go significantly beyond restating existing answers. There is no point in prescribing to the student what to do in each situation; because the expert in the research process is the researcher and not the teacher. But as the qualitative researcher gets to the communities for inquiry, the participants are the experts because they produce knowledge. This sums it all up. The procedure is not telling one what to do but letting them discover through the time of learning, listening and engaging, what God is calling them to do. Students are not to indiscreetly apply their lessons on their contexts but to use their knowledge to explore for themselves the path of theological wisdom in that context based on the unchangeable truth of the scripture. This requires time, intentionality, goal setting, impact assessment and visionary mentoring.

We reiterate, this is the actual working of God's mission in theological education. Qualitative research bridges the tower-top information with the ground reality of humans. This does not signify a distanced world of knowledge or the isolation of a person to create a body of human philosophical wisdom. Genuine qualitative research requires time to observe, explore and reflect; the task is never over with a hurried process of data collection and writing of a report.

Speaking in terms of the Kingdom of God narrative, qualitative research is like a mustard seed that starts with one contextual query but eventually attains phenomenal growth in God's eternal scheme of mission. Duly comprehending this plan, all that the learner does is, let the Spirit of wisdom and knowledge help him/her discover how such a broken, needy world could be reconciled and restored to God's reign. This process of learning presumes that the researcher's body, soul, and spirit is fully engaged.

BIBLIOGRAPHY

Abend, Gabriel. 'The biMeaning of Theory', Sociological Theory 26, 173-199, June 2008.

Alasuutari, Pertti. Researching Culture: Qualitative Method and Cultural Studies. London: Sage, 1995.

Anderson, Ray S. The Shape of Practical Theology: Empowering Ministry with Theological Praxis. Illinois: Inter Varsity Press, 2001.

Antaki, Charles. 'Discourse Analysis and Conversational Analysis' in Alassutari. P., Bickman L, and Brunnen J (eds), The Sage Handbook of Social Research Methods. London: Sage, 2008. Citation from https://dspace.lboro.ac.uk/dspace-jspui/bitstream/2134/5435/1/antaki%201.pdf on May 31, 2017.

Auerbach, Carl F. and Silverstein, Louise B. Qualitative Data: An Introduction to Coding and Analysis. New York: New York University Press, 2003.

Babbie, Earl. The Practice of Social Research, 10th Edition. Belmont, CA: Wardsworth/Thomson, 2004.

Ballard, Paul and Pritchard, John. Practical Theology in Action: Christian Thinking in the Service of Church and Society. London: SPCK, 1996.

Barsness, Roy E. and Kim, Richard D. 'A Pedagogy of Engagement for the Changing Character of the 21st Century Classroom' 89-106 in Theological Education, Vol.49, Number 2, 2015.

Bell, Nanci. Visualizing and Verbalizing for Language Comprehension and Thinking. CA: Gander Publishing, 2007.

Bernard, H Russell. Research Methods in Anthropology: Qualitative and Quantitative Approaches, 4th Edition. New York: Altamira Rowman and Littlefield Publishers, 2006.

Bernard, H Russell. Research Methods in Anthropology. Thousand Oaks, CA: Sage, 2004.

Bevans, Stephen B. Models of Contextual Theology. New York, Maryknoll: ORBIS, 2004.

Beyer, Janice M. 'Researchers are not Cats: They can Survive and Succeed by being Curious'65-72 in P J Frost and R E Stablein (Eds). Doing Exemplary Research. Newbury Park, C A: Sage, 1992.

Bhattacharya, K. 'Consenting to the Consent Form: What are the Fixed and Fluid Understandings between the Researcher and the Researched?' Qualitative Inquiry, 13(8), 2007, 1095-1115.

Blaxter, Loraine. Hughes, Christina and Tight, Malcom. How to Research, 2nd Edition. Buckingham: Open University Press, 2001.

Boeije, Hennie R. Analysis in Qualitative Research. London: Sage, 2010.

Booth, Wayne C. Colomb, Gregory G. & Williams, Joseph M. The Craft of Research. Chicago: the University of Chicago Press, 1995.

Boyer, Ernest L. Scholarship Reconsidered: Priorities of the Professoriate. San Francisco: Jossey Bass, 1997.

Bradley, Ann Palmer. 'Mentoring: Following the Example of Christ'. ICCTE Journal. Vol. 12, Issue 1, Spring, 2017.

Brookfield, Stephen D. and Hess, Mary E. 'How can We Teach Authentically? Reflective Practice in the Dialogical Classroom' 1-18 in Mary E Hess and Stephen D Brookfield (eds), Teaching

Reflectively in Theological Contexts: Promises and Contradictions. Florida: Krieger Publishing Company, 2008.

Bryman, Alan. Quantity and Quality in Social Research. London: Unwin Hyman, 1988.

Bryman, Alan. Social Research Methods, 4th Edition. Chapter 3 'Research Designs'. Oxford: Oxford University Press, 2012.

Burgess, R G. In the Field: An Introduction to Field Research. London: Allen and Unwin 1984.

Carmean, Colleen. Mapping the Learning Space. Referred from Patricia McGee, 'Learning Objects: Bloom's Taxonomy and Deeper Learning Principles' Paper at Department of Interdisciplinary Studies & Curriculum and Instruction, The University of Texas at San Antonio, USA. faculty. coehd.utsa.edu/pmcgee/nlii/LOBloomsMcGee.doc accessed on 20 April 2017.

Cartledge, Mark J. Practical Theology: Charismatic and Empirical Perspectives. Cumbria: Paternoster, 2003.

Cesa, Ian L and Frazer, Scott C, 'A method for encouraging the development of good mentor-protégé relationships', 125-128 in Teaching of Psychology, 16 (3).

Charmaz, Kathy. Constructing Grounded Theory. Thousand Oaks: Sage, 2006.

Chiroma, N H and Cloete, A. 'Mentoring as a supportive pedagogy in theological training', HTS Teologiese Studies/ Theological Studies 71(3), Art. #2695, 8 pages, 2015. http:// dx.doi. org/10.4102/hts. v71i3.2695 accessed on 06 May, 2017.

Christians, Clifford G. 'Ethics and Politics of Qualitative Research', 208-244. Chapter 5 in The Landscape of Qualitative Research: Theories and Issues, 2nd Edition. Norman K Denzin and Yvonna S Lincoln (eds). Thousand Oaks: Sage, 2003.

Clandinin, D. J. & Connelly, F. M. Narrative Inquiry: Experience and Story in Qualitative Research. San Francisco: Jossey-Bass, 2000.

Cohen, Louis and Manion, Lawrence. Research Methods in Education. London: Routeledge, 1994. Repr. 1995.

Cooperrider, David L. Whitney, Diana and Stavros, Jacqueline M. The Appreciative Inquiry Handbook: For Leaders of Change. Oakland, CA: Berrett-Koehler Publishers, Inc, 2008.

Corbin, Juliet and Strauss, Anselm. Basics of Qualitative Research: Techniques and Procedures for Developing Grounded Theory, 3rd Edition. Thousand Oaks, CA: Sage, 2008.

Costello, Patrick J M. Action Research. London: Continuum, 2003.

Creswell, J W. Research Design: Qualitative, Quantitative and Mixed Approaches. Thousand Oaks, CA: Sage, 2009.

Creswell, John W. Qualitative Inquiry and Research Design: Choosing Among Five Approaches. Thousand Oaks, CA: Sage, 2013.

Creswell, John W. 30 Essential Skills for the Qualitative Researcher, First Edition. Sage: London, 2015.

Creswell, John W and Cheryl N Poth. Qualitative Inquiry and Research Design: Choosing among Five Approaches. London: Sage, 2017.

Daloz, L A. Mentor: Guiding the Journey of Adult Learners. San Francisco, C A, Jossey-Bass, 1999.

Davies, Richard E. Handbook for Doctor of Ministry Projects: An Approach to Structured Observation of Ministry. University Press of America, 1984.

Dawson, Catherine. Practical Research Methods. New Delhi: UBSPD, 2002.

Denscombe, Martyn. The Good Research Guide for Small Scale Social Research Projects. Buckingham: Open University Press, 1998.

Denscombe, Martyn. Ground Rules for Good Research: A Ten Point Guide for Social Researchers. Buckingham: Open University press, 2002.

Denzin, Norman K. and Lincoln, Yvonna S. 'Introduction: The Discipline and Practice of Qualitative Research', 1-46 in The Landscape of Qualitative Research. Thousand Oaks: CA,

Sage, 2nd Edition 2003 & 3rd Edition 2008.

Engen, Charles Van. 'Biblical Theology of Mission's Research Method'113-118 in Edgar J Elliston, Introduction to Missiological Research Design. Pasadena: William Carey Library, 2011.

Estes, Daniel J. Hear, my Son: Teaching and Learning in Proverbs 1-9. Downers Grove, IL: Inter Varsity Press, 1997.

Farley, Edward. "Four Pedagogical Mistakes: A Mea Culpa", 200-203. Teaching Theology and Religion 8, No. 4, 2005.

Fetterman, David M. Ethnography: Step by Step, 2nd Edition. Thousand Oaks, CA: Sage, 1998.

Fink, Arlene. Conducting Research Literature Reviews: From Paper to Internet, Thousand Oaks, CA: Sage, 1998.

Frost, P. 'Principles of the Action Research Cycle' in R. Richie, A Pollard, P Frost and T Eaude (eds.). Action Research: A Guide for Teachers. Burning Issues in Primary Education, Issue No. 3, Birmingham: National Primary Trust, 2002.

Garfinkel, Harold. Studies in Ethnomethodology, First edition. Malden, MA: Blackwell publishers, 1967.

Gadamer, Hans-Georg. Truth and Method. New York: Continuum, 1975.

George, Alexander L. and Bennett, Andrew. Case Studies and Theory Development, Cambridge: MA: MIT Press, 2005.

Gerring, John. Case Study Research: Principles and Practices. Cambridge: University Press, 2007.

Glaser, Barney G., & Strauss, Anselm L. The Discovery of Grounded Theory: Strategies for Qualitative Research. New York: Aldine Publishing Company, 1967.

Glaser, Barney G. 'The Constant Comparative Method of Qualitative Analysis' Social Problems, Vol. 12, No. 4, Spring 1965.

Glaser, B G and Strauss, A L. The Discovery of Grounded Theory: Strategies for Qualitative Research. New York: Aldine De Gruyter, 1967.

Gnanakan, Ken R. "Postgraduate Theological Degrees" 53-60. AETEI Journal, Vol. 9, No. 1 Jan-June 1996.

Graham, Elaine., Heather Walton and Frances Ward, Theological Reflection Methods. London: SCM, 2005.

Grant, Cynthia and Osanloo, Azadeh. Understanding, Selecting and Integrating a Theoretical Framework in Dissertation Research: Creating a Blueprint for your "House" 12-26 in Administrative Issues Journal: Connecting Education, Practice and Research Vol. 4, Issue 2, 2014, 14, 15. DOI:10.5929/2014.4.2.9 accessed May 18, 2017. http://jolle.coe.uga.edu/wp-content/uploads/2015/02/89596_manuscript-file_249104.pdf

Guy, R F., Edgley, C E., Arafat, I and Allen, D E. Social Research Methods: Puzzles and Solutions. Boston: Allyn and Bacon, 1987.

Hammersley, Martyn and Atkinson, Paul. Ethnography: Principles in Practice, 3rd Edition. London: Routeledge, 2007.

Hansman, Catherine A. 'Navigators on the Research Path: Teaching and Mentoring Student Qualitative Researchers' Chapter 3, 41-66 in Research Methods: Concepts, Methods, Tools and Applications. IGI Global, Informative Resources Management Association: Hershey, PA, 2015.

Harkness, Allan 'Introduction', 7-22, in Tending the Seedbeds: Educational Perspectives on Theological Education in Asia, by Allan Harkness (ed.). Quezon City: Philippines: Asia Theological Association, 2010.

Have, Paul ten. Understanding Qualitative Research and Ethnomethodology. Thousand Oaks, C A: Sage, 2004.

Heidegger, Martin. The Basic Problem of Phenomenology, Transl. by Albert Hofstardter. Indiana: University Press, 1988.

Heitink, Gerben. Trans. By Reinder Bruinsma, Practical Theology: History, Theory, Action Domains. William B Eerdmans: Michigan, 1999.

Heckathrorn, Douglas D. 'Respondent-driven Sampling: A New Approach to the Study of Hidden Populations', Social Problems, 44:174-199, 1997.

Huang, Hilary Bradbury. 'What is good action research? Why the resurgent interest?' 93-109 in Action Research, Vol. 8 (1), 2010, 93. Sage Publications DOI: 101177/1476750310362435

Husserl, Edmund. Ideas Pertaining to a Pure Phenomenology and to a Phenomenological Philosophy, Trans. By F Kersten. Springer Science and Business Media: 1983.

Hutton, Peter F. Survey Research for Managers: How to Use Surveys in Management Decision-Making, 2nd Edition. Basingstoke: Macmillan, 1990, 8.

Hyden, Margareta and Overlien, Carolina. '"Doing" Narrative Analysis' 250-268 in Deborah K Padgett (ed.), The Qualitative Research Experience. Australia: Thomson Brooks/Cole, 2004.

Jaison, Jessy. Enjoy Your Research. Trivandrum: New India Publications, 2000.

Jaison, Jessy. Vital Wholeness of Theological Education: Framing Areas of Assessment. Cumbria: Langham Global Library, 2017.

Janesick, V. 'The Choreography of Qualitative Research Design: Minuets, Improvisations and Crystallization', 379-399, in N Denzin and Y Lincoln (Eds), Handbook of Qualitative Research, 2nd Edition. Thousand Oaks, CA: Sage, 2000.

Jenesick, V J. Stretching Exercises for Qualitative Researchers, 2nd Edition. Thousand Oaks, CA: Sage, 2004.

Kemmis, Stephen and McTaggart, Robin. 'Participatory Action Research', 567-607 in N K Denzin and Y S Lincoln Eds., Handbook of Qualitative Research, 2nd Edition. Thousand Oaks, CA: Sage, 2000.

Knowles, Malcolm. The Adult Learner: A Neglected Species, 3rd Edition. Texas: Gulf Publishing, 1984.

Knowles, Malcolm. Andragogy in Action. San Francisco: Jossey Bass, 1984.

Kothari, C R. Research Methodology: Methods and Techniques. New Delhi: Viswa Prakashan, 1990.

Kuhn, Thomas. The Structure of Scientific Revolutions. Chicago: University of Chicago Press, 1970.

Kvale, Stenier. 'Doing Interviews' in Graham R Gibbs (ed). Qualitative Research Kit. Woodland Hills, CA: Sage, 2007.

Kvale, Steinar and Brinkmann, Svend. Interviews: Learning the Craft of Qualitative Research Interviewing. London: Sage, 2009.

Lerum, K. 'Subjects of Desire: Academic Armor, Intimate Ethnography and the Production of Critical Knowledge' Qualitative Inquiry, 7(4), 2001.

Lewis, Jane and Nicholls, Carol McNaughton. 'Design Issues' 47-69 Chapter 6 in J Richie, J Lewis, C M Nicholls & R Ormston. Qualitative Research Practice, 2nd Edition. London: Sage, 2014.

Lincoln, Yvonna S and Guba, Egon G. Naturalistic Inquiry. Beverly Hills, CA: Sage, 1985.

Litosseliti, Lia. Using Focus Groups in Research. London: Continuum, 2005.

Longkumer, Limatula. 'Theological Education as Critical Engagement' 115-122 in Communion on the Move: Towards a Relevant Theological Education. Wati Longchar, P Mohan Larbeer (eds). Bangalore BTESSC, 2015.

Lose, David J. 'How do We Make Space for Students to Seek Truth? Teaching with Conviction' 19-31 Chapter 2 in Mary E Hess and Stephen D Brookfield (eds), Teaching Reflectively in Theological Contexts: Promises and Contradictions. Florida: Krieger Publishing, 2008.

Mabry, Hunter P. A Manual for Researchers and Writers, Bangalore: BTE-SSC, 1999.

Marshall, Catherine., and Rossman, Gretchen B. Designing Qualitative Research, 5th Edition. Thousand Oaks, CA: Sage, 2011.

Mason, Jennifer. Qualitative Researching. Thousand Oaks, CA: Sage, 1996.

Masterson, Patrick. Approaching God: Between Phenomenology and Theology. London: Bloomsbury, 2013.

Maynard, Douglas W. and Clayman, Steven E. 'The Diversity of Ethnomethodology' 385-418 in Annual Review of Sociology, Vol. 17, 1991.

McCarty, Doran C. Supervision: Developing and Directing People in Ministry. Florida: McCarty Services, 2001.

McKinney, Carol V. Globe-Trotting in Sandals: A Field Guide to Cultural Research. Texas, SIL International, 2000.

Merriam, Sharan B. Qualitative Research and Case Study Applications in Education. San Francisco, CA: Jossey Bass, 1997.

Miller-Mclemore, Bonnie J. "Practical Theology and Pedagogy" 170-194. For Life Abundant: Practical Theology, Theological Education and Christian Ministry. Dorothy C Bass and Craig Dykstra, Eds. Cambridge: William B Eerdmans, 2008.

Miller-McLemore, Bonnie. 'The Contributions of Practical Theology', in The Wiley Blackwell Companion to Practical Theology, Ed. Bonnie Miller-McLemore, Oxford, UK: Blackwell Publishing Ltd., Kindle Edition, 2012.

Mills, Lisa and Kotecha, Mehul. 'Observation'243-264, Chapter 9 in J Richie, J Lewis, C M Nicholls and R Ormston, Qualitative Research Practice, 2nd edition. London: Sage, 2014.

Milner, H R. 'Race, Culture and Researcher Positionality: Working through Dangers Seen, Unseen and Unforeseen 388-400. Educational Researcher, 36(7), 2007,

Morgan, David L & Krueger, Richard A. The Focus Group Kit, London: Sage, 1997.

Morse, Janice M. and Richards, Lyn. Readme First for a User's Guide to Qualitative Methods, 3rd Edition. Thousand Oaks, CA: Sage, 2002.

Moustakas, Clark. Phenomenological Research Methods. Thousand Oaks, CA: Sage, 1994.

Neuman, W. Lawrence. Social Research: Qualitative and Quantitative Approaches, 2nd Edition. Boston: Allyn & Bacon, 1994.

Nouwen, Henry J M. Reaching Out: The Three Movements of the Spiritual Life, 1966. Bantam Doubleday: New York, 1975 reprint.

Ogletree, Thomas W. 'Dimensions of Practical Theology: Meaning, Action and Self' 83-104 in Practical Theology: The Emerging Field in Theology, Church and World, Don S Browning (ed.). San Francisco: Harper & Row, 1983.

Oliver, Paul. Writing Your Thesis. Sage publications: London, 2008.

Osmer, Richard R. Practical Theology: An Introduction. Grand Rapids, MI: William B Eerdmans, 2008.

Orna, Elizabeth and Stevens, Graham. Managing Information for Research. Buckingham: Open University Press, 1999.

Ott, Bernhard. Understanding and Developing Theological Education. Cumbria: Langham Global Library, 2016.

Padgette, Deborah K. 'Introduction: Finding a Middle Ground in Qualitative Research'1-18 in The Qualitative Research Experience. Belmont, CA: Wadsworth/Thomson, 2004.

Padgette, Deborah K. Qualitative Methods in Social Work Research: Challenges and Rewards. Thousand Oaks: CA: Sage, 1998.

Palmer, Parker. To Know as we are Known: Education as Spiritual Journey. San Francisco: HarperCollins, 1993.

Pattison, Stephen. The Challenge of Practical Theology. London: Jessica Kingsley Publishers, 2007.

Patton, Michael Quinn. Qualitative Research and Evaluation Methods 3rd edition. Thousand Oaks, CA: Sage, 2002.

Paul, Richard and Elder, Linda. The Miniature Guide to Critical Thinking Concepts and Tools, 7th Edition. Foundation for Critical Thinking Publishing, 2014, 12. https://www.criticalthinking.org/files/Concepts_Tools.pdf accessed on June 2, 2017.

Peck, John and Strohmer, Charles. Uncommon Sense: God's Wisdom for our Complex and Changing World. Tennessee: The Wise Press, 2000.

Punch, M. 'Politics and Ethics in Qualitative Research' 83-97 in Handbook of Qualitative Research, N K Denzin and Y S Lincoln (Eds). Thousand Oaks: CA, Sage, 1994.

Radcliffe-Brown, A. R. Method in Social Anthropology. Chicago: Chicago University Press, 1958.

Ragin, Charles C. Constructing Social Research: The Unity and Diversity of Method. Thousand Oaks, CA: Pine Forge Press, 1994.

Reed, Jan. Appreciative Inquiry: Research for Change. Sage: London, 2007.

Reynolds, Paul Davidson. Ethics and Social Science Research. New Jersey: Prentice Hall, 1982.

Richardson, L. 'Evaluating Ethnography' in Qualitative Inquiry 6 (2), 253-255, 2000.

Richie, Jane., Lewis, Jane., Nicholls, Carol McNaughton & Ormston, Rachel. Qualitative Research Practice, 2nd Edition. London: Sage, 2014.

Roller, Margaret R. and Lavrakas, Paul J. Applied Qualitative Research Design: A Total Quality Framework Approach. New York: Guilford Press, 2015.

Rossman, G B. & Rallis, S F. Learning in the Field: An Introduction to Qualitative Research, 2nd Edition. Thousand Oaks, CA: Sage, 2003.

Rubin, Herbert J. and Rubin, Irene S. Qualitative Interviewing: The Art of Hearing Data. London: Sage 1995.

Ryen, A. 'Ethics and Qualitative Research' 416-438 in D Silverman (Ed.) Qualitative Research, 3rd Edition. London: Sage, 2011.

Saldana, Johnny. The Coding Manual for Qualitative Researchers, 2nd Edition. London: Sage, 2013.

Sampson, H. 'Navigating the waves: The Usefulness of a Pilot in Qualitative Research', 383-402 in Qualitative Research, 4(3), 383.

Schutz, Alfred. Phenomenology of the Social World. Illinois: Northwestern University Press, 1967.

Schutz, Alfred. On Phenomenology and Social Relations. University of Chicago Press, 1970.

Schwandt, Thomas A. 'Three Epistemological Stances for Qualitative Inquiry' 292-331 Chapter 7 in The Landscape of Qualitative Research: Theories and Issues, 2nd Edition. Norman K Denzin and Yvonna S Lincoln (eds). Thousand Oaks: Sage, 2003.

Shaw, Daniel R. Kandila: Samo Ceremonialism and Interpersonal Relationship. Michigan: The University of Michigan Press, 1990.

Shaw, R. Daniel. 'Qualitative Social Science Methods in Research Design', 141-151 in Edgar J Elliston, Introduction to Missiological Research Design. Pasadena, CA: William Carey Library, 2011.

Shelby, R D. Using the Mentoring Relationship to Facilitate Rigor in Qualitative Research, 315-327 Smith College Studies in Social Work, 702 (2). DOI: 1080/003773100009517595.

Shulman, Lee. 'Making Differences: A Table of Learning', in Change The Magazine of Higher Learning 34(6):36-44, November 2002.

Shulman, Lee S and Kieslar, E R. Learning by Discovery: A Critical Appraisal. Chicago IL: Rand McNally, 1966.

Shulman, Lee S. The Wisdom of Practice: Essays on Teaching, Learning and Learning to Teach, Edited by Suzanne M Wilson (ed). San Francisco: Jossey-Bass, 2004.

Silverman, David. Doing Qualitative Research: A Practical Handbook. Thousand Oaks, CA: Sage, 2000, 2010.

Smith, Gordon T. 'Faculties that listen, Schools that Learn: Assessment in Theological Education'

229-245 in Malcom L Warford (ed) Practical Wisdom on Theological Teaching and Learning, 3rd Edition. New York: Peter Lang, 2004.

Soble, Alan. 'Deception in Social Science Research: Is Informed Consent Possible?' Hastings Center Report, 40-46. October 1978.

Spears, Deanne. Developing Critical Reading, 9th Edition. McGraw Hill Companies Inc. 2012.

Strauss, C Levi. The Savage Mind, 2nd Edition. Chicago: University of Chicago Press, 1966.

Strauss, Anselm and Corbin, Juliet. Basics of Qualitative Research: Grounded Theory Procedures and Techniques, 2nd Edition. Newbury Park, CA: Sage, 1998.

Studebaker, Steven and Beach, Lee. 'Friend or Foe? The Role of the Scholar in Emerging Christianity' 43-56 in Theological Education, Vol. 48, Number 2, 2014.

Swanson, Richard A. Theory Building in Applied Disciplines. San Francisco, CA: Berrett Coehler Publishers, 2013.

Swinton, John and Mowat, Harriet. Practical Theology and Qualitative Research, 2nd Edition. London: SCM, 2016.

Taftee, The Association of Theological Education by Extension (TAFTEE)'s Research Guide. Archives at New India Bible Seminary Library, Kerala, 2000.

Taylor, Steven J., and Bogdan, Robert. Introduction to Qualitative Research Methods, 2nd Edition. New York: Wiley, 1984.

The Handbook of Accreditation Section Eight, Association of Theology Schools 'A Guide for Evaluating Theological Learning.' 14-17. http://cf2015.bhcarroll.edu/files/session-2-toward-a-learning-century/assessment/assessment-handbook-section8-ats-harris.pdf accessed on 25 June, 2017.

The Norvegian National Research Ethics Committee, Guidelines for Research Ethics in the Social Sciences, Humanities, Law and Theology, 4th Edition, June 2016, p. 17. https://www.etikkom.no/globalassets/documents/english-publications/60127_fek_guidelines_nesh_digital_corr.pdf accessed on 25 April 2017. https://www.etikkom.no/globalassets/.../60127_fek_guidelines_nesh_digital_corr.pdf

The University of Oxford, Document on 'Plagiarism' https://www.ox.ac.uk/students/academic/guidance/skills/plagiarism?wssl=1 accessed on April, 24, 2017.

Tracy, David. Blessed Rage for Order: The New Pluralism in Theology. Chicago: Chicago University Press, 1975.

Van der Ven, J A. 'Empirical Methodology in Practical Theology: Why and How?' Practical Theology in South Africa, 9 (1), 29-44, 1994.

Waller, Willard. 'Insight and Scientific Method', American Journal of Sociology 40:3 (November) 285-97, 1934. Weiss, C H. Evaluation, 2nd Edition. Upper Saddle River, NJ: Prentice Hall, 1998.

Webster, Stephen., Lewis, Jane., and Brown, Ashley. 'Ethical Considerations in Qualitative Research' Chapter 4 in Qualitative Research Practice: A Guide for Social Science Students and Researchers, 2nd Edition. Jane Ritchie, Jane Lewis, Carol McNaughton Nicholls and Rachel Ormston (eds). Thousand Oaks, CA: Sage, 2014.

Weil, Nolan J. Thinking beyond the Content: Critical Reading for Academic Success. Michigan: University of Michigan Press, 2008.

Weiss, C H. Evaluation, 2nd Edition. Upper Saddle River, New Jersey: Prentice Hall, 268.

Wellington, J. Bathmaker, A. Hunt, C. McCulloch, G. and Sikes, P. Succeeding with your Doctorate. London: Sage, 2005.

Wilkinson, T S & Bhandarkar, P L. Methodology and Techniques of Social research. Bombay: Himalaya Publishing House, 1996.

Wood, Charles M. An Invitation to Theological Study. Pennsylvania: Trinity Press International, 1994.

Wooffitt, R. Conversation Analysis and Discourse Analysis: A Comparative and Critical Introduction. London: Sage, 2005.

Yin, R K. Case Study Research: Design and Methods, 4th Edition. Thousand Oaks, CA: Sage, 2009.

Zachariah, George. 'Discernment, Vocation, and Commitment: A Call to Repentance and Transformation' 71-85 in Theological Education: Ploughing the Field for New Life to Sprout, Bangalore: BTE-SSC & CLS, 2014.

Zahavi, Dan. Husserl's Phenomenology. California: Stanford University Press, 2003.

Ziegenhals, Gretchen E. 'Faculty Life and Seminary Culture' 49-66 in Practical Wisdom on Theological Teaching and Learning, Malcolm L Warford (ed). New York: Peter Lang, 2004.